Jaap Sleifer · Planning Ahead and Falling Behind

Jahrbuch für Wirtschaftsgeschichte BEIHEFT 8

Im Auftrag der Herausgeber
des Jahrbuchs für Wirtschaftsgeschichte
herausgegeben von Reinhard Spree

Jaap Sleifer

Planning Ahead and Falling Behind

The East German Economy in Comparison with West Germany 1936–2002

Akademie Verlag

ISBN-10: 3-05-004201-X
ISBN-13: 978-3-05-004201-5

Printed on permanent paper in compliance with the ISO standard 9706.

Coverdesign: Ingo Ostermaier, Berlin
Setting, Printing and Binding: Druckhaus „Thomas Müntzer", Bad Langensalza

Printed in Germany

Contents

List of tables in text

List of graphs in text

Acknowledgements

This book examines the East German economy from 1936 to 2002 in comparison with West Germany. The research was carried out at the Faculty of Economics of the University of Groningen and was partly financed by the *Duitsland Instituut Amsterdam (DIA)*. The result was accepted as a thesis at the University of Groningen, in the Faculty of Economics. Insofar this book differs from the original thesis manuscript: changes, elaborations and improvements were made at the *Centrum voor Duitsland Studies (CDS)* at the University of Nijmegen.

The study benefitted from the comments of many collegues. First of all I want to express my gratitude to my supervisors at the Groningen Growth and Development Centre (GGDC): Bart van Ark, Rainer Fremdling, and Herman de Jong. The continuous supply of new ideas, their enthusiasm for doing research in general, and all their feedback on the chapters and on the outline were very stimulating. I am also grateful to Jan-Pieter Smits and Marcel Timmer for their advice and their comments during different stages of the research project and to Jan Oosterhaven and Erik Dietzenbacher who respectively commented on earlier drafts of Chapter 4 and of Chapter 2.

Furthermore I want to thank Udo Ludwig for making my stay at the *Institut für Wirtschaftsforschung Halle (IWH)* possible and also for his advice on various matters; the people at the *Bundesarchiv* in Berlin-Lichterfelde who assisted me in collecting the data for my 1936 benchmark and Andreas Cors of the *Deutsches Institut für Wirtschaftsforschung (DIW)* who sent me data-sheets which link up the pre- and postunification period. I also thank the editors and referees of the *Jahrbuch für Wirtschaftsgeschichte* and the discussants who provided helpful ideas when I presented papers on which this thesis is built. In this respect I particularly want to mention Steven Brakman, Patrick O'Brien, and Herman Hoen. I thank Hans-Jürgen Wagener for his detailed comments on the entire manuscript and Marc Schramm for his remarks on Chapter 7. Finally, I wish to thank Lies Fanoy for her loving support and encouragement.

Jaap Sleifer
Nijmegen, January 2005

Chapter 1: Introduction

1.1. The case of two Germanies

During the period from 1936 to 2002 the shape of Germany showed major changes, marked by (a) the expansion of the *Third Reich*; (b) the division of Germany into occupation zones in 1945; (c) the founding of the German Democratic Republic (GDR) and the Federal Republic of Germany (FRG) in 1949; (d) the unification of the GDR and the FRG in 1990. No matter what period is described, the analysis and estimates for East Germany in this thesis refer to the territory – associated with – the GDR, and for West Germany they refer to the territory – associated with – the FRG before unification.[1]

Before the expansion of the *Third Reich* the East German economy had the signs of a blossoming landscape. At that time per capita national income amounted to 103 per cent of West Germany, compared to a mere 31 per cent in 1991. In the industrial sector labour productivity dropped from 91 per cent of the West German level in 1936 to merely 31 per cent in 1991. Before the Second World War the level of East German labour productivity met high international standards, as it was ranked at a tenth position. After the fall of the Berlin Wall many countries achieved a higher labour productivity than in East Germany, leaving this region at a rank somewhere between Mexico and Chile.[2] During his re-election campaign in 1990 Helmut Kohl promised (the reappearance of) a 'blossoming landscape' in East Germany. Many researchers find challenge in predicting the time needed,[3] others wonder whether this day will ever come.[4]

This thesis looks backwards to investigate the relative wealth of East Germany around the mid-1930s, to analyse the economic gains and losses between 1936 and

---

1 This means that I imposed the boundaries of 1949 (for West Germany the boundaries of 1960) on the period from 1936 to 1945, including a division of Berlin. Other adjustments for geographical discontinuities include the areas lost after World War II and the Saar territory that was alleged to France until 1959. As a result statistics refer to the same geographical territory for different periods in time. See Annex D for a map of the German boundaries.

2 Maddison (1995); Maddison (2001)

3 Burda (1995)

4 Sinn and Westermann (2001)

1991. The withering East German landscape provides a special case study for a persistent theme in economic history: what are the causes of the wealth and poverty of nations?[5] Here is a case of an economy that was relatively wealthy, but lost out in relatively short time due to a complex interaction of political, social and economic events. It is my aim to measure the performance of the East German economy relative to that of West Germany, to shed further light on which factors were key to this process.

The analysis focuses on the production side of the economy and distinguishes between sectors (e.g. agriculture, mining, manufacturing) and manufacturing branches (e.g. food, machinery, textiles). The main indicators used are comparisons of the growth and relative levels of value added and labour productivity of the East German and West German economies from 1936 to 2002.

Obviously the changes of the German geographical constellation coincided with changes of the political, institutional and economic environment. The historical profession often uses such changes to mark the beginning or the end of a period. Most (economic) historians have therefore focused their study on the period from 1945 to 1989.[6] Similarly much of the economic research focuses on the post-unification period.[7] A major contribution of this thesis is that it covers the entire period from 1936 to 2002. Firstly the integration of pre-division and post-unification data are helpful in constructing a better data set for East Germany for the intermediate period from 1950 to 1989. Secondly there is a profound interest in the effects of (sudden) changes of the political, institutional and economic environment on the wealth and poverty of nations. Such 'shocks' are often believed to be important.[8] This study estimates the importance of these historical accidents for the East German economy falling behind.

In the following sections of this chapter I discuss the initial conditions (1936–1950), the economic systems of capitalism and socialism (1950–1989), and transformation and unification (1989–2002). Periodisation isolates the historical accidents around the Second World War and those related to the tumbling down of the Berlin Wall. Three possibilities may be put forward to explain for the East German economy falling behind relative to that of West Germany. Firstly, the initial conditions of East Germany were unfavourable in comparison with West Germany. Secondly, the performance of the East German economy was less successful than the performance in West Germany. Thirdly, the East German economy 'mismatched' with West Germany when the two economies integrated.

---

5 Landes (1999); Cameron and Neal (2003)

6 Heimann (1997); Ritschl, (1996); Schwarzer (1999)

7 Brakman, Garretsen, and Schramm (1999); Sinn (2000)

8 Maddison (1991) pp. 108 ff.

1.2. Initial conditions, 1936–1950

The issue of the initial conditions is often put forward as a paradox: was it a bad start or a bad performance that explains the East German backwardness relative to West Germany? Choosing between the two explanations, recent literature explains the East German hardship mainly by a failing economic performance due to the economic system. Steiner (2004) states that the bad start was certainly important, however the crucial explanation is the system of central planning.[9] After summarizing the main findings in recent literature, Abelshauser (2004) too concludes the East German problem was the backward economic policy that was ill-equiped for modern economies.[10]

In fact the two explanations of the paradox are closely related. On a mathematical level, the initial labour productivity level combined with the growth rates allow extrapolation to the current level of labour productivity. Given the low levels of labour productivity in East Germany relative to West Germany in the late 1980s, Wagener stated that: the better the initial conditions, the worse the growth rates must have been.[11] And *vice versa*.

Such 'derived' evidence on the East German growth rates is useful as in the literature the official East German growth rates are very much distrusted.[12] In Chapter 2 of this thesis I will elaborate further on the accuracy and on the comparability of the (official) East German statistics. Information on the East German initial conditions can provide supportive 'evidence' for the trustworthiness of the East German growth rates. In an elaborate attack on "western cold war propaganda" the East German author Barthel (1979) claimed that East Germany had a bad start in comparison to West Germany.[13] This can be seen as an implicit defense of the officially reported high East German growth rates: the East German growth performance had to be good, given the bad initial conditions (and given the contemporary estimates of the East German level of labour productivity).

On a theoretical level, 'initial conditions' show a window of opportunities for the period after 1950. This relates to the relative ease to imitate existing technologies in comparison to inventing new ones. Through the adoption of more advanced technologies and modern institutions the 'backward' country can catch up with more advanced countries. These ideas built on studies of Gerschenkron and Abramovitz,[14] whose main findings concern the advantages of backwardness and the conditions for the exploitation of these advantages respectively. Thus, quantitatively, a measure of economic perform-

---

9 Steiner (2004) p. 4

10 Abelshauser (2004) pp. 363–366

11 Wagener (1996) pp. 24, 25

12 Von der Lippe (1995); Melzer and Stäglin, (1991)

13 Barthel (1979) pp. 13–28

14 Abramovitz (1989); Gerschenkron (1962)

ance at the beginning of the period (and also the period since transformation and unification) provides an anchor for the statistics on the period from 1950 to 1989. If East Germany had a bad start: it possibly also had a good potential for growth.

However, the significance of examining the 'initial conditions' during the 1930s and 1940s goes beyond reexamining the period from 1950 onwards. It also gives insight in the economic impact of the complex developments at that time. What were the effects of the Second World War and the division of Germany on the East German and West German economies?

In Chapter 4 the economic growth performance of the two German economies between 1936 to 1950 are analysed in a growth accounting framework, which decomposes output growth into growth of labour inputs, growth of capital inputs and total factor productivity. The framework was developed as a tool of historical description emanating from the historical national income research program at the U.S. National Bureau of Economic Research during the early 1950s and since mainly builds on the pioneering work by Abramovitz and Solow.[15] Its use for the analysis of the two German economies from 1936 to 1950 is that it helps to identify the effects of widely varying issues such as war damage, dismantling, war casualties, migration, etceteras on capital and labour input.

Between 1936 and 1950 the two parts of Germany developed into two independent political and economic entities. This process was characterised by the introduction of their own monetary, fiscal and social policies. This can be seen as the opposite of economic integration: economic disintegration.[16] Due to the establishment of a new physical border labour and capital could not move as freely as before. In the case of the mobility of people (labour) the building of the Berlin Wall in 1961 has become a main symbol. However, already in the 1950s the mobility was sharply reduced through the closing down of the border (except for Berlin). People needed permission to travel to West Germany, and permission was less and less granted as East Germany faced the wandering off of many inhabitants. Besides a reduction of factor mobility there was also a reduction of the movement of commodities: trade between East and West Germany deteriorated. Before the Second World War a division of labour between the two parts of Germany may be expected; thereafter it disappeared.

In Chapter 4, I provide estimates of the level of East German labour productivity in the industrial sector relative to West Germany for two benchmark years: 1936 and 1954. These benchmarks provide important building stones for the debate on the initial conditions. Firstly it estimates the actual labour productivity level of the two German economies. Secondly it improves the knowledge on the industrial structure in East Germany and West Germany. Were there differences in patterns of specialisation in 1936? And if so, who inherited the most productive industrial structure: East Germany or West Germany? What were the effects of the division, i.e. economic disintegration?

---

15 Abramovitz, (1956); Solow (1956); Solow (1957)

16 On economic integration see: Balassa (1961)

1.3. Economic system and economic performance, 1950–1989

This thesis measures the economic performance in the two German economies by gross domestic product per capita and gross domestic product per worker. The two indicators relate as gross domestic product per capita may increase either through an increase of participation in labour (in per cent of the total population more people are employed), or through an increase of labour productivity (i.e. gross domestic product per worker). Importantly the increase of gross domestic product per capita based on a higher participation is not sustainable as it (ultimately) suffers from diminishing returns. Labour productivity may improve through the use of capital inputs instead of labour inputs, through new technologies, and through the reallocation of labour inputs from sectors with a low productivity level to sectors with a high level of labour productivity.

In the case of the East German and West German economies it is particularly interesting to examine how economic performance links up with the existence of different economic systems. There exists a *communis opinio* that for the period from 1949 to 1989 East Germany should be categorised as a centrally planned economy and West Germany as a market economy, even though literature on economic systems has much struggled with matters of definition.[17] A study of Elliott defined an economic system as "a set of relations among decision-makers and between decision-makers and economic variables. It consists of the sum of ideas, goals, methods, and institutions used in society to resolve these economic issues in some more or less organised or 'systematic' way".[18]

This relates very much to the ideas of North, who advocated the incorporation of institutions in economic analysis and stated the following.[19] (1) Economic models are specific to particular constellations of institutional constraints that vary radically both through time and cross sectional in different economies; (2) A self-conscious incorporation of institutions will force social scientists in general, and economists in particular, to question the behavioral models that underlie their disciplines; (3) Ideas and ideologies matter, and institutions play a major role in determining just how much they matter; (4) The polity and the economy are inextricably interlinked in any understanding of the performance of an economy and therefore we must develop a true political economy discipline.

How the economy works depends on its socio-institutional context. There is no theoretical reason to restrict ourselves to a dichotomy of two economic systems: socialism (or centrally planned economies) and capitalism (or market economies). For example,

---

17 See Pryor (1985); Wagener (1979)

18 Elliott (1985)

19 North (1990) pp. 110–112

referring to West Germany Giersch *et al.* speak of a "social market economy".[20] However, empirically it makes sense to distinguish between these two economic systems. During the *cold war* the political systems of communism and democracy opposed one another and in many respects so did the economic systems that more or less correspond to the political systems.[21] Studies on economic systems often explicitly state the major characteristics of capitalism and socialism, and obviously East Germany is considered as a centrally planned economy and West Germany as a market economy.

The differences between the two systems may be characterised by the structure of ownership and the degree of centralisation in decision-making. West Germany, as a capitalist country, mainly relies on private and individual ownership and control of the business enterprise, whereas in East Germany, as a socialist country, state enterprises were predominant. Regarding the degree of centralisation capitalism provides wide areas of discretion for freedom of individual choice, which leads to decentralisation of economic decisions, whereas socialism shows a more centralised approach towards economic decisions.

According to Eidem and Viotti the degree of centralisation and the ownership are two ways of expressing the same phenomenon.[22] They argue that ownership should be analysed in terms of the bundle of rights attached to the ownership: the "property rights", where unlimited private ownership allows the owners to use their property in any way they see fit. From this perspective the property rights define the discretion for decision-making autonomy that is attached to property.

How does the discretion for decision-making autonomy influence economic activities? To begin with it is useful to make this characteristic more concrete. It links up with theories of *economic regulation*, which can be defined as "a state-imposed limitation on the discretion that may be exercised by individuals or organisations, which is supported by the threat of sanction".[23] According to Viscusi *et al.* the three key decision variables controlled by regulation are price, quantity, and the number of firms. Less frequently controlled variables include product quality and investment.[24] Table 1.1. shows the actor autonomy on key decision variables in the Third Reich, in East Germany (1950– 1989), and in West Germany. Autonomy of actors are considered to be low if the decisions are made centrally – and high if the discretion of decision-making is very much decentralised.

---

20 Giersch, Paqué, and Schmieding (1994)

21 It is sometimes argued that a country may have capitalism and democracy or capitalism and dictatorship; similarly a country may have socialism and democracy or socialism and dictatorship. See: Zimbalist and Sherman (1984) pp. 15–23

22 Eidem and Viotti (1978) p. 76–79

23 Alan Stone, *Regulation and Its Alternatives* (Washington 1982), as quoted in: Viscusi, Vernon, and Harrington Jr. (1992)

24 Viscusi, Vernon, and Harrington Jr. (1992) p. 296–299

Table 1.1. Actor autonomy on key decision variables in the Third Reich, East Germany and West Germany

	Third Reich	East Germany	West Germany
Prices	Low	Low	High
Quantity	Moderate	Low	High
Number of firms	Low	Low	High
Product quality	High/Moderate	Moderate	High
Investment	Low	Low	High

Source: Schneider (1996)

Most of the literature on economic regulation primarily focuses on particular (regulated) industries in a dominantly 'capitalist' economy. In that sense the East German 'socialist' economy is a very extreme case of regulation, as it involves most industries. For instance, the East German producer who makes new cars had little decision autonomy on its price, quantity, and new investments. As entry and exit were up to the central government, it was not the producer's decision to stop production altogether.

Although the East German position was extreme, the decision variables that are distinguished in economic regulation provide a clear indication what kind of limitations can be put on the 'discretion of the decision-making autonomy' of actors. The effects of such limitations can be analysed in a static and in a dynamic model. In a static model that is presented by Yeager there are several necessary conditions that must be present to allow markets to function well, including good consumer information, a stable monetary system, secure property rights over the product both before and after the sale, and access to a third party system to enforce transactions.[25] Yeager concluded the following:

> "Socialist economies satisfied these criteria. Given that there was little or no choice in product selection, consumer information was not very important. East Germany had a stable monetary system, and property rights were specified and enforced by the state. Strict enforcement mechanisms were in place to oppress reactionaries. The result was that costs of transacting were low."

In my opinion Yeager simplifies the situation too much as he makes insufficiently clear the role of well-functioning markets with regard to increasing living standards and the support of the allocation of resources to its most productive uses. In a centrally planned economy shortages and surpluses arise at the same time. An example by Kornai shows that the producer's aim is to reach the targets for aggregate output set by the central planner, even at the cost of making far more green dresses and far fewer blue, far more baggy pants and far fewer tight ones than demanded by consumers.[26]

---

25 Yeager (1999)

26 Kornai (1992) p. 271

Despite this simplification concerning the static model, I agree with Yeager in his claim that the dynamic model is far more important. The dynamic model in Yeager is primarily based on the Schumpeterian concept of 'creative destruction'. Yeager wrote: "For intensive growth to occur, institutions must foster the process of creative destruction in which new technology destroys the old. This requires supply-side competition and profit-seeking behaviour. Socialist economies, by their very nature, do not promote competition".[27]

Whether socialist economies did or did not promote competition should be encountered with caution. Stiglitz already emphasised that the term 'competition' has a variety of meanings.[28] In the literature it has been argued that under communism there was a fierce competition between individual enterprises competing with each other for resources. Investment goods and different inputs necessary for production were allocated administratively and were scarce. Therefore state-owned enterprises had to compete with each other, most often in the process of increasingly multilateral bargaining, to force central planners to give them as much as possible (and demand as little as possible).[29] Therefore I think that the main difference is what the competition between firms is about rather than whether it is apparent. There is a point, however, whether competition was 'creative': whether it supported technological change, whether it satisfied demand and raised living standards, and whether it helped to allocate resources to its most productive use as to reduce potential wealth losses.

A dynamic model: factor reallocation

Schumpeter starts his narrative on the process of creative destruction stating that capitalism never is and never can be stationary. He discerns that the new consumer goods, new methods of production or transportation, new markets, new forms of industrial organisation incessantly revolutionises the economic structure from within, incessantly destroying the old one, incessantly creating a new one. This process he calls creative destruction.

It is a dynamic model for a society where a decentralised discretion for freedom of individual choice prevails. The introduction of a new commodity, a new technology or a new type of organisation involves concrete decisions. In a market economy there are several actors who may decide upon these issues, using their own (accesses to) means, and carrying their own gains and losses. Obviously profitable decisions might generate money, and therefore increase future means to effectuate new decisions. At the same time future means might be reduced due to unprofitable decisions. Consequently the

---

27 Yeager (1999) p. 72; see also Schumpeter (1961)

28 Stiglitz (1994) pp. 109–138

29 Jasiński and Ross (1999) pp 195, 196

relative positions of the different actors (firms) are repeatedly re-established, in other words they lead to a continuous reallocation of resources.

For each enterprise past decisions have effects on 'current' means. At the micro level of firms – where the process of creative destruction takes place – factors shift towards the most successful firms. Hence much of this reallocation reflects within-sector rather than between sector-reallocation. But even between sectors shifts of labour and capital from less productive to more productive sectors can accelerate growth.[30]

What can be expected of factor reallocation in a country where decision-making is centralised? In a centrally planned economy the central government sets production targets, allocates resources, and bears the risks. Because firms neither get the gains nor bear the risks there is no clear relationship between past-decisions and current means. The lacking relationship between past-decisions and current means is best described in Kornai: "What happens under the classical socialist system if a state-owned firm's spending exceeds its budget constraint? And what happens if this is a regular, not an isolated, occurrence? The observation then is that the constraint will be adjusted to the repeated overspending. The firm receives regular external assistance".[31] In the socialist system firms had soft budget constraints: to increase their budget they had to negotiate with the regime.

Due to the soft budget constraints inefficient firms could stay in business. Their losses could be compensated for through bargaining on (structural) state subsidies, lower taxation, favourable credits, or new (administrative) prices. Moreover, "soft budget constraints generated excess demand, unsatisfied (and unsatisfiable!) excess demand generated shortages, shortages aggravated supply uncertainty and – in order to insure themselves against late or missing deliveries – enterprises tried to hold as large input inventories as possible". The centrally planned economy produced "output that existed but should not".[32] Meanwhile the reallocation process is to a large extent the domain of politics. The system depended on the grants of the regime, which makes it a matter of political decision-making. Whereas in the decentralised model the economic structure changes 'from within', in the centralised model it changes 'from above'.

The different model for factor reallocation is the main (ultimate) explanation for the troublesome performance of the East German economy. Abelshauser (2004) elaborately addresses the loss of entrepreneurship in East Germany. He describes the importance of autonomous decisions made by individuals, of (personal) networks and information gathering, and of the institutional changes imposed by East German politics that drove East Germany away from its historically developed institutions. Steiner (2004) repeatedly points at crowding out effects on the "neglected" sectors as a result of prioritisa-

---

30 Chenery, Robinson and Syrquin (1986) p. 13; Foster, Haltiwanger and Krizan (1998)

31 Kornai (1992) pp. 140 ff.

32 Winiecki (2002); Literature recognises 'output that existed but should not' and also 'output that did not exist'. The latter refers to the earlier mentioned distrust in the East German statistics and will be discussed in Chapter 2 of this thesis.

tion of specific industries.[33] To understand the transformation of the East German economic structure it is therefore useful to examine the policy of the regime. Besides the development of some prioritised industries, what were the policy aims?

Firstly it was to some extent necessary to meet the demand of the consumers. According to Kopstein the East German population mirrored itself to West Germany, and thus demanded western living standards. Especially before the building of the Berlin Wall in 1961, when East German people could migrate relatively easy towards West Germany, this was important. For instance in 1958, Ulbricht declared that the chief economic task was overtaking West Germany in per capita consumption of all important food items and consumer goods by 1961.[34] Above, Kornai's example of green and blue dresses (baggy and tight pants) made clear that the regime did not manage to produce the proper amount of each category. While failing to satisfy consumer demand and raise utility and living standards, the firms mainly aimed to reach the production target. At the same time the example shows that the regime did bother enough to produce both colours of dresses and both types of pants.

Secondly East German employment policy set ambitious goals. In East Germany the people had a right to get a job (also there was an obligatory regulation for people who refused to work). It was the aim to establish full employment, and indeed official unemployment was almost absent. Even (partly) disabled persons were integrated in the labour process. The result of this social policy is that in addition to holding large inventories, firms also hoarded labour adding to their slowing productivity growth.[35] With hard budget constraints unemployment would have risen in East Germany. Therefore the budget grants the regime gave to the firms are in part related to labour market policy.

Thirdly it was important to satisfy the economic-political aims of the Soviet bloc. This is illustrated by the building of heavy industries – iron and steel – in *Eisenhüttenstadt* near the Polish border. This new industrial centre fitted into the pattern of 'socialist industrialisation', where according to the Soviet example an industrial structure was developed with a focus on heavy industries.[36] From an efficiency viewpoint it would have been more sensible to build these industries in Rostock, so that Swedish iron ore could be used. However, the location in Rostock was undesired by the Soviet Union – and the alternative of *Eisenhüttenstadt* made the East German industries much more dependent on Soviet ores.[37]

---

33 Steiner (2004) pp. 89, 149, 212 ff., 223; Steiner describes several examples that clearly refer to a crowding out hypothesis. His study lacks the data to (quantitatively) test this hypothesis, as will be done in the following chapters of this study.

34 Kopstein (1997) p. 43, 44

35 Hoffmann (2002) p. 115

36 Schultz (1999)

37 Gayko (2000)

A dynamic model II: innovation systems

New technology is regarded as a main driving force for productivity growth. It is claimed that the centralised or the decentralised organisation design do not only influence the process of factor allocation, but also the introduction of new technologies. Fritsch and Werker observed three main differences between innovation systems in centrally planned economies and innovation systems in market economies.[38]

Firstly the centralised innovation system, especially in East Germany, uses a linear innovation model that distinguishes the logical steps of the innovation process, i.e. invention, development, innovation and diffusion. These phases had to be passed successively one after another. The linear model was less widely applied in the decentralised innovation system, mainly because the model largely neglects a feedback process: what about the effects of consumers' preferences on the research activities?

Secondly the centralised system lacks a clear relationship between successful innovations and future resources. This links up with the previous section, where it was argued that in the decentralised system gains and losses are allocated corresponding to the firm that actually made the decision. Fritsch and Werker state that the lacking relationship between successful innovations and future resources leads to relatively weak incentives to generate innovations in the centralised system. This also links up with Gomulka, who finds that the severe limitations in the freedom of decision-making and resource reallocation lead to weak innovation incentives.[39] According to Gomulka in a centrally planned economy the main motivation for innovating firms is the need to overcome supply difficulties.

As a result process innovations rather than product innovations tend to dominate, i.e. the use of different intermediate inputs for making the same product. For East Germany this can be illustrated with the example of the 'basic and fabricated metal products' branch. After the Second World War this branch faced difficulties in retrieving the necessary inputs, which were produced insufficiently by East German mining. Hence the firms were motivated to overcome supply difficulties. The bottlenecks were solved by the use of alternative inputs, especially (metal) scrap.[40] But on the side of product innovations, 'new products' remained limited to variations on the same product.

Thirdly the "centralised" innovation decision was based on what they believed to be the most promising technological path. As a result there was little variety of alternative technologies. Whereas the communist regime regarded redundancy of innovation activities mainly as an unnecessary waste of resources, there are also major drawbacks. Fritsch and Werker mention the following:

---

38 Fritsch and Brezinski eds. (1999)

39 Gomulka (1986) pp. 42–61

40 Mühlfriedel and Wießner (1989) pp. 245–258; Unger (2000) pp. 147–169

- In cases where decisions for technological paths turn out to be wrong alternative technologies were not readily available;
- The relatively poor variety of technology options could result in difficulties if the environmental conditions changed and technologies that were inferior in the short-run could provide important solutions;
- A lack of variety implies only very limited opportunities for competition between different solutions in order to discover the best alternative.

In a cynical view of Bentley, espionage in Western countries by East Germany's secret service was an important channel of the latest developments in technology.[41] Bentley distinguishes three phases in the East German technological history. From 1945 to 1962 the decision-making on innovation and diffusion was centralised. According to Bentley the central plans for new technology tended to be less the result of active project selection than simply a compilation of proposals from below. From 1963 to 1971 the decision-making was becoming more decentralised. This coincides with the introduction of the *new economic system* in East Germany between 1963 and 1967. Although this concept promised theoretically to stimulate industrial innovation and diffusion more efficiently than before, it was not allowed very long to prove itself. From 1971 onwards management of the economy was recentralised.

1.4. Transformation and unification

After 1989 East Germany was transformed from a centrally planned economy into a market economy and in 1990 East and West Germany (re) unified. As was the case with the period before the division of Germany, the period after unification provides a second anchor for the years that the two 'Germanies' were separated (1950–1989). Moreover, after the shock effect of unification had petered the East German economy seemed in worse condition than before. Why did transition at first lead to crisis? How well did the East German economy do after 1991? And what are the future prospects?

During the transformation from a centrally planned economy to a market economy the soft budget constraints were replaced by hard budget constraints. Firms that were held in business through aid of the regime had to close down. The demand for large inventories disappeared. In short: the economy got rid of 'output that existed but should not'.[42] However, different processes were set into motion simultaneously. Besides the transformation of the economic system, the East German economy integrated into the West German (and the West European) market, and politically the two German states unified. It is not so easy to separate the transformation to a market economy from other

---

41 Bentley (1992)

42 Winiecki (2002)

processes. The East German experience does not only show the effects of a change from a centrally planned economy to a market economy. It also shows the readiness of East German firms to compete on the new German market.

Transformation improved the autonomy of firms in decision-making on prices, quantity, quality and investment. The introduction of West German market based institutions changed what competition was about: rather than the favour of central planners, firms were now primarily interested in the favour of consumers. However, unification gave firms little time to adapt to the new institutional environment. The integration of the East and West German markets brought all kinds of new (West German) products to East Germany. Whereas the East German economy was under massive reconstruction, the struggle for market shares had already started.

Transformation and unification refers to processes related to a shift from a centrally planned economy, but also to processes related to the integration of markets. During these changes the East German economy was supported to invest in a modernisation of the existing capital stock and also to improve its infrastructure through financial transfers from West Germany to East Germany.

Convergence of the East German economy, in particular of East German labour productivity, to West German levels is a dominant theme in the literature since unification. When will East Germany catch up with the West German level? Estimates vary from about 2060 by Barro and Sala-i-Martin[43], to somewhere between 2003 and 2010 by Burda.[44] The convergence hypothesis states that the existence of a technological gap points at an extra growth potential.[45] If followers are able to imitate superior technology, they can catch-up to the leader. In the case of the two German economies this means that East Germany should adopt those technologies that are already used in the (more advanced) West German economy.

In order to do so, there is need for technical congruence. That is a compatibility of the natural resource endowment and the market size of a country on the one hand, and the characteristics of the technologies to be adapted on the other hand. Furthermore a country needs the ability to assimilate advanced countries technology effectively, i.e. "social capability".[46] Social capability can be defined as a set of requirements: adequate levels of human capital; appropriate institutions; openness; and a political system that does not block reform or impede innovative activity.[47] After the transition between 1989 and 1991 East Germany fulfilled these requirements. Transition provided East Germany of adequate institutions, openness and the required political system. Levels of

43 Barro and Sala-I-Martin (1991)
44 Burda (1995)
45 Gerschenkron (1962)
46 Abramovitz (1989)
47 Crafts (2000)

human capital are usually seen as good, so that superior technology might be successfully implemented.[48]

Social capability is a necessary condition for catch-up. It does not automatically imply that if East Germany adopts new – superior – technologies it will converge to the West German level of labour productivity. This is particularly stressed by Fremdling, who stated that what is superior technologically need not be superior economically.[49] Since convergence levelled off after 1995, more attention is paid to the question whether East Germany will catch-up at all. In a study of Boltho, Carlin and Scaramozzino, East Germany was compared with Mezzogiorno (Southern Italy), a region that did not converge to Northern Italian levels. They concluded that given East Germany's great *social capability* for growth, and provided that investment continues to be encouraged, the prospects for convergence are more promising in East Germany than for Mezzogiorno.[50]

More recently, Sinn and Westermann concluded that East Germany faces the Mezzogiorno scenario. They rejected the convergence hypothesis and observe a drifting away.[51] East Germany is located at the outskirt of the European Union, lacks adequate quality of the local infrastructure, has – therefore – a location disadvantage. The analysis may differ since the enlargement of the European Union. Still, due to the integration of the East and West German markets the core and the peripheries are new defined. Location preferences are as important as access to technological knowledge, and may be decisive in matters of convergence. It is noted that the enlargement of the European Union may have a positive impact on the East German economy, as it makes it a less peripheral region.

Still, for the period from 1991 to 2002 the story goes that the expectations based on transformation (i.e. convergence) may have done their job for some years but in the end processes that were initiated by the unification and the integration of markets (i.e. location theories) prevent a further catching up. Support for this idea is also found in Brakman, Garretsen and Schramm, who concluded that relocation of industries to the core (West Germany) was strongest for industries with the strongest economies of scale.[52] This thesis will discuss the effects of intertemporal transformation and spatial integration for the transition between 1989 and 1991, and also for the period thereafter in Chapter 7.

---

48 It is noted that some authors are critical with regard to East German skill levels; see Hitchens, Wagner and Birnie (1993)

49 Fremdling (1990)

50 Boltho, Carlin and Scaramozzino (1997)

51 Sinn and Westermann (2001)

52 Brakman, Garretsen, and Schramm (1999) p. 18

1.5. Outline

This thesis aims to explain the divergence of the East and West German economies between 1936 and 1991. How much and when did East Germany fall behind the west, and what were the main causes? For this purpose I distinguish the initial conditions, the growth performance from 1950 to 1989, as well as the unification of the two economies in 1990. A follow up question that will be examined concerns convergence of the East German economy to West Germany between 1991 and 2003, as well as prospects for further convergence thereafter.

Important innovations in this study are new time series for the total economy, as well as for some of the underlying sectors and manufacturing branches. It presents two new estimates for the relative level of labour productivity in the industrial sector of 1936 and 1954, again split up for manufacturing branches.

The analysis in this study is very much oriented towards quantitative approaches and methods, as can be seen in the short introduction to the chapters below. Chapter 3, after starting with an overview for the entire period from 1936 to 2000, deals with the East German growth performance from 1950 to 1989 in comparison with West Germany of the total economy. The main argument is that the observed East German performance based on Gross Domestic Product (GDP) per capita hides underlying problems of the East German economy that become apparent when looking at GDP per person employed.

Chapter 4 analyses the effects of the initial hardship on the relative level of labour productivity in the case of the industrial sector. The analysis includes two benchmark comparisons (1936 and 1954) that differentiate for the major industrial branches, which provides information on the East and West German economic structure and also on structural changes between 1936 and 1954. Labour productivity does not only differ between sectors and branches, but also between regions. Therefore the analysis of the initial conditions in Chapter 4 includes a comparison of the labour productivity performance of East and West German regions before and after separation.

I examine the East German growth performance in the industrial sector in Chapter 5. This chapter first compares the comparative performance of labour productivity in industry and manufacturing (industries, except mining) in East Germany and West Germany. A main question is: how did structural change contribute to economic growth? Based on the different economic systems that prevailed, structural change is expected to contribute less to economic growth in East Germany than in West Germany. Another issue related to differences between capitalism and communism is the quality of products. Whereas East German producers aimed to meet the production targets, West German producers wanted to reach the consumer. As a result quality differences may be expected. Therefore I will also compare the quality of East and West German products. The performance of the non-industrial sectors is discussed in Chapter 6. This Chapter looks in more detail to the comparative developments in agriculture, public utilities, construction and transports and communications.

Transformation and unification did not only release processes related to a shift from a centrally planned economy to a market economy, but also processes related to the integration of markets. Chapter 7 looks at the economic development from 1989 to 2003. It aims to explain the collapse of the East German economy between 1989 and 1991, and it indicates the probability of convergence to West German levels of labour productivity in the near future.

Many of the official East German statistics, i.e. the statistics of the German Democratic Republic, have been criticised for lacking reliability and lacking comparability with western statistics. Chapter 2 discusses backgrounds to the East German statistics in general, to the data that were used in this research in particular, and also the main alternatives provided in the literature.

Chapter 2: The political economy of the GDR statistics

2.1. Official growth rates

During the forty years that East Germany existed as an independent nation the GDR bureaucracy produced numerous statistics, of which the statistics on economic growth were a cornerstone. Growth was based on "five year plans" that gave production targets for enterprises. At the same time growth could be used for propaganda to stress the accomplishments of the *regime*. Consequently the statistics on the actual growth performance were important in two ways. First as a mechanism of control whether economic plans were actually fulfilled; and second as some kind of justification of the *communist* authorities.

Based on the official statistics on national product the East German growth rates were very impressive. However, as it will be shown in following chapters the actual performance was not that impressive at all. Centrally planned economies are known for their notorious overstating of economic growth. It is shown that the official statistics for the Soviet Union and in East Germany showed much higher growth than the economies of the 'West'. The literature refers to the overstating in the official statistics as 'output that did not exist', or as a 'phantom economy'.[53] In the following I will examine where the phantom economy comes from: how does it appear in the statistics? Thereafter it will be examined how the phantom economy element can be filtered out of the statistics.

During the 'cold war' the countries east of the iron curtain were sometimes suspected of double book keeping in the sphere of information. One – falsified – set was for the people and public, the other one was for the country's leadership. What is the status of the statistics that were published in the East German statistical yearbooks? Von der Lippe claims that in East Germany there was a clear distinction between statistics that were published and statistics that were only provided to a very exclusive group within the communist party.[54] This emphasises the importance of statistics as an instrument for propaganda and suggests that the high growth is explained by its lacking reliability.

---

53 The term 'phantom economy' comes from A. Besancon, *Anatomie d'un spectre. L'économie politique du socialisme réel* (Warsaw 1984) as quoted in: Winiecki (2002)

54 Von der Lippe (1995) p. 1979

Table 2.1. Official growth estimates of gross output in constant prices in East Germany in comparative perspective from 1950 to 1989 (1950 = 100)

	East Germany (official)	Soviet Union (official)	West Germany	United States of America	Western Europe
1950	100	100	100	100	100
1960	262	261	219	141	161
1970	401	523	336	212	259
1980	638	850	439	291	347
1989	902	1,107	516	392	426

Sources: Statistisches Jahrbuch der Deutschen Demokratischen Republik 1990; Statistisches Bundesamt (1991); Kudrov (1998); Maddison (2001)

As a narrative the idea of double book keeping offers an exciting story. Instead of examining the statistical yearbooks that were made public, a *quest* for the statistical information for the country's leadership could be proclaimed. In the case of the Soviet Union after the collapse of communist power it was officially revealed that there was no such exclusive statistical economic information for the leadership.[55] According to Melzer and Stäglin in East Germany the economic leaders were responsible for "using coefficients to obtain wrong valuations of fixed assets and exports and imports, [for] double counting in production figures, [for] changing definitions without explanation [...] and [for] giving up the publication of certain detailed data".[56] Still there is some debate whether the published East German statistics were false equivalents for the true statistics available to the regime. Elaborating on the foreign trade statistics Van Brabant criticises the position of Melzer and Stäglin, as he stated: "calling these statistics deliberately falsified [...] is an exaggeration on an almost colossal scale, to put it mildly".[57] Instead Van Brabant points at the 'habit' and 'inertia' of the statistical reporting systems.

Instead of looking at the *reliability* of the East German statististics it is more fruitful to examine the *comparability* of these statistics to standards in the 'West'. As in other centrally planned economies East Germany used the *Material Product System* rather than the *Systems of National Accounts*. There are several studies that study the differences between the statistics in Eastern Europe and the western world in great detail.[58] Marer (1985) mentions three reasons why the official growth rates of most centrally planned economies cannot be compared to growth rates in market economies:

1. The lack of meaningful prices (in centrally planned economies)
2. Methodological shortcomings
3. Lack of coverage of the "nonmaterial" services

---

[55] Kudrov (1998)

[56] Melzer and Stäglin, (1991) pp. 407–449

[57] U.S. Bureau of Labor Statistics and Eurostat (1991) p. 452

[58] U.S. Bureau of Labor Statistics and Eurostat (1991); World Bank (1993); Marer (1985)

The literature shows several attempts to deal with these problems of data comparability. In the following sections it will be discussed how the differences between the two statistical systems hamper the comparability between for instance the East- and West German data, how it results in the overstating of East German growth, and what can be done to solve these problems.

2.2. The lack of meaningful prices

Whereas in a pure market economy prices are determined by demand and supply, in a pure centrally planned economy prices are set by the planning authorities. Prices in a market economy are supposed to reflect the relative scarcities; prices in a centrally planned economy are the outcome of the governmental decision making process. As a result it is not clear what prices mean, or as Marer put it: there is theoretical uncertainty as to what is being measured. This section deals with this particular problem, starting with a brief discussion how prices were established. Thereafter this section discusses the conclusions of Dietzenbacher and Wagener regarding the outcomes of the East German decision making on prices, and finally it is discussed how this study dealt with this problem.

How prices were established

The system of calculating prices in East Germany has been more or less the same since 1953. Although there were minor changes in the calculation of profits, from 1953 onwards most prices were based on the so-called *Selbstkosten*. The *Selbstkosten* reflected wages, depreciation, and the costs of intermediate inputs for each particular product. Following this method of determining prices, factor costs are a main ingredient of the cost price.

Depending on the method for calculating the profit mark-up East Germany distinguished three different types of prices: the *lohnbezogenen Preistyp*, the *kostenbezogenen Preistyp* and the *fondsbezogenen Preistyp*. In short the *lohnbezogenen Preistyp* calculated the profit mark-up as a percentage of labour costs, i.e. wages. Clearly this type stimulates labour intensive industries and may have hindered the substitution of labour for capital. Therefore the *kostenbezogenen Preistyp* was considered as more appropriate, as it included the use of material inputs and depreciation into the calculation. The most appropriate mark-up system according to East German specialists of the time, however, was the *fondsbezogenen Preistyp*. The *kostenbezogenen Preistyp* did not account for the financing of capital, which introduced a disadvantage of capital-intensive industries relative to other industries. This problem was solved in the *fondsbezogenen Preistyp*.[59]

59 For more details see: Hartmut Zimmerman ed. (1985) pp 422, 423; Maier (1997)

In theory an efficient economy with profit-maximising enterprises hires each factor of production to the point where the value of its marginal product equals the price (or wage) of the factor. As the East German price system was very much based on factor costs, does this mean that it could have provided a good representation of the relative scarcities in the country? The outcomes of the East German decision making on prices are discussed later in this section. Here it is stressed that in a centrally planned economy besides prices also the amount of products to produce were set by production targets in the economic plans. Furthermore factor markets were very inflexible. Wage rates and decisions on investment were to a large extent influenced by government, just as prices.[60]

Not all prices were calculated according to the same method. Until 1953 prices were fixed at the price level of 1944, but these differed across regions and companies. In 1953 it was attempted to obtain fixed product prices for the entire country, based on *Selbstkosten*. However, in 1955 the prices of identical products from different plants were still – according to the *Selbstkosten* of the particular plant – set at different prices. In a speech by Ulbricht it is referred to six different plants that produce the wheel N-13 262a. For twenty such wheels the works price, including material, basic cost, and overhead is as follows:[61]

VEB[62] "8 Mai"	338.31 DM-Ost	VEB "W. Friedel"	443.00 DM-Ost
VEB "F. Heckert"	492.37 DM-Ost	VEB "Modul"	675.43 DM-Ost
VEB "Kratos"	472.41 DM-Ost	VEB "Schleifmaschine"	771.79 DM-Ost

Other examples for this failure to fix prices per type of product include several products in the branch "food, beverages, tobacco".[63] Beside the failures to fix prices it is also noted that even since 1953 not all prices were based on *Selbstkosten*. Especially prices for 1944 were frequently used as an alternative. Table 2.2 gives some examples of prices which were not based on *Selbstkosten*.

Until the introduction of the "New Economic System" many prices, especially for raw materials, were not based on factor costs. Most of these products were frozen at prices of 1944. Consequently it is unlikely that East German prices did reflect relative scarcities very well.[64] Firstly there were inconsistencies between prices based on *Selbstkosten* on the one hand and prices based on e.g. prices of 1944 on the other hand. Secondly the product prices based on *Selbstkosten* may have no longer reflected relative scarcities correctly, as via the use of raw materials and semi-fabrics the system of *Selbstkosten* was infected. Some of the prices for material inputs were inconsistent with

---

60 Wilczinsky (1970)

61 Walter Ulbricht, "Die Rolle der Deutschen Demokratischen Republik im Kampf um ein friedliches und glückliches Leben des deutschen Volkes", in: *Neues Deutschland* (1955) October 30th, No. 255, p. 5; as quoted in Stolper (1960) p. 70

62 VEB = "Volkseigener Betrieb" (nationalised plant).

63 Maier (1997)

64 See also: Steiner (2002) pp. 187–190

Table 2.2. Prices for selected East German products 1953–1963/67

Black Coal and Cokes	Based on prices for imports
Brown coal	Based on prices of 1944
Energy	Largely based on prices of 1944
Basic non-ferrous metals	Based on prices of 1944, except for Copper and Aluminium
Metal Scrap	Based on prices of 1944
Stone, Clay, Glass	Based on prices of 1944
Wood, Wood Products	Based on prices of 1944

Source: Maier (1997)

the prices based on *Selbstkosten*, so that differences in the use of material inputs were not properly accounted for.

The "New Economic System" which was introduced in three stages between 1964 and 1967 improved the characteristics of the East German price system in several respects. First of all the *Selbstkosten* system became the basis for all prices.[65] As a result prices reflected factor costs better than before. It is noted that there were also changes in the calculation of the *Selbstkosten*, in particular for the part of depreciation. This was related to major recalculations of the East German capital stock.[66] Finally the "New Economic System" somewhat loosened central planning of the economy and shifted from directive to indicative management. However, in 1971 this part of the reform was abolished. A detailed description of this "decentralisation" (and "recentralisation) can be found in Leptin and Melzer.[67] But factor costs, i.e. *Selbstkosten*, remained the basis for East German prices, albeit that prices were re-established periodically.[68]

Did prices reflect relative scarcities?

After this examination of how prices were established in East Germany, the question arises whether these prices reflected relative scarcities or not. For the period before the "New Economic System", the answer is negative. Considering how the prices were constructed according to different methods it is not likely that there has been much

65 Steiner (1999) gives an elaborate account of the price reform. He also concludes that since the reform the consistency of prices has improved, which is related to the "einheitlichen methodischen Basis". According to Steiner consistency could still be further improved after 1967 for political objectives in the determination of prices, profits and subsidies, and the static character of the reform.

66 An inventarisation of the total capital stock was made, which led to a revaluation of fixed capital. See: Melzer (1980); Maier (1997); Steiner (2002)

67 Leptin and Melzer (1978)

68 The main problem which made periodical price revisions necessary concerned the imports from other countries. Because East Germany depended to a considerable extent on foreign (natural) resources the East German internal price policy was influenced by the "external environment".

consistency in this respect. It also relates to conclusions on the input/output relationship in Chapter 6. There it is found that changing input output ratios between 1960 and 1970 based on official statistics in current prices account for a new price structure rather than (or besides) a new input output relationship.

For the period since 1967, when the *Selbstkosten* (factor costs) system became the basis for all prices, the answer is still inconclusive. On the one hand theories of perfect competition suggest a clear relationship between efficient markets, the prices for products, and the prices for factors. On the other hand Chapter 5 shows that in East Germany the substitution of capital and labour was not very price elastic. Even though the measure is good, in the case of East Germany the conditions are problematic.

Dietzenbacher and Wagener compare the 'given' East German prices with the 'actual' relative scarcities for 1987. The estimation of these relative scarcities are based on a calculation of Seton's eigenprices.[69] This method of eigenprices derives two sets of data that are brought together to obtain one set of prices. The first set of data is based on factor costs for each commodity. It also contains 'indirect factor costs' such as raw materials and other intermediate inputs. Clearly this first set of data resembles the *Selbstkosten* of products, albeit that Seton does not yet aggregate the costs of the different factors. The second set of data derives the contribution of factors (and commodities) to final use for all final commodities. After solving these two sets of data mathematically a set of prices for factors and products emerges which have been named the 'eigenprice' set of the system.

After comparing West German eigenprices with West German actual prices and East German eigenprices with East German actual prices Dietzenbacher and Wagener conclude that "East German data deserve a similar treatment as West German data, since, on the whole they are not worse than West German data".[70] The result does not imply, however, that East German pricing was more or less guided by relative scarcities. The crucial part in the explanation of Dietzenbacher and Wagener is that a sizeable part of West German GDP is not produced under competitive market conditions either. Therefore, according to my interpretation of the conclusion of Dietzenbacher and Wagener, we should appease with the fact that price data are not ideal.

Thus Marer was right about the uncertainty to what is being measured, especially for the period until 1967. For the period since the 'new economic system' there is some reason to relax upon this uncertainty, because East German relative prices proved of similar quality as West German prices.

---

[69] Seton (1992)

[70] Dietzenbacher and Wagener (1999) p. 145

Dealing with East German prices

The output series in this thesis are based on physical quantity indicators. Price data were used as weights to aggregate the change in quantities of physical products to the level of branches, from branches to sectors, and when sectors were aggregated to total GDP. According to Marer the administered prices may affect the growth indexes if the component volume indexes are dispersed and there is a correlation between the extent of price distortion and the relative growth of the volume indexes.

In this research I weighted my series at East German unit values, branch value added and sector value added in 1991, which is the first year after the unification of the two German economies.[71] At that time East Germany was a market economy, so that there is less 'uncertainty as to what is being measured'. Even though on the whole East German prices were found not all that less accurate as West German prices, within the sectors where the market prevailed, West German prices were of better quality. This is particularly the case for the industrial sector, which is the core of this thesis' research.

As indicated by Gerschenkron growth rates based on physical indicators depend on the year for which the weights are chosen.[72] The choice for only one year, the end year 1991, makes the series a fixed-weight index of the Paasche-type. A disadvantage of the use of a fixed-weight index is that it ignores changes of relative prices in the periods remote from the base-year. As a result of this bias the series of this study may be downward biased. Generally chained index series, with annual weights for the physical products, are considered to be most appropriate. In the case of East Germany – at least for the period before 1967, and to a lesser extent also for the industrial sector – relative scarcities need not be better represented in prevailing East German prices than in the base year used in this study.

Other approaches that are based on quantity indicators also dealt with the problem of weighting. In a two step aggregation Alton first aggregates physical quantity indices to branch series using prices, and thereafter aggregates branches (and sectors) using adjusted factor cost weights. This method was inspired by the ideas developed by Bergson (1961) for estimating the production potential of the Soviet Union.[73] The same valuation standard has also been applied by the CIA, which makes it the dominating approach for "western" statistics on centrally planned economies.

Adjusted factor costs are based on the rewards for labour, capital and land.[74] Rewards for labour are based on branch statistics on employment and average annual earnings. Using these data total earnings per branch are calculated, which after a mark-up for social security contributions gives an estimate for the total returns to labour. Rewards

[71] See Annex A and Annex B for more details on the aggregation procedure.

[72] Gerschenkron (1962)

[73] Bergson (1961)

[74] The following is based on a calculation of adjusted factor cost weights for East Germany in 1975 in Alton, *et al.* (1981)

for capital are based on the estimates on the depreciated value of fixed capital and working capital. In the case of agriculture the return to land is estimated on the assumption that the return to land equals the net return to all other agricultural fixed and working capital.

Alton reweights his index several times, confined to the industrial sector using adjusted factor cost weights for 1958, 1968, and 1975. Even if prices reflected relative scarcities during the 1980s fairly well, the use of adjusted factor cost weights rather than official East German prices clearly improved the series. Methods for calculating prices in East Germany changed several times and especially before the 1960s several prices were still fixed at their 1944 level. However, there is an important drawback as well. Because prices for 1958 were absent, Alton used Hungarian prices for the first step of aggregation. For later years Alton assumed similarities between the East German and the Czechoslovak wage structure, and he applied Czechoslovak and Hungarian branch ratios of net depreciated versus full replacement values of fixed capital assets for his calculation of the adjusted factor costs.

Such assumptions, in the words of Wilkens, carry boldness to the pitch of heroism.[75] East Germany was more advanced in its industrial structure than Hungary and Czechoslovakia, in particular during the 1950s and 1960s. This can, for example, be illustrated by a higher production of electricity per million inhabitants, which in 1966 amounted to 3332 GWh in East Germany, 2565 GWh in Czechoslovakia, and 1165 GWh in Hungary. Even though Hungary and Czechoslovakia were on the same side of the iron curtain, I doubt whether such a similarity of wage structures, depreciation rates and prices existed.

Instead of using East German prices or East German (adjusted) factor costs for aggregation, it is also possible to use West German prices or prices of the German *Reich* before the two parts were split up. Stolper, who claims that for the 1950s West German prices reflect East German relative scarcities relatively well, follows this approach.[76] The use of a base-year before the two parts of Germany were divided, i.e. 1936, very much resembles the procedure of this study, where a base-year after unification of East Germany and West Germany was used. However, Stolper based the calculations on prices of the German *Reich*, i.e. figures for total Germany in 1936. This study uses *East German* prices in 1991. For this purpose it should be recognised that regional price structures, in particular between East Germany and West Germany, differ.[77]

The approaches that start from the official series (Merkel and Wahl, Schwarzer, Wilkens, and Sturm) made no serious attempt to deal with the 'meaning' of East German prices. Of these approaches the one of Merkel and Wahl is probably most frequently quoted. However, there are other scholars who state more clearly why they refrained

75 Wilkens (1981) p. 67

76 Stolper (1960) pp. 85–88

77 Müller (1999)

from doing anything about the East German prices. According to Wilkens it is important to bear in mind for what purpose the figures are used. He argues the official statistics are suitable to "gauge the macroeconomic significance of the various sectors, but not without reservations for intertemporal efficiency comparisons".[78] Sturm follows the path to legitimise the use of official data by criticising the alternatives. He argues that the alternative "indices are ill-suited to a correction of the valuation bias" and "thus" accepts the official NMP index.[79] His type of reasoning is not followed here. Disbelief that the problem of administered prices can be solved adequately does not logically imply that the official series are the best series available.

The more positive adherence to the official statistics as can be found in Schwarzer argues that the official statistics were not so bad after all.[80] He refers to experts who believe that despite distorted prices for particular products, with regard to the "productive sectors" the official East German statistics were as good as in the west.[81] This is a similar positive sound as was found in the above mentioned analysis of the East German price structure in comparison with West Germany by Dietzenbacher and Wagener. However, Dietzenbacher and Wagener as well as the experts Schwarzer referred to, confined their conclusion to the late 1980s. What about the earlier periods?

In a search for the 'phantom economy' it should be noted that the East German growth rates might be overstated by the choice of early base-years. By using an early base-year the rapid growth of fairly new products accounts for a (too) large share in total growth, as new products are often characterised by high prices and high growth rates. However, the series used in Merkel and Wahl and also in Schwarzer are based on the prices and the economic structure of 1985, which is a late base-year.

2.3. Methodological shortcomings

In the discussion of methodological shortcomings there are two problems that need to be addressed. Firstly there is a "reporting" bias. This refers to the fact that enterprise managers and officials at all levels in the administrative hierarchy were judged and rewarded on the criterion whether or not they are increasing production. Thus nearly everyone had a material interest in reporting high production figures. Marer categorises this problem as a system-induced bias.[82] As a result the figures were biased upward. At

78 Wilkens, (1981) p 76–83

79 Sturm (1974) pp. 154–160: To be more precise Sturm accepts the official NMP index after adjusting it for the exclusion of depreciation allowances and adding an estimate for value added in the "non-productive" sectors of the East German economy.

80 Schwarzer (1999) p. 110

81 Schwarzer refers to Ludwig and Stäglin (1996) p. 96

82 Marer (1985) p. 167

the same time the regime provided some effective safeguards in the law – which were actively supervised – therefore in general statistics reported by enterprises are reliable.[83]

The second problem is related to the method of deflation for computing growth rates at constant prices. For this purpose "double-deflation" methods were used: deflating inputs and outputs separately by means of the appropriate price index. The necessary statistics to enable these calculations were provided by the enterprises, which gave production figures in current prices and *also* in prices of the previous year.[84] It should be emphasised that the method for deflation as described above is "perfectly acceptable".[85] Nevertheless two deflation-biases occur in these series; one due to the absence of fixed prices in the 1950s, and the other due to the introduction of new products.

> For the 1950s, when prices for specific products differed per plant, in the calculation of an index in supposedly constant prices different prices were used for the same product. As a result "production" can increase simply because a good is produced by an inefficient firm instead of an efficient one and hence is counted at a higher price.[86] At the same time "production" decreases if a good is produced by an efficient firm instead of an inefficient one.
> For "new" products there are no constant prices of the previous year, because at that time they were not in production. The constant price of a new product is often the temporary price set for it in the current period of its production. As there was no agreement on the definition of what a new product was, this allowed enterprises to blow up their production in constant prices with some slightly redesigned products, just so that they could be labelled new products.

On the whole these methodological shortcomings give the official East German growth rates an upward bias. In order to avoid the introduction of this bias into the new series it is possible to make some adjustments or to simply ignore the official growth rates and start from different data. Merkel and Wahl revaluate the East German production data in West German currency by means of a "specific exchange coefficient". This coefficient was developed by them using several indicators such as quality of the products, price disturbances, productivity differences with West Germany, but also the official exchange rate of the two currencies. According to Merkel and Wahl this revaluation shows East German product according to "western" quality standards.[87]

Unfortunately the series of Merkel and Wahl suffer of ill documentation regarding the conversion of the estimates in East German currency into West German currency. The main problem is that the consistency and importance of the underlying indicators

---

83 Ludwig and Stäglin (1997) p.61
84 Collier (1985) pp. 11–13; Heske (1993) pp. 58–61
85 Marer (1985) p. 167
86 Rumen Janakieff, "Kritische Bemerkungen zur Anwendung der Kennziffer Bruttoproduktion für die Einschätzung der Produktionsarbeit des Industriebetriebes" in: *SP*; as quoted in Stolper (1960)
87 Merkel and Wahl (1991) p. 50

remain unclear. For this reason the series were criticised by Schwarzer.[88] He suggested that it concerns a major interpolation between the exchange values for 1946 and for 1990.[89] As an alternative for the "specific exchange coefficient" Schwarzer proposed to apply several "exchange rates" in order to arrive at a range of outcomes which set the boundaries. For this purpose Schwarzer uses indicators based on the terms of trade, the *Rentenüberleitungsgesetz*, the value of *valutamark* versus *DM-Ost*, and a price comparison with West Germany. The central question for this section is whether these 'exchange rates' filter out the methodological shortcomings, i.e. the introduction of new products and the absence of fixed prices in the early period.

Without going into the details of these 'exchange rates' it is clear that the procedure involves a deflation which adjusts for varying product prices. This applies for the introduction of slightly modified 'new' products as well as for the absence of fixed prices in the 1950s. This can be illustrated with the terms of trade. Suppose East Germany tries to sell these modified products abroad, will it get the same price increase as within East Germany? Only insofar the modification is really an improvement.

However, the results are still misty as they rely on macroeconomic package-information. The example of terms of trade only refers to the goods that are traded – the valutamark versus the *DM-Ost* also refers to traded goods – and the *Rentenüberleitungsgesetz* relates to social security that needed to be transposed into West German currency in 1991. A drawback of the trade related 'exchange rates' is that these indexes only refer to tradable and also that they include other changes than the required deflation for the methodological shortcomings, such as international competitiveness. With regard to the social security I am not sure that a law of 1991 – aimed to ascertain that social benefits in East Germany would not fall below the existence minimum in the 1990s – adequately filters out the observed shortcomings.

The series in this thesis need no such adjustment as they ignore the official growth rates and start from different data. They are entirely based on physical quantity indicators, which by their nature make no distinction whether products are produced at a plant with high or low prices. Thus the methodological problem of the absence of fixed prices in the early period has no effects on the series. Furthermore the physical quantity indicators are by nature deflated for the price increases that followed only minor product modifications. A litre of milk is accounted for as a litre of milk, a bicycle is accounted for as a bicycle, and a fridge is accounted for as a fridge. Series based on physical quantity indicators filter out the methodological shortcomings, though are often criticised for filtering out too much as they supposedly ignore the 'real' quality improvements of products. In theory this would give these series a downward bias, though it is stated in

---

88 Schwarzer (1999) pp 155–168

89 Schwarzer (1996) p. 184; This also makes clear that the plausibility of the data for the beginning and the end of the period, which Ritschl and Spoerer consider as the main advantage of the Merkel and Wahl series, does not say anything about the soundness of the methodology. See Ritschl and Spoerer (1997) p. 35

Chapter 5 – where the quality issue is discussed in more detail – that for the centrally planned East German economy the effects are probably smaller than for the West German market economy.

In the series of Alton the East German growth rates were also based on physical quantity indicators. However, Alton does not ignore the official growth rates altogether as he uses a mixed sample including several products in East German currency at constant prices. Instead of filtering these products out of the sample, Alton preferred to include these products to increase the size of his sample.[90] Furthermore the Alton series are also criticised because it does not adequately measure quality improvements and the introduction of new products, which gives the growth rates a downward bias. It has been argued that the inclusion of value indicators includes quality improvements and thus offsets this particular bias.[91] As it is discussed above, however, besides quality improvements these value indicators encompass a bias due to measurement issues. Therefore it is concluded that the upward bias of the unadjusted value indicators probably offsets the downward bias because of the quality improvements, leading to an upward bias of the series.

Here it is also important that the use of value indicators is concentrated in particular branches, i.e. 'machinery and transports', 'electrical equipment', 'textiles and wearing apparel'. Other branches such as for example 'chemicals, plastics, rubber, oil refining', 'paper and printing', and 'food, beverages and tobacco' are only based on quantity indicators. As the direction of the bias – and also the extent of the bias – in the sample of Alton differs across branches, the appropriateness of his data when dealing with for instance structural change has been reduced. It is therefore preferate to construct series that only use physical indicators, as was done in this thesis. This is shown in an example of the 'machinery and transports' branch.

The example of Machinery and Transports

The example is confined to the 'machinery and transports' branch during the 1980s. There are good reasons to focus on this particular period and branch. Regarding the period it is generally believed that the 1980s are the most problematic decade for the *reliability* of the East German statistics. According to Von der Lippe data were left out of the statistics owing to a fall in output.[92] Although this can be legitimate if the importance of this particular product becomes negligible, it potentially introduces a selection bias with regard to the representativity of data. In this respect the examination of another period would lead to less pronounced results. Furthermore the almost complete overview of what was produced in East Germany during the last decade of its existence

---

[90] Alton *ed.* (1972) p. 40

[91] Paul Marer (1985) pp 173–178

[92] Von der Lippe (1995)

as an independent nation in a publication of the (West) German statistical office after the reunification offers a good standard of evaluation.[93]

In comparison with other branches the sample of 'machinery and transports' is most appropriate to compare different sources of data. Firstly it is possible to use the available quantity data for products that were produced. Secondly one can extend the sample based on quantity indicators by adding products for which the East German statistical office only gave data at constant (East German) prices. Thirdly the estimate can be based on the official gross output series at constant prices. Obviously these three different samples relate to the constructed series of respectively this thesis, Alton, and Merkel and Wahl. Whereas this thesis only uses quantity indicators, the Alton-series are based on the mixture of quantity indicators and data for products at constant prices. Merkel and Wahl started at the official series in constant prices. It should be emphasised that this merely concerns the underlying data of these series, as for the actual series additional calculations were carried out.

To determine the appropriateness of the three sources, each particular product – or in the case of the official gross output series each particular industry – was indexed to 1980. The sample of quantity indicators only used all 11 products for which the East German statistical office showed the produced quantity of 1980 and 1989. For the sample with both quantity indicators and value indicators the East German statistical yearbook contained 37 products, and the third source – the official gross output series – distinguished 18 industries. The percentage distribution of index outcomes is shown for these samples and for the data of the (West) German statistical office after reunification, which is seen as the evaluation standard.

The spreading of index outcomes for 57 products in the 'machinery and transports' branch that were found in a publication of the West German statistical office were used as a standard of evaluation. It is believed that the West German statistical office had no interest in leaving out data owing to a fall of production for propagandistic purposes, so that a comparison with the East German statistics gives an indication whether a selection bias was apparent.

The sample based on quantity data resembles the spread of outcomes according to the West German statistical office most. It shows only a minor bias towards the higher growth indices, which becomes also apparent in the unweighted average (mean) of 101 versus 95 according to the post-unification data.

A main drawback of a pure quantity indicators sample is that the size of the sample is relatively small in comparison to a sample elaborated with value indicators. For this reason the Alton series included German *mark* value series to represent a given subgroup, especially for machinery.[94] The result of the elaboration is a mean of 131, which is 36 percent points above the data of the West German statistical office after

93 Statistisches Bundesamt (1993)

94 Alton ed. (1972) p. 40

Graph 2.1. Spreading of index outcomes for 1989 (1980 = 100), percentage of outcomes per index range

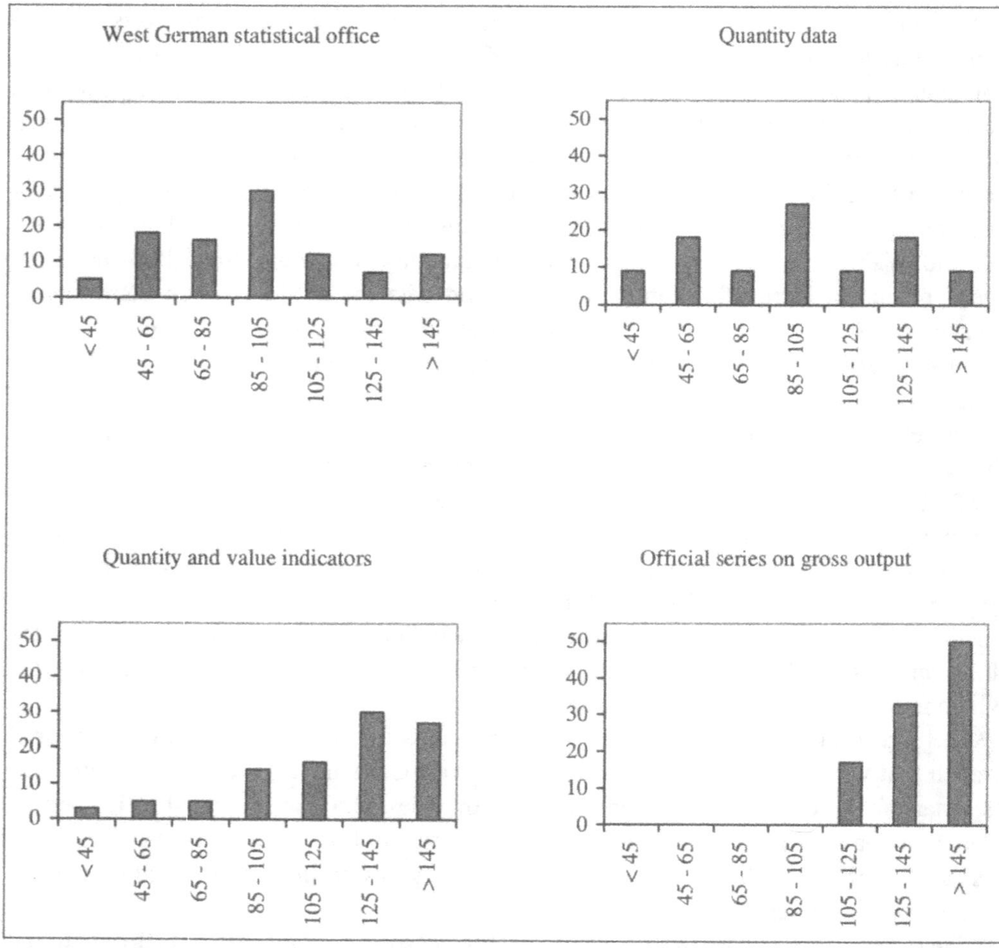

Sources: Statistisches Bundesamt (1993); Statistisches Jahrbuch der Deutschen Demokratischen Republik 1990 (1990)

unification. According to the graph the spread of the observations of this sample has an upward bias, which makes clear that the problem is not caused by some outliers.

Clearly the third example based on official series on gross output, where the mean amounts to 157, overestimates the actual development even more. The cause of this deviation is related to the methodological shortcomings that were discussed earlier in this section. Without any adjustment the sample solely based on quantity indicators is clearly most appropriate. In the case of the Alton series no adjustment was made for the harm that was done due to the elaboration of the sample with value indicators. Therefore the data set of Alton is bound to lead to an upward bias.[95] In the case of the series by Merkel and Wahl it is more complicated to draw a conclusion here, as they did make an adjustment for the methodological shortcomings.

To end up with, there are several serious problems concerning the East German statistics that need to be solved. Despite the confusion these problems may cause, the evidence is not sufficient for the harsh accusation of falsification. Therefore it seems reasonable to follow the conclusion of the (West) German statistical office that there is little evidence that East German data was directly falsified.

2.4 Coverage of the 'nonmaterial' services

The final difference between the statistics in East Germany and in West Germany originates from the concept of macroeconomic bookkeeping that was used. As in other centrally planned economies East Germany used the material product system (MPS) whereas West Germany used the system of national accounts (SNA). As a result East Germany excluded the "non-productive services" and depreciation from the measure of aggregate output, i.e. net material product (NMP).[96]

According to the vocabulary of the MPS there is a distinction between "productive" or "material" services and "non-productive" or "nonmaterial" services. Material services such as transports and communications and trade were distinguished in the statistics. Among the excluded nonmaterial services are for example public administration, health care and education.

The coverage of the "nonmaterial" services affects the statistics on production, as well as the statistics on employment. For production the exclusion of nonmaterial services underestimates the actual production at the time. Whether this gives a downward or an upward bias of the growth rates depends on the increase of production in the nonmaterial services relative to the increase of production in the covered sectors. Furthermore there is some uncertainty whether nonmaterial services are accounted for as intermediate inputs. Issues regarding the input output relationship are discussed in Chapter 5.

For employment it is important to find out if the nonmaterial employees were not mentioned at all or whether they were hidden in some other categories. Using the statistics of the former Soviet Union it proved to be a difficult problem to estimate the nonmaterial employment figures.[97] As employment data also provides the main source for estimates on the production in the East German nonmaterial sector, the classification of these services seems to be of particular interest.

---

95 See also: Fink and Havlik (1989)

96 World Bank (1993) p. 8

97 Kouwenhoven (1997)

Employment

After the reunification of the two parts of Germany in 1991, the statistical office (Statistisches Bundesamt) published a study on the East German employment statistics. This study examines into detail what data on employment were included and what data were excluded from the official statistics.[98] Firstly the statistics did not provide figures for the so-called "X-bereich", which means that employment statistics for e.g. the army, police, *stasi*, (political) party's and organisations, SDAG Wismut and Zentrag were omitted. Most of these belong to the nonmaterial employment, however, SDAG Wismut (uranium) and Zentrag (publishing) are a part of the material sectors.

Secondly the East German employment concept "Berufstätige" exclude women on maternity leave, whereas these women are included in the concept of "Erwerbstätige". For time series there is clearly more to it than simply look at the fluctuation in the number of births, as regulation on the duration of this leave is important as well. The trend of the number of births was decreasing, whereas the duration of the leave increased. For the employment indices from 1950 to 1989 the effect of this difference is probably minor.

The third difference concerns the definition of a sector. Some parts of a sector according to the East German statistics should be attributed to another sector according to the West German statistics. This is also important for the continuity of the statistics before and after reunification. For this purpose the (West) German statistical office calculated a matrix which shows the amount of people employed into one sector according to the East German "Berufstätige" and to another according to the West German "Erwerbstätige". As the "Berufstätige" of a specific sector primarily cover employed persons of that sector, it can be held representative for the development of employment in that specific sector for the period from 1950 to 1989. The table below distinguishes sectors according to the "Berufstätige" concept and shows the percentage of employed persons in the same sector according to the "Erwerbstätige" concept, as well as the percentage that should be attributed to another sector.

For most sectors the representativity of data on 'Berufstätige' for 'Erwerbstätige' seems acceptable, however, for the remaining services and to a far lesser extent for trade this is clearly problematic. For agriculture, industry, construction and transports the number of people attributed to the same sector indicates that employment data did not – at least not systematically – hide nonmaterial employees in these sectors. At the same time there were some differences for the classification of workers within manufacturing across different industries.[99]

---

98 Statistisches Bundesamt (1994)

99 See Görzig (1991)

Table 2.3. Comparison of the East German employment concept 'Berufstätige' and the West German employment concept 'Erwerbstätige' in 1989

Berufstätige (MPS)	Erwerbstätige (SNA)	
	Attributed to the same sector	Attributed to another sector
Agriculture[a]	99.3%	0.7%
Industry[b]	99.7%	0.3%
Construction[c]	98.4%	1.6%
Trade[d]	90.9%	9.1%
Transports[e]	96.0%	4.0%
Remaining (Material) Services[f]	82.1%	17.9%
Nonmaterial Services[g]	95.9%	4.1%
Education, Health[h]	98.0%	2.0%
Government[i]	100.0%	0.0%

Source: Statistisches Bundesamt (1994)
Notes: [a] MPS: Land- und Forstwirtschaft; SNA: Land- und Forstwirtschaft, Fischerei; [b] MPS: Industrie; SNA: Energie- und Wasserversorgung, Bergbau, Verarbeitendes Gewerbe; [c] MPS: Bauwirtschaft; SNA: Baugewerbe; [d] MPS: Handel; SNA: Handel; [e] MPS: Verkehr, Post- und Fernmeldewesen; SNA: Verkehr und Nachrichtenübermittlung; [f] MPS: Sonstige Zweige des Produzierenden Bereiches; SNA: a category which in total corresponds to the MPS categories (f), (g), (h), (i), i.e. Dienstleistungen von Unternehmen und freien Berufen, Gebietskörperschaften und Sozialversicherung, Kreditinstitute und Versicherungsgewerbe, Organisationen ohne Erwerbszweck und private Haushalte; [g] MPS: Dienstleistende Wirtschaft; SNA: see (f); [h] MPS: Wissenschaft, Bildung, Kultur, Gesundheits- und Sozialwesen; SNA: see (f); [i] MPS: Staatliche Verwaltung, gesellschaftliche Organisationen; SNA: see (f)

Production

Due to lack of appropriate data estimates on the production of the 'non productive sectors' are based on employment or employment related data. Despite the common source the differences are substantial. Whereas Stolper assumes labour productivity to remain the same in this sector, Sturm assumes that labour productivity in the non-productive sectors was similar as in West Germany. The assumption of Sturm is clearly inappropriate, as the structure of this sector was very different in the two parts of Germany. Underdeveloped services in East Germany in comparison with West Germany were banking, insurances, advertising agencies, travel agencies, and lawyers.[100]

As far as the other approaches are concerned the conclusions are too much mixed. Clearly the use of wages as in Wilkens is a common practice for western countries. However, as the East German statistics only showed information on the productive sectors these estimates were built on an assumed correlation of the wage and salary

[100] Merkel and Wahl (1991)

structures in East and West Germany. This implied that the estimates on East German incomes in the non-producing sector are based on East German incomes in the producing sector extrapolated with the West German wage structure. Although Wilkens found such correlations between the East and West German wage and salary structures for the productive sectors in his empirical testing, it might be argued that the extension to the non producing sectors stretched this evidence too far. Therefore the alternative of Stolper and Alton, assuming a constant labour productivity in this sector, may prove more useful. Their assumption has been commonly made in Western countries just as the assumption of using income as in Wilkens.[101]

Another example from the literature, the estimates of Merkel and Wahl, were based on information on productivity growth in the 1980s from statistics that became available after the fall of the Berlin Wall in 1989, which were linked up with employment statistics. As a result they showed a minor change in labour productivity over this period. Unfortunately their precise method and data were not clearly documented.

If all these estimates are linked up with employment or employment related data; how useful are the statistics on employment for such a purpose? A major drawback of having to rely on employment data is that any estimate on production ultimately requires an assumption on the increase of labour productivity. Moreover, the exclusion of the "X-Bereich" might introduce some difficulties as the increase of employment of the nonmaterial production that is not covered might differ from the increase of employment that is covered.

However, what is the alternative? This thesis opted to focus on material production as did the centrally planned economies. The nonmaterial part was derived from the aggregates for material production that were linked up with Gross Domestic Product (in 1991). The implicit assumption is that nonmaterial production increased the same as material production. For labour productivity this led to a modest increase in the nonmaterial sectors, as was the case in Merkel and Wahl.

Finally, this section provides an overview of the estimates on East German growth of the authors that have been discussed. It shows the name of the author in alphabetical order, the period that is covered in the particular research, and the methods that have been applied.

---

101 U.S. Department of Commerce, *U.S. Income and Output*: as quoted in: Thad P. Alton (1975)

Table 2.4. Overview of estimates on East German growth

Author	Coverage	Methodology
Alton (1972, 1975, 1980, 1983, 1990)	1950–89	The non-productive sectors are estimated using employment data and assuming a constant labour productivity. The series are largely built up from quantity indicators. At the level of sectors and branches the series were aggregated using "adjusted factor cost" weights.
Merkel and Wahl (1991)	1950–89	The non-productive sectors are estimated using employment data and assuming a minor increase of labour productivity. The series depart from the official growth series at constant prices for the productive sectors. The outcomes are revalued in West German DM by means of a "specific exchange coefficient".
Schwarzer (1999)	1950–89	Departs from Merkel and Wahl estimates before revaluation in West German DM. Uses various "exchange rates" to show a range of different outcomes in West German currency.
Stolper (1960)	1936–58	The non-productive sectors are estimated using employment data and assuming a constant labour productivity. The series on the other sectors are built up from quantity indicators. The sectors and branches were aggregated using 1936 and 1950-prices and/or West German prices.
Sturm (1974)	1950–70	The non-productive sectors are estimated using employment data and assuming a similar labour productivity increase as in West Germany. The series on the productive sectors are built up from official growth series at constant prices.
Wilkens (1976)	1960–76	The non-productive sectors are estimated using data on the incomes of personnel. These incomes were estimated from data on the productive sector, assuming the same differentials between the producing and non-producing sector as in West Germany. Official growth rates at constant prices are used for the productive sectors.

Chapter 3: East German GDP

3. 1 International perspective

Before the Second World War East Germany's economic performance was somewhat above the West German level. Grünig estimated the East German gross domestic product (GDP) per head of the population in 1936 at 103 per cent of West Germany, and per person employed at 102 per cent of West Germany.[102] Calculations on data in the *Statistisches Handbuch von Deutschland 1928-1944* suggests that East German GDP per head of the population was even higher, at 107 per cent of West Germany.[103]

Estimates for 1932 and 1934 arrive at similar results,[104] even though the 1930s are very much influenced by the economic crisis so that annual statistics on GDP are volatile. Nevertheless it appears that the cyclical variations did not change the relative GDP per capita of East Germany in comparison with West Germany. According to Ritschl (2002) the depression of the 1930s was more severe in Germany than in other European countries. However, by 1936 Germany surpassed its pre-depression levels of national product.[105]

In 1991, the first year after the unification of the two German economies, the East German economy comes out badly in comparison with West Germany. During this year East German GDP per head of the population and also per person employed amounted to merely 31 per cent of the West German level.[106] What explains for the East German falling behind relative to West Germany? Was it a bad start after the ending of the Second World War; was it a bad growth performance from the early 1950s to the 1980s; or was it related to the unification of East Germany and West Germany in 1990?

Table 3.1. compares the expansion of East German GDP from 1950 to 1989 with some western European countries. It shows that growth of East German GDP was higher

---

102 Grünig (1948)

103 Länderrat des Amerikanischen Besatzungsgebiets (1949) pp. 600, 601; I divided Berlin into two equal parts of 50 percent.

104 Idem

105 Ritschl (2002) p. 561, 562

106 Statistisches Bundesamt

Table 3.1. East German GDP in 1989 (1950 = 100) in comparison with West Germany, Belgium, France, Netherlands, and United Kingdom

	East Germany	West Germany	Belgium	France	Netherlands	United Kingdom
1950	100	100	100	100	100	100
1989	341	491	353	454	409	270

Sources: Annex B; Maddison (1995)

than in the United Kingdom and comparable with Belgium. The underlying series for East Germany were discussed in more detail in Chapter 2. Intuition might suggest that the growth performance, and perhaps also economic policy and the economic system, were not so bad after all. In my view such a conclusion would be inappropriate, as for the purpose of comparing the performance of economic policies or the economic systems the criterion of the growth rates should be related to the growth potential.

Supposedly the East German initial conditions had been good, than the expansion of its GDP as shown in Table 3.1. could also be considered good. Especially if one bears in mind that the size of the East German population was declining. However, in 1950 the relative level of GDP per capita (and also per worker) was already relatively low. As will be discussed more elaborately in Section 3.3. and the following chapters, in my view it is *because* of the bad initial conditions that the growth of East German GDP can be seen as troublesome.

Chapter 2 already discussed alternative estimates of the East German growth rates. The East German growth performance as shown in Table 3.1. is based on this study's estimates. Series of Maddison, which are based on the Alton series of the Research Project on National Income in East Central Europe, show a similar picture for the initial and end year – though a somewhat different development inbetween. Table 3.2. shows that Merkel and Wahl arrived at a much worse growth performance of the East German economy.

Table 3.2. East German growth rates of GDP according to different series

	East Germany			West Germany
	This study	Merkel & Wahl	Maddison	ICOP
1950–1989	3.1	2.3	3.3	4.3
1950–1960	6.7	3.6	5.5	8.0
1960–1970	2.7	2.5	2.9	4.4
1970–1980	2.6	2.5	2.8	2.8
1980–1989	0.3	0.5	1.6	1.9

Sources: ICOP [107], Merkel and Wahl (1991), Maddison (1995), Annex B

[107] The International Comparisons of Output and Productivity (ICOP) project was set up at the University of Groningen under the direction of Angus Maddison in 1983. It carries out industry of origin comparisons of sectoral output and productivity across countries, and now covers about 30 countries in Asia, East and West Europe, and North and South America.

No matter what set of data is used, in all cases the growth estimates of East German GDP are below West German growth. Especially for the 1960s and 1970s the various estimates for East German growth are very similar. However, estimations differ more during the 1950s and the 1980s. A closer look at the underlying methodologies of the series, which I discussed in Chapter 2, sheds light on the origin of the different estimation results. In my view the explanation for this is the method of deflating the productive sectors, as the estimates for the non-productive sectors (which relate to the adjustment for the deviant systems of national accounting) are not too different in these three sets of data. In all cases production of the non-productive sector is based on employment data. The Alton series that are used by Maddison assume a constant labour productivity, Merkel and Wahl and this study arrive at a modest increase of labour productivity.

Stolper (1960) estimated East German annual growth from 1950 to 1958 at 6.3 per cent (based on prices of 1950) and 5.8 per cent (based on prices of 1936). This is close to the estimates of this study and the estimates of Maddison respectively, though much higher than the figures of Merkel and Wahl. Estimates of Sturm (1977) arrived at the highest East German growth during the 1950s: 7.4 per cent.[108]

3.2. GDP in East and West Germany

The previous section showed that from 1950 to 1989 GDP rose faster in West Germany than in East Germany. This section focusses on the comparative performance of the East and West German economies in terms of per capita income and labour productivity. Graph 3.1. extrapolates relative GDP per capita and relative GDP per person employed in 1991. To indicate the importance of the development between 1936 and 1950, the graph includes Grünig's benchmark for 1936, which I consider to be accurate.[109] It should be emphasised that – except for a few years only (in particular between 1944/1945 and 1989/1991) – throughout this period East Germany realised an increase in GDP, GDP per capita, and GDP per person employed. The graph hides these actual increases, as growth in West Germany was faster.

Relative to West Germany the East German GDP per worker drops between 1936 and 1950, continuously declines from 1950 to 1989, and declines fast between 1989 and 1991. After the reunification East Germany shows a rapid convergence towards the West German level. GDP per capita shows a similar movement between 1936 and 1950: that is a sharp decrease during the German break up. Also immediately after the fall of the Berlin Wall East German GDP per capita drops relative to the West German level, followed by convergence after 1991.

---

108 Sturm (1977) p. 22

109 In 1936 the East German and West German economies were still in the same statistical system.

During the separation of the two parts of Germany from 1950 to 1989 GDP per capita in East Germany was constant at approximately 56 per cent of the West German level. The divergence between the two German economies is divided into three subperiods: from 1936 to 1950; from 1950 to 1989; and from 1989 to 1991. Most of the divergence between East Germany and West Germany occurred in the first period from 1936 to 1950. Furthermore there was a sharp decline of East German GDP per capita (and to a much lesser extent of East German GDP per worker) relative to West Germany between 1989 and 1991, and convergence thereafter.

Based on GDP per capita the East German economy performed well from 1950 to 1989, there is only little falling behind relative to West Germany. At the same time, based on GDP per worker, the East German economy performed badly. To shed light on the peculiar combination of a decreasing relative GDP per worker and a stable GDP per capita it is useful to examine the underlying elements, i.e. GDP, employment and population. Their relationship can be shown as: Y/P = Y/L * L/P; where Y stands for GDP, P

Graph 3.1. East German GDP per capita and per person employed from 1936 to 2000 (West Germany = 100)

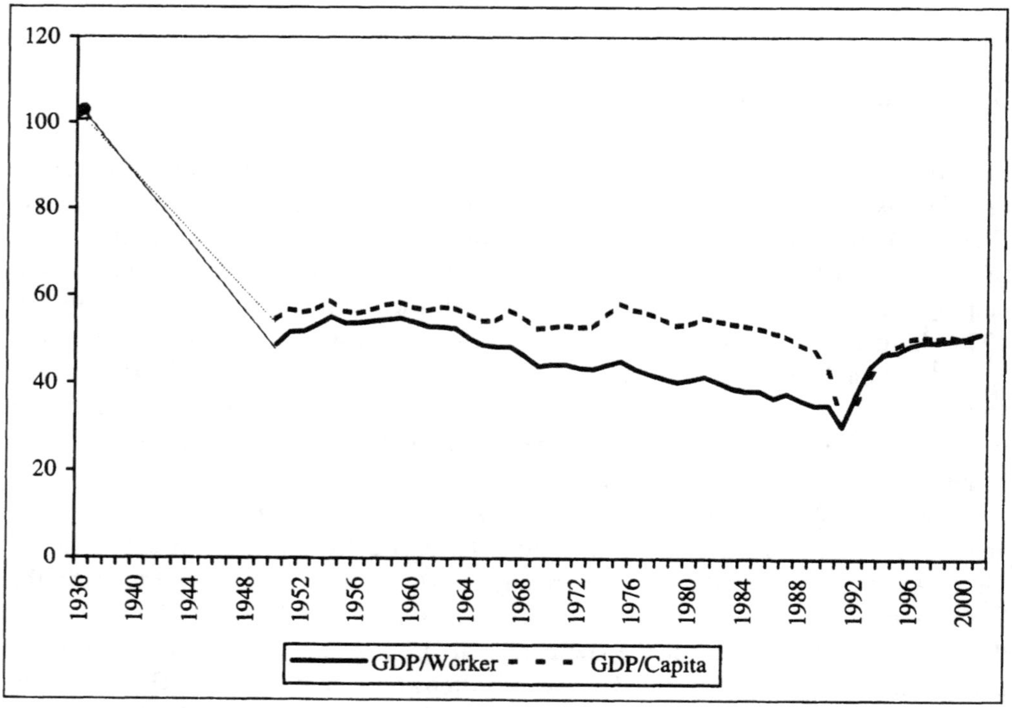

Notes: For 1936 Berlin was divided into two parts of 50 per cent; for the period after 1991 Berlin is included in West Germany

Sources: Annex B; Grünig, (1948); ICOP; Stat. Landesamt Baden-Württemberg, http://www.statistik-bw.de/VolkswPreise/ArbeitskreisVGR/tab02.asp (08-14-2002)

stands for population, and L stands for employment. As I will show below, in East Germany the relatively low growth of GDP per worker was compensated for by an increasing participation of labour, i.e. the share of employed people in per cent of the total population.

A comparison of the underlying series on population and employment in the two parts of Germany shows that East Germany combined a declining population with an increasing number of employed persons. West Germany realised a stable number of employed persons whereas the population increased. After the unification in 1990 the East German population decreased even faster than before, whereas West Germany had a higher increase. This reflects the migration from East Germany towards West Germany. At the same time the East German participation ratio – calculated as the percentage of employed persons as a percentage of the total population – converged to West Germany.

Table 3.3. Population (millions) and participation of labour (per cent); 1950–1998

	1950	1960	1970	1980	1989	1998
Population						
East Germany	18.4	17.1	17.1	16.7	16.4	15.3
West Germany	50.0	55.4	60.7	61.6	62.1	68.0
L/P						
East Germany	45.3	49.2	51.3	56.6	59.4	39.6
West Germany	41.3	47.0	43.8	43.8	44.8	41.0

Note: Participation of labour under 1998 actually shows participation ratio for 1997.
Sources: ICOP database; Statistisches Bundesamt (1994)

In the following pages of this section I will focus on the period from 1950 to 1989. During this period East Germany shrunk from a country with 18.4 million inhabitants in 1950 to 16.4 million in 1989. This is to a large extent explained by the migration of almost 3 million East Germans to West Germany between 1950 and 1961, when the Berlin Wall was built. In spite of a decreasing population more people got employed. To some extent this is related to the fact that given the age composition of the population within sub-periods the workforce population actually increased. Moreover East Germany achieved a very high participation of women in the working process of more than 82 percent of the female workforce population in 1983. At that time participation of women in West Germany was 55 percent of the female workforce population.[110] Finally it can be observed that participation of males was also higher in East Germany (88 percent versus 79 percent), which marks a lower unemployment rate. After 1990

110 Bundesministerium für innerdeutsche Beziehungen (1987) p. 277

East Germany faced high unemployment; so that the actual participation ratio became much lower than before the unification.[111]

For East German standard of living during the 1970s and 1980s – here measured as GDP per capita – the high participation ratio compensated for the relatively low labour productivity. High levels of labour productivity are sometimes associated with hard working; growth of labour productivity is confused with increasing work intensity. Especially in the case of former communist countries there is some appeal of low work intensity as an explanatory factor for low productivity levels. In the words of Landes: "When did the people in the queues work? The joke had it, they made believe they worked, and the state made believe it paid them".[112] Kopstein argues that "within the confines of the command economy" a new kind of German working class was created, "with different habits and expectations – with a different moral economy – than those characteristic of its predecessor or developing in the West".[113]

Besides work intensity many factors are at stake; factors that are more important in explaining the different performance of labour productivity than work intensity. The production function considers value added (Y) as a function of labour inputs (L) and capital inputs (K):

$$Y = f(K, L)$$

Looking at a growth accounting framework three main sources determine growth of value added: growth in labour inputs, growth in capital inputs, and total factor productivity. This can be shown as follows:

$$\Delta Y = \alpha \Delta L + \beta \Delta K + \Delta TFP$$

For the development of labour productivity this means that improvements may result of higher capital intensities (i.e. the amount of capital per worker) or of a better total factor productivity (which include technological change, and processes of factor reallocation).

Labour inputs

In the calculations of this study – unless otherwise specified – labour productivity is defined as value added per person employed. The number of persons that are employed is a rough indicator for the *quantity* of labour inputs, i.e. human resources. A more sophisticated measure for the quantity of labour inputs takes into account the actual hours worked.[114]

---

111 The period after the (re) unification of East Germany and West Germany in 1990 is analysed in Chapter 7.

112 Landes (1999) p. 496

113 Kopstein (1997) p. 21

114 Chapter 5 examines actual working hours for the industrial sector.

The *quality* of these labour inputs can be measured in several ways. A method that has been applied by Ritschl looks at the costs of formally recognised schooling and training.[115] Ritschl concluded that East German human capital was generally at a high level. Statistics for 1995 confirm that East German human capital was at a high level. In East Germany over 91 percent of the population completed formal education, against 82 per cent in West Germany.[116] On the other hand Hitchens, Wagner and Birnie found the East German skill levels well below that of West Germany, after comparing the performance of individual manufacturing plants. Nevertheless they concluded that general education was good and that the basic stock of East German human capital was high.[117]

Participation in primary, secondary and tertiary education as a percentage of the age group from 6 to 25 years old appears to be below the West German level. This links up with the high participation of labour as shown in Table 3.3. On average, East Germans ended their education – and started working – at a younger age than in West Germany.

Enrolment in education in East Germany was lower than in West Germany. Especially the age group from 20 to 25 years old shows a remarkable difference. It suggests that particularly the enrolment in tertiary education must have been relatively low in East Germany in comparison with West Germany. In primary and secondary education differences were less pronounced, although in 1982 enrolment in education of 15 to 20 years old is about 10 percent points higher in West Germany than in East Germany.

In comparison with West Germany, paradoxically, a higher percentage of the East German population had completed formal education in 1995, whereas education enrolment in the 1970s and 1980s was lower. The following considerations can explain the paradox. To begin with there are people who have enroled education though have not completed it. Completion as a percentage of enrolment was higher in East Germany.[118] Secondly, the figures on completed formal education in 1995 give a percentage of the total population. It is likely that the relatively low West German result on completed formal education is partly due to immigrants with no (or unrecognised forms of) education.

Table 3.4. Enrolment in education as a percentage of the population for age groups from 6 to 25 years old

	1973			1982		
Age-group	6–15	15–20	20–25	6–15	15–20	20–25
East Germany	93	71	7	93	71	7
West Germany	96	74	15	92	82	22

Source: Bundesministerium für innerdeutsche Beziehungen (1987) p. 321

115 Ritschl (1996)

116 Statistisches Jahrbuch 1997 (pp 383) These figures are based on a voluntary part of a questionaire.

117 Hitchens, Wagner and Birnie (1993) p. 115

118 At least this is the case for the employed people in East Germany. See: Müller (2000) p. 11

Capital inputs

The "extensive growth hypothesis" is a dominant theme in the literature on economic growth in Eastern Europe. It is stated that a main reason for the growth decline is the pattern of extensive growth, which is defined as a rising capital/output ratio.[119] According to the neo-classical model, a rising capital/output ratio implies capital deepening during the transition to a higher steady state. This capital deepening will sooner or later run into diminishing returns that will cause growth to slow or stop.

This view was rejected by Easterly and Fischer, who argued that the major problem of socialist economies was substitution between capital and labour. Easterly and Fischer suggested that "under an autocratically directed economic system, they accumulated a narrow rather than a broad range of capital goods [...]. It is more difficult to substitute more and more drill presses for a laborer than it is to substitute a drill press plus a computerized inventory and distribution system for a laborer".[120]

It indicates that there was capital widening (increase of the capacity) rather than capital deepening (increase of capital per worker). East Germany increased the production capacity; extensive industrialisation was a means to guarantee a high level of employment.[121] It is obvious that the effects on labour productivity are minimal. Building on the example of Easterly and Fischer: the purchase of an extra drill press increases the capacity and may allow for hiring a new labourer. Although total production may rise, it seems unlikely that production per worker increases. If, alternatively, investments were directed to a drill press plus a computerised inventory, machines may take over what was previously done by man. As a result production per worker would increase.

The production function framework demands for an investigation of the capital stock in the two parts of Germany. For the measurement of the size of the (East German) capital stock lots of information is needed, such as an initial benchmark estimate of the capital stock; statistics on gross fixed capital formation extending back to the benchmark, or, if no benchmark is available, back over the life of the longest-lived asset; asset price indices; information on the average service lives of different assets; information on how assets are retired around the average service life (mortality functions).[122] Especially the desired information on price indices proves to be problematic in the case of a centrally planned economy.[123] Looking at investment in capital stocks in proportion to national income, the following picture emerges.

Without the desired information on prices it is difficult to address the meaning of such a comparison. For the industrial sector it is known that for the capital stock the

---

119 Ofer (1987)
120 Easterly and Fischer (1994)
121 Abelshauser (2001) p.132
122 OECD (2001a) pp. 40 ff.
123 See Chapter 2

Table 3.5. Gross investment in capital stock in per cent of national income, current prices

	1950	1955	1960	1965	1970	1975	1980	1985
East Germany	10	14	23	24	31	30	29	26
West Germany	19	24	24	26	25	20	22	19

Notes: For East Germany gross investment not only includes machinery and dwellings, but also related charges
Sources: Baar, Müller and Zschaler (1995); Statistisches Bundesamt (1991)

suggested low investment during the 1950s was compensated for by the favourable vintage of the capital stock. Similarly high investment during the late 1960s was partly offset by high retirement of assets.[124] Looking at the total economy, it seems that gross investment relative to GDP in the East German capital stock was particularly high in the 1970s, but also in the 1980s.

According to estimates for 1991 the East German capital intensity, i.e. capital stock per worker, was much lower than in West Germany. Based on machinery only, for the private sector it was estimated at 29 per cent. Much of the East German capital stock has been regarded as technically backward and worn off.[125] This links up with Baar, Müller and Zschaler, who found that from the 1970s onwards investment focussed too much on expansion of traditional economic industrial structures and an ignorance of modernisation as well as a deterioration of infrastructure.[126] In other words, investments were directed into the wrong sectors and into the wrong capital inputs. In Chapter 4 a provisionary estimate of the East German industrial capital stock is made to indicate the components of growth in the industrial sector.

Dynamic efficiency: technological change

Technologically East Germany performed badly. Bentley wrote: "In a word, the GDR could neither keep up with the pace of Western technological developments nor could it prevent the technological gap with the FRG from becoming wider".[127] In literature there are two indicators to estimate the technological level that are used frequently: the number of patents and the expenditure on research and development. Without information on prices, the use of expenditure in research and development in per cent of national income, obviously has similar drawbacks as discussed above for the investment in capital stock.

---

124 Melzer (1980) pp. 42–44
125 IWH (1999) pp. 17–19
126 Baar, Müller, Zschaler (1995) p. 55
127 Bentley (1992)

Table 3.6. Expenditure in research and development in per cent of national income, current prices

	1970	1975	1980	1985	1989
East Germany	4.2	3.8	4.1	3.9	4.7
West Germany	2.3	2.2	2.6	2.7	2.8

Notes: Table 1970 shows 1971 (East Germany) and 1972 (West Germany)
Sources: Statistisches Jahrbuch der Deutschen Demokratischen Republik (1990) p. 111; Schwarzer (1999); Statistisches Jahrbuch für die Bundesrepublik Deutschland (various issues); Statistisches Bundesamt (1991)

A comparison of the amount of patents makes clear that the number of patents was much higher in West Germany.[128] In the period from 1970 to 1980 the number of patents in East Germany – and registered in East Germany – was on average less than 15 per cent of the number of patents in West Germany – and registered in West Germany. A comparison of the number of patents in the period from 1950 to 1980 registered in West Germany shows that East Germany had fewer patents than Switzerland, Japan, the Netherlands, and Sweden, but more than Italy, Austria, the Soviet Union and Belgium.

The East German expenditure in research and development was impressive. For the period from 1950 to 1970, that is not included in Table 2.6., Bähr and Petzina conclude that "die Betriebe in der SBZ/DDR auf vielen Gebieten noch bis in die fünfziger Jahre hinein technologisch mit der Entwicklung in Westdeutschland Schritt halten konnten". Thereafter East Germany lost track. According to Bähr and Petzina the following peculiarities determined the bad performance of East German technological growth: (a) Concentration of investments on *Schwerpunktprogramme*. This made it very difficult for other sectors to get the material resources; (b) Research and Development was oriented towards short term production objectives rather than long term development of new products, even though East Germany spent relatively a lot in R and D; (c) Low quality and availability of the products of suppliers.[129]

It is difficult to measure the benefits of technology on economic growth, though it is widely recognised as an important source for economic growth. Difficulties are particularly apparent in the economic system of the centrally planned economies. Within the confines of the growth accounting framework technological progress is included under the heading total factor productivity. This means that the contribution of technology is not purely based on measurement as it is in the basket of growth that remains unexplained by growth of labour inputs and growth of capital inputs.

Research has shown impressive results in improving the accuracy through subdividing total factor productivity into the various contributing components. Below I will

[128] Buck (1983)
[129] Bähr, Petzina eds. (1996) p. 17, 18

discuss the contribution of structural change to productivity growth. Before discussing the structural change component of total factor productivity, there is a point of Brada (1989) regarding the utilisation of factor inputs. Brada makes a distinction "between the effects of improvements in technical know how and in the application of new technologies to production and the effects of changes in the efficiency with which available factors of production are utilised".[130]

This means that the estimation of total factor productivity (and thus technological progress) is affected by the hidden unemployment component in labour inputs and the capital underutilisation component in capital inputs. I will deal with this problem in more detail in Chapter 4, in my provisional growth accounting estimate for the industrial sector.

Dynamic efficiency: factor reallocation

Some sectors achieve higher levels of labour productivity than others do. As a result it makes a difference for aggregate labour productivity in what sector people are employed. If labour is shifted from a relatively low productivity sector to a sector where labour productivity is higher, this has also positive impact on aggregate labour productivity. Therefore it is important to get a clear view on the relative *level* of sectoral labour productivity and on *changes* of the employment structure in the economy. Table 3.7 shows the employment structure in the two German economies.

The reallocation of labour inputs shows the same direction in both countries – i.e. increase or decrease of the employment shares in total – for all sectors, except mining. However, the magnitude of these changes, and the actual employment shares in total employment, show some remarkable differences. This is particularly the case in agricul-

Table 3.7. Employment structure of the two German economies, 1950–1989 (in per cent)

	East Germany			West Germany		
	1950	1970	1989	1950	1970	1989
Agriculture	25.0	11.8	10.0	23.6	8.5	3.7
Public Utilities	0.9	1.2	1.5	0.7	0.9	1.0
Mining	1.8	2.1	2.1	2.9	1.2	0.7
Manufacturing	29.9	37.4	35.0	32.3	38.1	31.4
Construction	6.6	7.3	6.4	7.4	8.7	6.6
Transports	4.8	5.8	6.8	4.7	5.3	5.6
All other sectors	31.0	34.4	38.2	28.4	37.3	51.0
Total	100.0	100.0	100.0	100.0	100.0	100.0

Sources: Annex B, ICOP database, http://www.eco.rug.nl/ggdc/index-dseries.html

130 Brada (1989) p. 434

ture and the rest-category "all other sectors" which includes "wholesale and retail trade", "finance, insurance and real estate", "community social and personal services", and "government services".

What explains the productivity performance over time, for instance between 1950 and 1989? On the one hand labour productivity improved in each sector. These sector differences are here referred to as "intra sector" and its contribution to the aggregate increase of labour productivity is called the "intra sector effect". On the other hand the aggregate increase can be the result of the so-called "shift effects". This refers to changes in the composition of production between sectors with different productivity growth rates or levels, for example whether there are more people employed in agriculture or in manufacturing.

An examination of the relative level of labour productivity across sectors shows that agriculture was a low-productivity sector and the rest-category "all other sectors" was a high-productivity sector. As Table 3.7. shows East German labour inputs moved out of agriculture and into the category "all other sectors" at a slower pace than in West Germany, and manufacturing, which is a high-productivity sector, declined less. Shift share analysis allows the estimation of the structure effect and the shift effects. Pioneers in this type of analysis were Fabricant, Kuznets, Chenery and Syrquin. The following equation was derived from Timmer, where LP = Labour Productivity and S_i = Share of employment in particular sector.[131]

$$LP^T - LP^0 = \sum_{i=1}^{n} (LP_i^T - LP_i^0)\, S_i^0 + \sum_{i=1}^{n} (S_i^T - S_i^0)\, LP_i^0 + \sum_{i=1}^{n} (S_i^T - S_i^0)\,(LP_i^T - LP_i^0)$$

After dividing both sides of the equation by LP^0, on the right hand side of the equation increases of labour productivity between 1950 and 1989 are decomposed into an intra sector effect, a static shift effect and a dynamic shift effect. The intra sector effect, which is the first term, accounts for improvements of the sector productivity levels. The static shift effect is the second term and accounts for productivity growth caused by a shift of labour towards sectors with a higher productivity level at the beginning of the period. The third term, the dynamic shift effect, measures shifts towards more dynamic sectors, i.e. sectors with higher labour productivity growth rates. If these calculations are carried out it appears that the magnitude of the different effects were somewhat different in the two economies.

Chapter 2 discussed the underlying series in more detail. Here I want to discuss the main findings. The decomposition of productivity growth between 1950 and 1989 shows a higher contribution of the combined shift effects to the aggregate productivity growth in East Germany than in West Germany. Especially the dynamic shift effects in East Germany were relatively high. This can be explained as a consequence of econo-

---

131 Marcel Timmer, *The Dynamics of Asian Manufacturing: A Comparative Perspective, 1963–1993* (Eindhoven 1999) pp. 102–105

Table 3.8. Decomposition of productivity growth from 1950 to 1989 in East and West Germany

	Annual labour productivity growth	Percentage of labour productivity growth explained by:			
		Intra sector effect	Static shift effect	Dynamic shift effect	Total effect
East Germany	2.7%	82.6	8.5	8.9	100.0
West Germany	3.6%	84.2	9.9	5.9	100.0

Source: Calculations from Annex B

mic planning. As it was shown in Chapter 1, in a centrally planned economy for firms there is no clear relationship between past decisions and current means. Instead the government allocates resources.

Regarding the investments in research and development there was a concentration on particular *Schwerpunktprogramme*. Assuming that the priority sector in terms of investment in R and D was also the priority sector for investments in capital inputs and that labour inputs were directed towards such a sector, high dynamic shift effects are a probable outcome. For instance, if the regime had a focus on (heavy) industries many investments in capital stock and technology were spent in this particular part of the economy. Within the production function framework – considering the substitutability of capital and labour – the investments in capital improve labour productivity. Investments in R and D might generate technology which also improves labour productivity. It is likely that such a priority sector achieved a high growth of labour productivity in comparison with other sectors.

Especially if defining priority sectors led to crowding out effects for non-priority sectors, i.e. non-priority sectors had great difficulties to acquire the resources for investment in capital stock and technology. It is emphasised that the high shift effects do not mean that structural change was more successful in East Germany than in West Germany; the decomposition refers to the percentage of labour productivity growth that is explained by within-sector intra effects or between-sector shift effects. For both effects the contribution in absolute terms was higher in West Germany than in East Germany. Hence East Germany needed less factor reallocation to arrive at the same structure effect.

So far it has become clear that the East German falling behind of aggregate labour productivity – GDP per worker – relative to West Germany largely took place in two sub-periods: between 1936 and 1950, and between 1950 and 1989. In the following section of this chapter I will discuss what the periodisation means for the (causal) explanation of the lag of the East German economy.

3.3. High growth of an underachiever?

In spite of a declining population, growth of East German GDP was high. Per capita GDP was at a more or less constant distance from the West German level. Only per worker GDP showed a decrease relative to West Germany, however, not as much as it had decreased between 1936 and 1950. Here I want to answer a dominant question in the literature on the origin of the East German troubles: was it a bad start, or was it a bad performance?

Chapter 1 already showed that recent literature explains the East German troubles as a result of the economic system rather than as a result of the initial conditions. How does this relate to the periodisation of the falling behind relative to West Germany? As it was stated earlier in this chapter, for the purpose of comparing the performance of economic policies or the economic systems the criterion of the growth rates should be related to the growth potential. This relates to a study of Abramovitz (1989) who found that countries "that are technologically backward have a potentiality for generating growth more rapid than that of more advanced countries, provided their social capabilities are sufficiently developed to permit successful exploitation of technologies already employed by the technological leaders".[132] Therefore the East German falling behind during the initial period can in fact be supportive to the view that the performance was bad.

The key concept in this study on catching-up, i.e. social capability, will be discussed later in this section. Before doing so, I want to address an implication of the theoretical perspective of catching-up on the debate of "a bad start" versus "a bad performance" of the East German economy. Empirical evidence for the bad initial conditions of the East German economy, emphasizing the war damage and the reparations to the Soviet Union can be found in Baar, Karlsch, and Matschke (1995), and Karlsch and Laufer (2003). Chapter 4 compares the industrial labour productivity in the two German economies in 1936 and in 1954 and shows an East German falling behind relative to West Germany.

Unaware of the theoretical perspective of Abramovitz one could easily arrive at a conclusion that "a bad start" rules out a "bad performance". The implication of the theory is that the two explanations do not rule each other out. On the contrary, as the bad initial conditions can be looked upon as a potential for high growth. This also means that the periodisation of on the one hand the years 1936 to 1950 (examining the initial conditions of the East German economy) and on the other hand the years from 1950 to 1989 (examining the economic performance) does not isolate excuse from bad policy.

From the theoretical perspective of Abramovitz one could condemn economic policy (or economic system) either for its adverse effects on social capability or for its failure to live up to the potential. The East German case shows a country that was familiar with

---

132 Abramovitz (1989) p. 225

modern institutions and acquainted with the state of the art technology before the Second World War. The experience of war, division and reparations showed a development of a 'reverse diffusion' of (or a retreat from) modern technologies. Bombing and reparations layed down (or transferred) some of the modern industries and constructions. Minjuk (2002) shows that in the automobile industries parts of the industrial equipment were transported to the Soviet Union. A study by Mühlfriedel and Wießner (1989) made clear that the division created bottlenecks that among other things hindered production in the machinery and transports branch as the requirements for inputs of basic and fabricated metal products that were formerly obtained from West Germany, were no longer guaranteed.

Thus, after the Second World War, the division of Germany, and the reparations to the Soviet Union in theory there were great opportunities for East Germany to boost productivity growth. Firstly, through a re-diffusion (or a re-implementation) of the modern technologies that it had used before. Secondly, productivity could be boosted through the diffusion of the American recipe for success. Sectors with high capital intensity and where scientific management were particularly important, such as iron and steel, transport equipment, and non-electrical machinery, could be further developed.

The "potentiality" for productivity advance

After the Second World War the East German economy imitated the institutions of the Soviet Union, not exactly an advanced economy. Surely, as follows from Gerschenkron (1962) the Soviet Union had already proven that their institutions were able to lead their country into an industrial society and support high growth. However, did it also provide the adequate conditions for further modernisation? To answer this question it is useful to give a clearer definition of what is meant with adequate conditions, i.e. social capability.

To begin with it is emphasised that social capability refers to the potentiality for productivity advance by way of catch-up. The pace at which the potentiality is realised will be discussed later in this section. Two elements of the social capability stand out: the adaptability to change and the obstacles to change. Adaptability to change refers to the constraints to the choice of a technology by the knowledge of a nation's population and its existing institutional arrangements. Obstacles to change refer to vested interests, established positions, and customary relations among firms and between employers and employees.

Surely, the East German regime knew that chances for modernisation were present. Not only had the (East) Germans worked with modern technologies before (and during) the Second World War, they could also witness the further diffusion of American technology in West Germany.[133] To a large extent Soviet ideology stimulated grasping these

---

133 See e.g. Stokes (2000) who examined the meaning of the trade fairs of Hanover and Leipzig

opportunities for advance. The heritage of Lenin who advocated mass production through electrification and scientific management was still present, although Stalin's concept of 'socialist industrialisation' had added ideological priority to heavy industries (as opposed to light industries).[134]

Knowing that opportunities lay ahead and knowing how these could be implemented are two different things. In response to the shift to communism – and in response to the expropriations of private property – many (highly educated) East Germans fled to the West, notably those who exhibited entrepreneurial skills.[135] Thus, when it comes down to experience with the organisation and management of large-scale enterprises the shift to the communist regime did bring about a loss of social capability.

Meanwhile East Germany did maintain a good system of education and it invested in research and development, thus it improved the knowledge of its population. Whether or not the gains of potential by means of education (and also research and development) were sufficient to compensate for the outflow of human capital through migration is not clear. There are qualitative differences between the type of knowledge that was gained and the type that was lost. Until the erection of the Berlin Wall in 1961 there remained a steady outflow of East Germans who migrated to West Germany.

After monitoring the constraints to the introduction of new technology by the knowledge of the East German population, the constraints by the institutional arrangements needs further discussion. Could the institutional arrangements be held sufficient for their facilitating task to mobilise capital for individual firms? According to Gerschenkron, under the circumstances of industrialisation in the Soviet Union, the allocation by the regime was a worthy alternative for creditors. However, what about the East German regime in the late 1940s and the early 1950s, constrained by the burden of reparations? At that time West Germany already benefited from the facilities created by the Marshall Aid, and being a market economy it was an interesting country for foreign direct investment. Obviously, in the early 1950s mobilisation of capital by the East German regime was problematic.

The East German organisation of the financial market has been clearly described by Gutmann (1999) who made clear that credits and economic planning were closely integrated. This indicates that mobilisation of capital was very much related to policy. Some problems might have occurred in the 1970s and 1980s. At that time the state increasingly used up the available credits for investment, as it was directed towards the construction of houses and for different kinds of subsidies.[136]

The second element of Abramovitz' concept of social capability points at the obstacles to change raised by vested interests, established positions, and customary relations among firms and between employers and employees. One way of analysing this exa-

---

134 See: Schultz (1999) for a more elaborate account of the concept of socialist industrialisation

135 Hefele (1998) pp. 87 ff.

136 Buck (1999); Baar, Müller, Zschaler (1995)

mines the openness to competition, the establishment and operation of new firms, and the sale and purchase of new goods and services. As it was shown in Chapter 1, however, in East Germany this was very much an issue of the political economy. On the one hand the dominant existence of central planning and state enterprises brought about little openness to competition and to the establishment and operation of new firms, etcetera. On the other hand the East German government did have the power to break through vested interests and established positions of the operating firms.

It should be stressed that the case of East Germany shows that the power to break through vested interests as a "positive" contribution to the potentiality for productivity advance clearly has a mirror image. The power can be used to create something good – it can also be used to destroy something valuable. Whereas the power to break through vested interests creates chances as it removes obstacles to change, it also creates risks as it upsets the existing system of checks and balances. In East Germany, when communist rule was established, the regime was very dedicated in replacing former interest groups. Doing so, in the view of Abelshauser, the country lost its historical strengths of the "korporativen Marktwirtschaft".[137]

It can be argued that the very ideology of 'socialist industrialisation' with its emphasis on investment and its postponement of consumption too inhibits the ignorance of other interests. Meanwhile the mass demonstrations in 1953, when East German industrial labourers demanded higher wages, show that collective action was not banned altogether. Although the demonstrations were broken down by force, as it is claimed by Kopstein (1997), the regime did become more aware of living standards thereafter.

Whereas the East German government could easily break through the vested interests of the operating firms, and with more difficulty through the interests of its people, it had little chance to do so regarding the interests of the Soviet Union. Their demand for reparations, their ideas on participation in the Marshall-programme, and their involvement in location decisions[138] could be major obstacles to change, thus reducing the potentiality of East German productivity advance.

In short, the development of East German potential for productivity advance shows elements of expansion and elements of erosion. The adaptability to change benefited of education and research and development, and suffered from the outflow of human capital (until 1961). Although the financial system was able to mobilise capital, during the 1970s and 1980s government increasingly used up the available credits for investment. Moreover, in the 1950s reparations put a heavy burden on budgets, and throughout the period from 1950 to 1989 the Soviet Union repeatedly were a major obstacle to change.

---

137 Abelshauser (2004) is very much in favour of this system and prefers evolving institutions above a radically new (human) design.

138 In Chapter 1 the location decision to built up steel industries in Eissenhüttenstadt near the Polish border rather than in Rostock is given as an example. See: Gayko (2000).

Did East Germany live up to the potential?

Having the "potential" for productivity advance through catch-up is one thing, to actually "realise" such an advance is yet another. The crowding out hypothesis clearly suggests that as a result of the decisions to prioritise specific industries the economic performance of the East German economy as a whole remained below its potential. Still, it is my impression that during the 1950s East Germany achieved what it was capable of. At that time the main constraint was to mobilise capital, which resulted in a relatively low rate of investment. This also explains why East German growth remained high throughout this decade, as to a large extent it concerns a belated and spread restoration boom that West Germany had already experienced in the late 1940s. The East German economy expanded at a pace that relates to the lifting of major constraints as bottlenecks and the rate of investment.

If the period of the West German restoration-boost is taken into account, the difference with the East German growth performance in the initial period becomes more visible.[139] From 1946 to 1960 the average yearly growth amounted to 10.9 per cent in West Germany. Estimates for East Germany arrive at a mere 6.2 per cent a year.

The more innovation became disconnected with memory, the more it concerned the implementation rather than the reimplementation of modern techniques, the more difficulty East Germany had to realise potential. On the one hand the East German innovation-weakness relates to the allocation of resources. According to Steiner (2004) the prioritised sectors of the late 1960s, the so-called "strukturbestimmende Industrie", absorbed more than 50 percent of all investments in science and technology.[140] On the other hand it is clear that this weakness also relates to the relatively isolated international position of East Germany. In East Germany the facilities for the diffusion of knowledge were limited. In many respects the world behind the iron curtain was an entity of its own. As other Eastern European scientists, the East German scientists had a low attendance at international conferences where they could exchange knowledge with scientists from the west. Diffusion via multinational corporations or through direct capital investments were incompatible with the institutional structure of public enterprises. The main channels that helped to increase knowledge were international trade, and perhaps also (see Chapter 1) the acquisitions of the intelligence service, the *Stasi*.

Table 3.9. Growth of GDP in East and West Germany

	1945–60	1950–60	1960–70	1970–80	1980–89
East Germany	6.2	6.7	2.7	2.6	0.3
West Germany	10.9	8.0	4.4	2.8	1.9

Sources: Annex B; ICOP; Ritschl and Spoerer (1997)

139 Figures on the period from 1946 to 1950 were derived from Ritschl and Spoerer (1997)

140 Steiner (2004) p. 145

Table 3.10. East German import and export intensity, percent of national income

	1950	1955	1960	1965	1970	1975	1980	1985	1989
Import intensity	2.5	5.0	7.6	6.3	6.9	11.0	14.5	14.1	10.7
Export intensity	2.2	5.5	7.6	6.7	6.5	9.8	13.1	16.2	10.2

Source: Statistisches Jahrbuch der Deutsche Demokratischen Republik, Schwarzer (1994)

Within the economic bloc of the Soviet Union and Eastern Europe, at least during the late 1940s and early 1950s East Germany was the "technological leader" in many areas of knowledge. No coincidence that the reparations to the Soviet Union involved the compliance of East German scientists to work in the Soviet Union.[141] Being the socialist technological leader, in terms of transfers of knowledge, trade relations with Comecon (the eastern trade bloc) were not very beneficial. To realise catch-up potential, East Germany had to import from the technologically more advanced countries in the west.

Until 1975 East German import intensity was at a comparable level as in West Germany, thereafter its expansion did not keep up with the increased participation in international trade in West Germany. Most of the East German trade was with Comecon-countries, and there was also considerable trading with third world countries. Even though international trade was such an important source of knowledge diffusion, the required trade relationships with the advanced countries of the western world were weakly developed.

East German trade with the West was troubled by the lack of foreign currencies. Steiner (2004) describes the desperate attempts to acquire these currencies through the *Intershops*, the *Mindestumtausch*, and through arbitrage – selling cheaply bought Russian oil to the West. In my view Steiner is right when he states that the underlying problem was the failing East German competitiveness, and ultimately the East German problems to increase productivity.[142] Still, as it will be discussed in Chapter 4, the retreat from the international division of labour is also a cause of the East German productivity problem. In this respect the shift in the early 1960s from the German technical standards DIN to the Soviet GOST system must have had negative effects as it (even further) reduced the flexibility to incorporate western (high technological) semi-fabrics in East German products.[143]

Maier (1999) shows that in 1980 about 35 per cent of East German imports came from the relatively advanced OECD countries, of which imports from West Germany were most important. What could East Germany learn from its technological content? A closer examination shows that the largest part of East German imports consisted of raw

---

141 Judt and Ciesla (1996)

142 Steiner (2004) pp. 196, 215

143 See Abelshauser (2004) pp. 370–378; especially p. 373 where he argues that in the 1950s West Germany benefited from the imports of high-technologies from the United States; as East Germany first needed to develop such technologies the rate of innovation was relatively slow.

materials, agricultural products, and food and beverages. Products that inhibited the progress of new technology, such as for instance computers, were not imported in large amounts.

Examples of the difficulties East Germany had with advancing beyond restoration include the failure to build a modern engine in the automobile industry during the late 1950s (Bähr and Petzina, 1996), the steel industries (Unger, 2000), and also the technological quality of East German computers was lagging behind western standards throughout the 1980s (Bentley, 1992). To a considerable extent the East German lack of technological progress relates to the bipolar world order, where East Germany stood relatively isolated from the "technology leaders" in the west. In Chapter 1 it was discussed that in addition also the centralised innovation system had serious drawbacks.

Chapter 4: The industrial sector, 1936–1954

4.1. Output and productivity growth, 1936–1954

The main part of the total East German falling behind relative to West Germany between 1936 and 1991 occurred between 1936 to 1950. During this initial period the level of East German labour productivity worsened in all sectors of the economy, except in public utilities (See Chapter 6). The complexity of the (East) German history of this period incorporates casualties, war damage, reparations to the Soviet Union, changes in the political-institutional system, and the division of Germany.

This chapter starts examining the effects during this period on the German economies in a growth accounting framework. I elaborate on changes of labour inputs, capital inputs and total factor productivity in the relatively well documented industrial sector. At that time this sector was the largest sector in both German economies and it was particularly affected by the systemic change towards central planning in East Germany. Furthermore the production- and employment structure in the industrial sector of the two economies will be compared in benchmark comparisons for 1936 and 1954.

Gross output in the industrial sector

In 1950 the industrial sector, defined as manufacturing and mining, covers about a third of all employment in both German economies. At the end of World War II there was a drastic fall of output in both East Germany and West Germany. Thereafter production increased so that West Germany attained the same production volume as it had done in 1936 as early as 1950. Its pre-division peak of 1944 was surpassed as early as in 1951. In East Germany the recovery phase took more time. Whereas in 1953 East Germany produced as much as in 1936, the level of 1944 was reached no earlier than in 1958.

Graph 4.1. Gross output in the industrial sector, 1936–1954 (Index 1936 = 100)

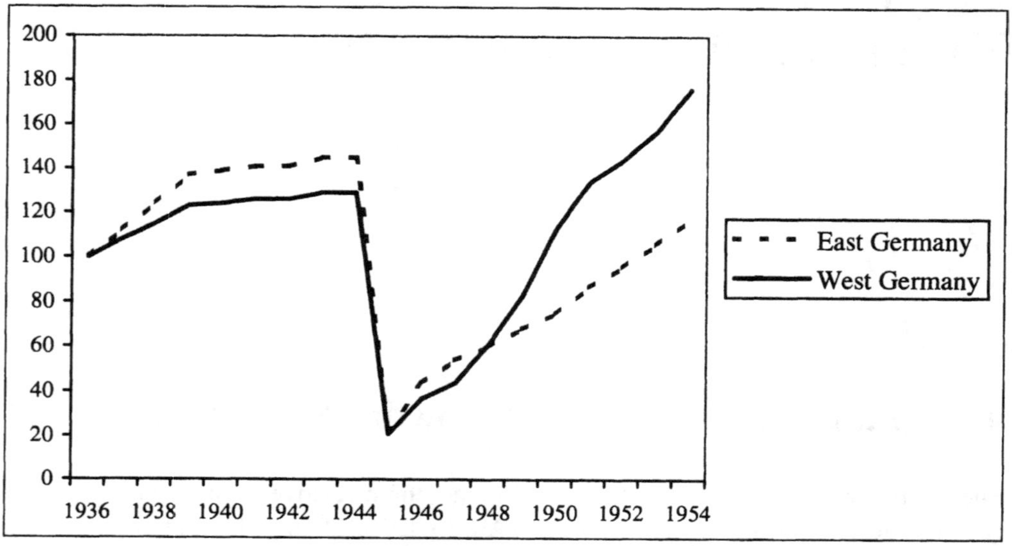

Sources: Own series of Annex A; Abelshauser (1983); Gleitze (Berlin 1956); Overall Economic Effects Division (1945); Stolper (1960)

The East German series on industrial production are based on physical quantity indicators to link up 1936 to 1950 and after.[144] For the period from 1936 to 1944 series are built on estimates of Gleitze and the years from 1945 to 1949 were derived from Abelshauser.[145] Between 1936 and 1944 East German industrial output improved its share in the total output of the *Third Reich*. At that time a large industrial centre was built on East German soil, which was considered to be a military strategic location, outside the reach of bombers.[146] Efforts were made to make industries less dependent on foreign intermediate inputs: new production capacities, particularly in the chemical industries, were aimed to provide substitutes for all kinds of raw materials.

Graph 4.1. shows gross output in East German and West German industries from 1936 to 1954, which is the year that the reparations to the Soviet Union had ended. The most remarkable development is clearly the drastic fall of output in 1944 and 1945. Obviously this relates to the final phase of the Second World War.

But over the whole period, overall growth of industrial output has been much higher in West Germany than in East Germany. Additional data on the growth of labour- and capital inputs allows estimation of the contribution of labour and capital to the growth of industrial output between two benchmark years 1936 and 1950 using the growth

144 See Annex A

145 Gleitze (1956); Abelshauser (1983)

146 Wagenführ (1963) pp. 16–24

Table 4.1. Percentage point contribution to industrial output growth of labour, capital, and TFP, 1936–1950

	Relative weights	East Germany		West Germany	
		1936–1950	*1936–1944*	1936–1950	*1936–1944*
Industrial output		–2.1	*2.7*	0.9	*1.8*
Labour inputs	0.45	0.5	*0.9*	0.6	*1.0*
Capital inputs	0.55	–1.3	*1.3*	0.8	*1.2*
TFP		–1.3	*0.4*	–0.5	*–0.4*

Note: Weights for labour inputs were based on the wage share in value added in 1936; weights for capital inputs are complementary; labour inputs in East and West Germany in 1944 are based on extrapolations from 1939.
Sources: Same as Graph 3.1. and also: Baar, Karlsch and Matschke (1995); Gleitze, (1951); Krengel (1956); Länderrat des Amerikanischen Besatzungsgebiets, (1949); Zank (1987)

accounting framework which was explained in Chapter 3. The non-explained part is referred to as total factor productivity (TFP) and reflects the increased efficiency of capital and labour.

The East German decrease of industrial output between 1936 and 1950 occurred through a reduction of the capital stock and an efficiency loss in the use of capital and labour inputs, despite an increase of the number of workers. In West Germany there was also an efficiency loss, though here industrial output increased through the increase of labour and capital inputs. In addition to the development of industrial output from 1936 to 1950 Table 4.1. separates out the period from 1936 to 1944. I will not analyse the findings for this period in more detail; the purpose for showing it in this thesis is to indicate that the negative contribution of East German TFP was (largely) due to the postwar period. In the following pages I compare developments of factor inputs (mainly capital inputs) and total factor productivity.

Factor inputs

In 1950 the East German population was about 10 per cent larger than in 1939, compared to an increase of 16 per cent in West Germany. During the late 1940s there was an enormous migration towards the territories of East Germany and West Germany from the lost provinces of Pommerania, Silesia, and East Prussia, and of ethnic Germans from all over Eastern Europe. Hence immigration offset the loss of prime-age males in the war. As a result both parts of Germany were able to raise the amount of labour inputs. Meanwhile East Germany also faced the wandering off of parts of the East German population towards West Germany.

What if migration led to a brain drain? Perhaps one extra engineer would have been more useful for East German production than two unskilled workers. Ritschl suggested that "the westward route to individual freedom" led to a loss of human capital in East Germany.[147] In the growth accounting framework labour inputs and capital inputs isolate the quantity of factor inputs only. If migration actually led to a brain drain, this implies that the quality of labour input in East Germany declined. As I do not account for this in my measure of labour input, this effect shows up in lower TFP growth (or faster decline). TFP will be examined in more detail later in this section.

The estimates on the East German industrial capital stock shortly after the Second World War shows a wide variation. Whereas Harmssen (1951) estimated the East German capital stock in 1946 at 50 per cent of the 1936 level, studies of Melzer (1980) and Zank (1987) arrived at 89 per cent and 80 per cent in 1948 respectively.[148] A main problem in estimating the East German capital stock concerns the dismantling under Soviet occupation. Recently Baar *et al.* have improved information on this issue, using material from the archives. They found that the East German industrial capital stock in 1948 was at 69 per cent of the level in 1936.[149]

After 1944 the East German and the West German industrial capital stock show a strongly divergent development. Firstly the decrease of the capital stock between 1944 and 1948 was much more severe in East Germany than in West Germany. This is largely explained by the dismantling of industrial capital stock by the Soviet Union, and not by larger damage due to war activity. According to Baar *et al.* in East Germany dismantling reduced the industrial capital stock about 30 per cent of its size in 1944, versus about 4 per cent in West Germany.[150] Secondly, since 1948 the West German growth of the industrial capital stock was at a higher pace as its investment climate improved rapidly due to the currency reform of 1948. East Germany, however, was forced to pay reparations to the Soviet Union, mainly through deliveries out of current production. These reparations put a heavy burden on the economy's capacity for new investment. Chapter 3 showed already that East German investment (in percent of its GDP) was relatively low in comparison with West Germany in 1950.

Table 4.2. Industrial capital stock, 1936–1950 (Prices of 1938, index 1936 = 100)

	1936	1944	1948	1950
East Germany	100	138[a]	69	72[b]
West Germany	100	136	113	122

Sources: Krengel (1956); Baar, Karlsch and Matschke (1995)
Notes: [a] Based on Zank (1987); [b] Extrapolated from Baar, Karlsch and Matschke (1995) using series of Melzer (1980)

---

147 Ritschl (1996) pp. 507, 508
148 Harmssen (1951); Melzer (1980); Zank (1987)
149 Baar, Karlsch and Matschke (1995) pp. 913–915
150 Baar, Karlsch and Matschke (1995) p. 916

Table 4.3. War damage, dismantling, reparations and occupation costs until 1953 (*Reichsmarks* of 1944)

	Total (million RM)		Per Capita (RM)	
	East Germany	West Germany	East Germany	West Germany
(a) War Damage	12,700	40,500	686	839
(b) Dismantling	7,100	2,900	384	60
(c) Reparations	19,700	1,120	1,065	23
(d) Occupation costs	12,000	33,300	649	689
Total	51,500	77,820	2,784	1,611

Note: The per capita estimates are based on the average population for the period from 1945 to 1953, i.e. 18.5 million for East Germany and 48.3 million for West Germany
Source: Baar, Karlsch and Matschke (1995)

The burden of the reparations on the East German economy is best illustrated by calculations of Baar *et al.* on the sum of war damage, dismantling, reparations and occupation costs for the total economy. It is noted that these estimates are larger than the industrial capital stock lost, as it does not only refer to losses of machinery, equipment and buildings in the industrial sector, but also to losses of dwellings and infrastructure. Similarly dismantling also affected non-industrial sectors, particularly the transport sector.

As a percentage of national income the reparations (including occupation costs) in East Germany amounted to more than 18 per cent in 1950. This was much lower than the 30 per cent of national income for the period from 1945 to 1949,[151] but well above the West German burden of the occupation costs (plus reparations) which was never more than 15 per cent of national income and was less than 6 per cent in 1950.

Total Factor Productivity (TFP)

Between 1936 and 1950 in both German economies TFP growth contributed negatively to growth of industrial output. Table 4.1. suggests that in the case of West Germany the negative contribution of TFP largely originated during the Second World War, whereas in East Germany it originated after 1944. What are the reasons for the decrease of productivity per unit of capital and/or per unit of labour?

Firstly it is noted that East Germany and West Germany did not achieve full capacity utilisation. Between 1945 and 1948 the West German economy faced bottlenecks in the flow of raw materials and fuels. Bottlenecks were caused by the "almost complete paralysis of the transport system and a mismatch between labour and jobs due to the loss of

151 Karlsch (1993) pp. 232 ff.

housing stock".[152] After the clearing of bottlenecks improved business confidence by the inclusion of the Western zones in the Marshall Plan, the currency reform in 1948 helped to re-establish market incentives and to reduce barter trade. Not until the Korea boom (1951) the capacity reserve was lifted, as it enabled West Germany to take advantage of the spurt in foreign demand. According to Wallich, exporters in other western countries were at a disadvantage because they were operating at full capacity and had to compete with rising domestic arms production.[153]

East Germany also faced bottlenecks, particularly shortages of raw materials and some other intermediate inputs. According to Barthel these bottlenecks were a result of separation from West Germany: the economic structure of East Germany was disproportionally endowed – with mainly light and relatively few heavy industries.[154] As a result of lacking intermediate inputs part of the capital stock in (light) industries was not utilised. For the calculation of TFP such an underutilisation of the capital stock shows up in TFP, as the contribution of capital inputs to industrial output growth was based on the total capital stock rather than the utilised capital stock. For the period from 1936 to 1950 this means that the contribution of capital inputs is overestimated, leading to rather pessimistic estimates for TFP.

Sometimes it is argued that the costs (in terms of slower productivity growth) were the result of policies during this initial period rather than the result of an unbalanced inherited structure.[155] East Germany could have avoided these bottlenecks if it had not been so reluctant to participate in international trade. As the East German economy was so much guided by central planning, did it lead to resource misallocation? The answer to this question has major influence on the interpretation of this part of the productivity loss, and the implications for the post-1950 productivity performance of East Germany. To put it simple: has the political economy eroded the autonomy of decision-making at the level where allocation of resources matters most for realising efficiency; or were inherited bottlenecks a reflection of bad luck.

A straightforward approach to deal with this issue is to explore the policy options of the East German government at that time and compare it to what was actually done. Government policy aimed to build up production capacity in the bottleneck industries; which are mainly industries in the basic and fabricated metal products branch. This can be referred to as 'socialist industrialisation' as it fits into a pattern that can be observed in all East European countries, and which is characterised by its focus on heavy industries and autarky.[156]

Let alone the political autonomy of the East German authorities to deviate its policy of Moscow's desires, it could have purchased the needed intermediate inputs on West-

---

[152] Carlin (1996), pp. 463–465
[153] Wallich (1955) pp. 79–87
[154] Barthel (1979)
[155] E.g. Stolper (1957) pp. 522, 523
[156] Helga Schultz (1999) pp. 110–116

ern markets or on Eastern markets. The context of the cold war provides rationality to a decision not to engage into a division of labour with Western economies. This is illustrated by the events in 1948, when Soviet military forces started a blockade of West Berlin in response to the West German currency reform. In order to deliver the necessary supplies in West Berlin, the United States and the United Kingdom started an impressive airlift. Furthermore the United States boycotted several deliveries out of the territory of West Germany towards the territory of East Germany. A memorandum for president Truman by the Central Intelligence Agency reports a complete stoppage of production in East German sugar refineries for lack of 50,000 meters of steel piping on order in the Western zone; almost a complete closing down of canneries since the entire raw material was received from the West; a certain discontinuance of the Baltic fishing fleet within a short time because of lack of machinery parts.[157] Furthermore heavy industries, particularly the steel mills in Hennigsdorf, could not produce without the West and other heavy industries in the Eastern Zone would be equally affected.

Within the context of the cold war – with the ever-eminent threat of a real war – the bottlenecks showed the vulnerability of the East German economy. Obviously there was a desire of the government not to become too dependent on the presumed enemies. The alternative was to buy the necessities on Eastern European markets. However, the Soviet Union produced insufficient raw materials and heavy industry products to supply Eastern Europe. Therefore there is some point in Mühlfriedel and Wießner, who stated that to solve the problem of the bottlenecks East Germany needed to increase its own production capacity in the basic and fabricated metal industries.[158]

The combination of the inability of the Soviet Union to deliver the wanted raw materials and heavy industry products and the cold war rationality to avoid too much dependence on the West limited the policy options for East German authorities. Moreover, the lack of hard currency – East Germany was not allowed to participate in the Marshall programme – made it difficult to purchase (Western) products as a temporary measure until socialist industrialisation was completed. Therefore it is my impression that East German bottlenecks – and the resulting production below the production possibilities curve – was not so much the result of bad policy, but more the outcome in a delicate and unfortunate situation.

Other factors that explain the negative East German TFP are the economically inferior technology and the outflow of human capital. Education and skills lead to higher productivity; and a decrease of human capital will therefore have negative effects on productivity. Indeed East German migrants who arrived in West Germany during the 1950s were particularly well educated.[159] Also during the late 1940s migration meant a

---

157 Memorandum, dated June 30, 1948, by U.S. Central Intelligence Agency, to President Harry S. Truman, http://www.trumanlibrary.org/whistlestop/study_collections/berlin_airlift/large/cia/bal48-2.htm (10/06/2002)

158 Also: Mühlfriedel, Wießner (1989) p.213

159 Giersch, Paqué and Schmieding (1994) pp. 68, 69

loss of human capital. Among other East German migrants many 'owners' with entrepreneurial skills left shortly after expropriations that started as early as 1945.[160]

The idea that compared to its technology level in 1936 East German technology was inferior from an efficiency viewpoint in 1950 suggests a contrasting development with West Germany. According to Krengel in comparison with 1939 the West German industrial capital stock in 1948 was not only of a more favourable age structure, but also technically more advanced.[161] The new capital stock in East Germany – built at the eve of World War II – aimed to provide substitutes for different kinds of raw materials. On the one hand these substitutes lessened the adverse effects of the disproportioned industry structure, thus minimise the negative TFP due to bottlenecks.[162] On the other hand the use of substitutes rather than the 'original' raw materials that were used in 1936 negatively affected TFP: not only was autarky never fully accomplished (so that some bottlenecks remained in existence), but more important its pursuit was negative for productivity.[163]

4.2. Level comparisons of industrial labour productivity[164]

About 36 per cent of the East German decline in labour productivity relative to West Germany between 1936 and 1991 occurred during the relatively short period from 1936 to 1950. The analysis of growth rates of the industrial sector for this period shows that the East German industrial sector indeed developed unfavourably in comparison with that in West Germany. This section estimates levels of East German and West German labour productivity in the industrial sector in 1936 and 1954, and aims to explain the rising gap between the industrial sectors of both economies by looking at the underlying branches.

A benchmark of industrial labour productivity in 1936

Before World War II both 'Germanies' were still a part of the same country and had the same statistical system. Hence the data for East- and West Germany are fully comparable, in contrast to most of the data after the separation. I use a benchmark for 1936 to shed light on the industrial structure that East Germany inherited. Several scholars have

---

160 Hefele (1998) pp. 87 ff.

161 Krengel (1958)

162 Ritschl (1996) pp. 504, 505

163 Wagenführ (1963) pp. 16–24

164 Parts of this section have been published in: Sleifer (2001)

compared the East and West German economies of 1936 before. They conclude that the East German labour productivity in manufacturing was below the West German level. For instance Van Ark estimated the East German level of labour productivity in manufacturing at 83.9 per cent of the West German level, Melzer estimated it somewhat higher at 87.5 per cent.[165]

There are several sources that can be used to obtain the data. Firstly the official publication of the results from this census: *Die deutsche Industrie.* Secondly, after the Second World War the 'Länderrat des Amerikanischen Besatzungsgebiets' published statistics on German industries in 1936, which by means of interpolations of the 'Nichtlandwirtschaftliche Arbeitsstättenzählung' of 1939 updated the official publication on the census.[166] This is the source used by Van Ark. Thirdly Gleitze published statistics on the industrial sector in 1936, using the official publication and also archive material of the actual census to improve (or extend) the data.[167] This is the source used by Melzer.

In all cases the ultimate source for these productivity estimates is the 'actual' industrial census of 1936, which has also been used for this study. In the 1930s the industrial census was seen as an instrument in rearmament planning with particular interest in the issue of raw materials and also the regional structure of German industry.[168] On the one hand this means that the census provides detailed information on the location of German industries, which allows for a division of East Germany and West Germany. On the other hand this means that much of the census data was classified and therefore left out of the official publication. Therefore I will use the original data of the census obtained from the archives in Berlin-Lichterfelde.[169]

The census provides regional data on gross output and employment for 300 industries. To arrive at value added additional calculations were made, assuming the overall German input output relationship for each particular industry in 1936. This is described in more detail in Annex C. The industries were classified into 13 more or less homogeneous branches as is common in research of the ICOP project (International Comparisons of Output and Productivity) at the University of Groningen.[170] It shows that in 1936 the industrial structures in the two parts of Germany were rather different. In West Germany many people were employed in 'mining' and 'basic and fabricated metal products', in East Germany the branches 'textiles, wearing apparel' and 'machinery, transports' were relatively large. Furthermore it shows that East German labour productivity was somewhat below the West German level in all branches except for 'mining'.

---

165 Van Ark (1996); Melzer (1980)

166 Länderrat des Amerikanischen Besatzungsgebiets (1949)

167 Gleitze (1956)

168 Tooze (2001) pp. 189–199; See also Fremdling and Stäglin (2003) who are working on the (re-) construction of the input-output tables for 1936.

169 BArch R3102/3309; BArch R3102/3651; BArch R3102/5922

170 Van Ark (1993)

Table 4.4. East (EG) and West German (WG) labour shares and labour productivity in the industrial sector in 1936 (in 1936 *Reichsmarks*)

	Employment share		Value added per person employed		
	East Germany	West Germany	East Germany	West Germany	EG (WG = 100)
Mining	4.6	9.4	4,746	3,777	125.6
Manufacturing	95.4	90.6	3,896	4,381	88.9
Food, Beverages, Tobacco	8.3	9.0	5,711	6,198	92.1
Textiles, Wearing Apparel	24.1	13.9	3,231	3,305	97.8
Leather Products, Footwear	2.4	3.3	3,403	3,587	94.8
Wood Products, Furniture	5.3	5.1	2,762	2,940	94.0
Paper and Printing	6.7	5.1	3,549	3,949	89.9
Chemicals, Rubber, Plastic, Oil Refining	5.8	5.5	6,510	7,692	84.6
Stone, Clay, Glass	8.3	7.4	2,864	3,243	88.3
Basic and Fabricated Metal	9.3	19.4	4,066	4,458	91.2
Machinery and Transports	15.7	12.1	4,291	4,834	88.8
Electrical Equipment	3.8	5.1	4,496	4,614	97.4
Optics, Fine Mechanics	5.8	4.7	2,839	2,865	99.1
Total Industry	100.0	100.0	3,935	4,324	91.0

Sources: BArch R3102/3309; BArch R3102/3651; BArch R3102/5922; see Annex C

In comparison with other branches 'textiles, wearing apparel' attains a low labour productivity level in absolute terms in both countries, and 'basic and fabricated metal' attains a high labour productivity level (although the level in chemicals, plastics, rubber and oil refining is even higher). In the 1930s 'basic and fabricated metal' was a key branch in the apparent 'technology regime', which encompassed the electrification of industry, transport, and the home.[171] It provided core inputs such as steel, copper, and metal alloys. As such the small size of the 'basic and fabricated metal' branch could lead to bottlenecks in East Germany after the division of Germany as discussed in the previous section.

Furthermore the concept of 'technology regimes' gives an impression of the modernity of the East and West German industrial structure. Following Freeman and Louçã there are five constellations of technical and organisational innovations: (1) water-powered mechanisation; (2) steam-powered mechanisation; (3) electrification; (4) motorization; and (5) computerisation. In 1936 technology was in the phase of electrification, and there were also signs of the breakthrough of motorization. Linked up with the different industry structure in the two parts of Germany, it appears that the West German structure was somewhat more modern than in East Germany.

171 Freeman and Louçã (2002) pp. 139 ff.

The relatively large branch 'textiles, wearing apparel' in East Germany and the relatively large coal dominated 'mining' sector in West Germany are associated with mechanisation, thus in a sense are a remnant of an old technology regime. In the heart of the prevailing technology regime was a branch that employed a relatively large share of the West German labour force: 'basic and fabricated metal'. Finally East Germany had a relatively large employment share in 'machinery, transports'. Some of the products in this branch relate to the steam-powered mechanisation, such as steam engines and machine tools. Other products relate to the announced motorization phase, for instance automobiles, trucks, tractors, diesel engines, aircraft and refineries. Looking at the products that relate to the motorization phase the aircraft industries employed a relatively large share in East Germany, and automobiles was much more developed in West Germany. On balance the relatively high labour share in 'machinery, transport' was employed to produce traditional products rather than the state of the art.

A different 'modernity' of the industrial structure may be important for explaining the different levels of labour productivity between East and West Germany, and also for the potential labour productivity trends after 1950. However, it is stressed here that the productivity gap in 1936 was merely 9 per cent. The bottom line is that East German industries attained a high level of industrial labour productivity – though a little below the West German level. And also, that the East German industrial structure was modern – though a little less modern than West Germany. Below the industrial labour productivity levels in the two German economies are compared in more detail, using shift share techniques.

Industrial Labour Productivity in 1954

From 1936 to 1954 the relative level of industrial labour productivity of East Germany in comparison with West Germany worsened. Ritschl linked a benchmark for 1936 to time series for this period and estimated East German industrial labour productivity in 1950 to range between 61 to 87 per cent of the West German level.[172] The upper bound of 87 per cent is probably too high, as it is based on the official published figures of industrial production.[173] The lower bound extrapolates the 1936 benchmark using time series of Stolper, who based his series on various physical indicators. Therefore this estimate is much more reliable. Similarly Van Ark estimated East German labour productivity in manufacturing in 1950 by linking a benchmark for 1987 to available time series.[174] Van Ark estimated East German labour productivity between 39 and 60 per cent of the West German level. Here the lower bound extrapolates the relative labour

---

172 Ritschl (1996) pp. 508–511

173 For a more detailed discussion, see Chapter 2.

174 Van Ark (1995)

productivity in 1987 according to a value added concept, whereas the upper bound refers to relative labour productivity based on gross output.

None of these estimates comes close to the level comparison of Grünig, whose estimates imply that East German industrial labour productivity in 1947 was at almost 100 per cent of the West German level.[175] At that time the two parts of Germany were still using the same currency – their monetary policy had not yet set a different course. Grünig shows estimates of national income, and also value added and employment of sectors, for the distinctive occupation zones and for Berlin.

As a result the issue of the relative labour productivity in the 1950s is misty. Extrapolations resulted in a wide range of outcomes. The level comparison for 1947 is too early a year to get a clear view on the relative labour productivity in the 1950s, as particularly the late 1940s are believed to have led to divergence (see section 4.1.). Therefore I provide a new estimate of the East German and West German industrial labour productivity in the early 1950s, i.e. 1954. For this purpose I relied on the "quantity approach" of international comparisons.[176] This approach is also applied in other comparisons of the two German economies, for instance by Sturm who estimated the relative labour productivity in 1964.[177]

The quantity approach uses physical output data for the two countries. For the comparison a total of 83 East German industrial commodities were matched with West German quantity and value data for corresponding commodities.[178] These products (j) were classified into industrial branches (i), as was the case in the 1936 comparison above. Within each branch relative East German gross production was estimated in two steps. Firstly the matched value (m), i.e. the value of the 83 products that were made in both parts of Germany, was estimated:

$$V_i^{E(m)} = \sum_j (Q_{ij}^E / Q_{ij}^W)\, V_{ij}^{W(m)}$$

where Q stands for physical quantity of output, V for sales value, j for product j, and the superscripts E stands for East Germany, and W for West Germany. After the estimation of the gross output of the matched products, the total branch value was estimated:

$$V_i^E = V_i^{E(m)} * (V_i^W / V_i^{W(m)}$$

The second equation hides the major underlying assumption of this method: the weighted quantity ratio of matched output between East Germany and West Germany is assumed representative for non-matched output. This implies that the West German coverage ratios (matched output as a percentage of total output) are the same as the East

---

175 Own calculations on Grünig (1948)

176 A pioneer of this approach is Rostas (1948)

177 Sturm (1974)

178 The use of West German prices introduces a bias known as the Gerschenkron effect. The estimates below are adjusted for it as is described in Annex C.

German coverage ratios, which allows the use of West German coverage ratios to aggregate the East German matched output to a branch total.

It is stressed that the representativity of matched output for non-matched output is an assumption, not a fact. *In casu* the East German coverage ratio is probably higher than the West German coverage ratio, estimating East German production too high. As the coverage ratio shows the matched output as a percentage of the total output, a high ratio indicates that few products are produced outside the range of the matched sample. At least the coverage ratio was higher for East Germany than for West Germany in benchmark comparisons for 1987 and 1992.[179]

In Table 4.5. the relative East German labour productivity in comparison with West Germany is shown for two different assumptions on the East German coverage ratio. First it shows labour productivity when the East German coverage ratio is the same as the West German coverage ratio; second it shows labour productivity for an East German coverage ratio that is 2 per cent above the West German ratio. This is much lower than the coverage ratio of 8 per cent above the West German ratio, as it was found in Van Ark's benchmark for 1987.[180]

In my view the West German ratio provides a good lower-bound and the ratio that is 2 per cent above the West German ratio provides a realistic upper-bound, although there is no hard evidence. In 1936 most industries that were apparent in West Germany were also apparent in East Germany.[181] The period after the Second World War is often characterised as a period of recovery. For the consumer goods it is known that product variety in West Germany increased from the mid-1950s onwards, but especially during the 1960s.[182] Unless East Germany stopped producing the products that it produced in 1936, there is little reason to expect that the coverage ratio differed more than 2 per cent of the West German ratio.[183]

In 1954 the employment shares across branches show several differences between East Germany and West Germany. West Germany had a relatively large share in 'mining', and 'metal, machinery, transports', East German 'food, beverages, tobacco', 'textiles, wearing apparel', 'wood products, furniture', and 'electrical equipment' were relatively large. In 1954 East German labour productivity only surpassed the West German level in mining, which was already at a higher level in 1936. In all manufac-

---

179 Van Ark (1995); Unpublished results of a benchmark comparison for 1992 by Bart van Ark and Erik Monnikhof

180 Van Ark (1995); If the East German coverage ratio were 8 per cent above the West German ratio in 1954 already, industrial labour productivity would be about 54 per cent of West Germany.

181 Annex C

182 Bundesministerium für innerdeutsche Beziehungen (1974) p. 254

183 Of course industries have been dismantled by the Soviet Union. However, except for some typical military-industries (weapons, munition) the balance with newly built capacities in the early 1950s suggests a reduction of the capacities, not a disappearance of the products. See: Karlsch (1993) pp. 87–93

Table 4.5. East (EG) and West German (WG) labour shares and labour productivity in the industrial sector in 1954 (in 1954 DM)

	Employment share		Sales per person employed		
	East Germany	West Germany	East Germany	West Germany	EG (WG = 100)
Mining	5.9	10.6	20,715	12,029	172.2
Manufacturing	94.1	89.4	14,699	24,600	59.8
Food, Beverages, Tobacco	9.0	6.7	38,759	55,442	69.9
Textiles, Wearing Apparel	17.1	14.3	16,789	18,871	89.0
Leather Products, Footwear	3.2	2.7	5,866	18,207	32.2
Wood Products, Furniture	7.5	5.6	9,896	16,499	60.0
Paper and Printing	3.6	4.6	15,367	22,394	68.6
Chemicals, rubber, plastic, oil refining	8.6	7.8	23,956	35,943	66.7
Stone, Clay, Glass	4.9	6.2	8,648	15,827	54.6
Metal, Machinery, Transports	27.8	32.9	8,875	23,705	37.4
Electrical Equipment	9.2	6.7	10,094	19,630	51.4
Optics and Fine Mechanics	3.2	2.0	3,685	12,986	28.4
Total	100.0	100.0	15,054	23,264	64.7
Total (Coverage ratio adjustment)					*61.6*

Sources: See Annex C.

turing branches East German labour productivity was below the West German level. Especially 'leather products, footwear', 'metal, machinery, transports', and 'optics and fine mechanics' show relatively low levels productivity. Compared to other manufacturing branches East German 'textiles, wearing apparel' only had a minor labour productivity gap relative to West Germany. This is particularly explained by East German wearing apparel – as this occupation required manual skills particularly available in traditional centres of textile production such as Sachsen.[184]

Concluding, the East German industrial labour productivity in 1954 reached at least 61.6 per cent, and at most 64.7 per cent of the West German level. In manufacturing East German labour productivity was between 56.8 and 59.8 per cent of the West German level. This is about 30 percentage-points below the relative productivity in 1936, which is fairly close to the estimates – based on extrapolations from 1936 – by Ritschl. It is noted that my estimates for 1954 are based on sales value. Van Ark estimated gross manufacturing output in East Germany at 59.6 per cent of West Germany, which also corresponds to this study's estimate. However, based on value added Van Ark arrived at

184 Heimann (1997) p. 153 Heimann argues it is plausible that in the early 1950s East German wearing apparel attained a higher level of labour productivity than in West Germany.

Graph 4.2. Relative level of East German industrial labour productivity, 1936 to 1954 (West Germany = 100)

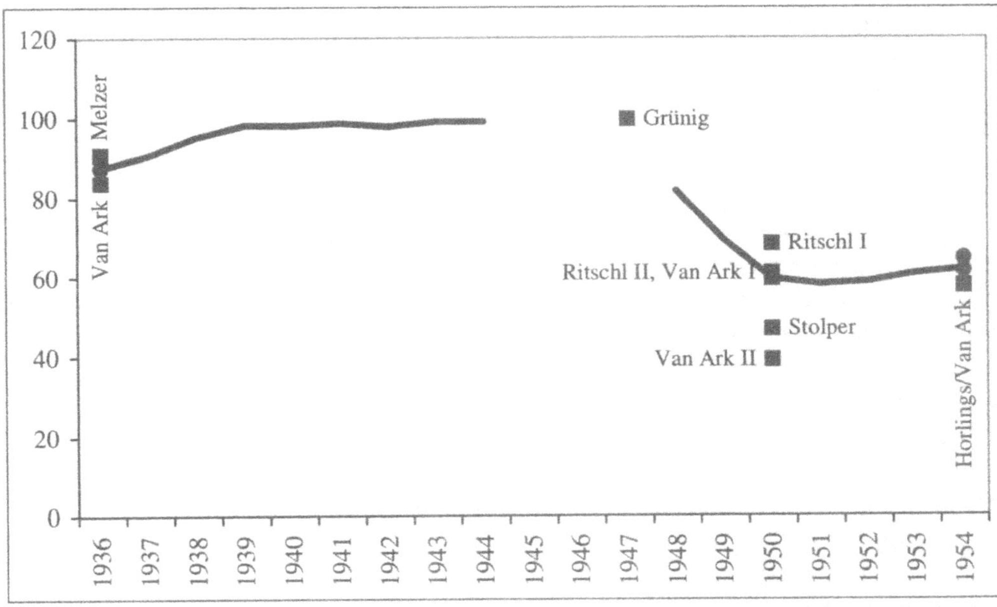

Notes: Dots show estimates of this study; Line links up the comparison for 1936 to available time series; boxes show estimates of other studies (see text).
Sources: See Annex A, Annex C

an East German manufacturing labour productivity of 39 per cent of the West German level.

Before going into some details of the share of intermediate inputs in gross output, I will confront my benchmarks for 1936 and 1954 with other estimates in the literature. Therefore I link up time series to the gross output estimate of the relative level of East German industrial labour productivity in comparison with West Germany for 1936.

To begin with it is observed that extrapolation from this study's benchmark for 1936 fits with the estimated relative productivity level in 1954. Other estimates for the relative level of industrial labour productivity in 1936 are not too different from my estimate of the East German productivity at 87.6 per cent of West Germany.[185] Similarly the estimated productivity level in 1954 is approximately the same as the level that could be derived from Horlings and Van Ark.[186] The benchmark of Grünig[187] for 1947 is located in a blank of the time series. For as much as the series suggest his estimate of

185 For 1936 the graph only shows estimates on relative labour productivity based on gross output.

186 Horlings and van Ark (1996); This paper compares both East and West German labour productivity with the level in the United States of America in 1954.

187 Grünig (1948)

the relative productivity level is possibly accurate. This would imply that East German labour productivity in the industrial sector started to deteriorate in comparison with West Germany after 1947.

Estimates for 1950 show very different results. The highest estimate is of Ritschl (I), who linked Melzer's estimate for 1936 to time series on national income (!) of Barthel.[188] A linkage of the 1936 estimate by Melzer to time series of industrial production by Stolper gave Ritschl (II) the more accurate estimate of East German industrial labour productivity at 61 percent of the West German level. At almost the same level, namely 59.6 percent, stands an estimate by Van Ark (I). However, there are two major differences between the estimates of Ritschl and Van Ark. Firstly, the coverage of these estimates differ. Van Ark confines to the manufacturing sector, whereas Ritschl refers to the total industrial sector (plus mining). Given the high productivity level in East German mining relative to that of West Germany, it is no surprise that Ritschl's estimate is somewhat higher.

Secondly, the estimate of the relative industrial labour productivity at 59.6 per cent by Van Ark (I) is based on gross output estimates. Based on value added Van Ark (II) arrived at the much lower level of 39.2 per cent of West Germany. Ritschl's estimate at 61 per cent, however, also aims to reflect the relative productivity level based on value added. The huge difference between their estimates based on value added originates in the benchmark year from which they extrapolated. Whereas Ritschl extrapolated from 1936, when the use of intermediate inputs in the two parts of Germany was almost the same, Van Ark extrapolated from 1987, when East Germany had relatively high input/output ratios.

An important question to resolve this issue therefore is whether the intermediate input/gross output ratio in 1950 was relatively close between East and West Germany (i.e. Ritschl's assumption) or already much higher in East Germany (i.e. Van Ark's assumption). According to the West German statistical office West German industries realised an input output ratio, or "Materialquote", of 51 per cent. This means that value added was 49 percent of gross output value. The material inputs include raw materials, semi-manufactures, energy, fuel and electrical energy, and parts, all valued at in-factory prices. Ideally the definition of material inputs which are used for the calculation of the use of intermediate inputs are exactly the same in both countries. The East German statistics that correspond the most to the West German definition of material inputs are those on 'Verbrauch von Material und Produktiven Leistungen'. This category consists of raw materials, semi-manufactures, energy, fuels, repairments and transport costs. It is one of the two sub-categories of 'Verbrauch an Produktionsmittel'. The other subcategory is 'Abschreibungen, Mieten, Pachten und Nutzungsentgelte' which contains

188 Ritschl (1996) p. 509; Barthel (1979) p. 145

rents and depreciation.[189] In current (East German) prices of 1954 the East German input output relationship was the following:

	Current Prices	Percentage
Gross Output	59,369	100.0
Material Inputs	27,666	46.6
Value Added	31,703	53.4

This implies that according to the official statistics the East German input/output ratio in 1954 was more or less the same as it was in 1936, and somewhat below the West German ratio. If one accepts the input output relationship of the official statistics, the value added estimate of Van Ark is too low. The same applies to the estimate of Stolper.[190] However, the interpretation of the official statistics on this matter is hazardous. The reliability and comparability of the official statistics was discussed in Chapter 2; developments of the input/output ratios will be discussed in more detail in Chapter 5.

Shift share analysis

Now that we have two benchmarks it is possible to examine the productivity gap between the two parts of Germany in more detail by decomposing into various components. On the one hand the relative East German industrial labour productivity in comparison with West Germany shows differences within each branch. These branch differences are usually referred to as "intra branch" and its contribution to the aggregate relative productivity difference is called the "intra branch effect". On the other hand the aggregate difference can also be the result of so called "structure effects". This refers to the part of the gap that is caused by differences in the composition of output, for instance whether a larger share of persons are employed in textiles or in chemicals. Since some branches realise higher productivity levels than others the composition, or structure, affects the aggregate outcome of the relative productivity level.

Shift share analysis allows the decomposition of the aggregate productivity gap into structure effects and intra branch effects. Pioneers in this type of analysis were Fabricant, Kuznets, Chenery and Syrquin. The following equation was derived from Timmer

189 Statistisches Jahrbuch der Deutschen Demokratischen Republik 1955 (1956) p. 91; Statistisches Jahrbuch der Deutschen Demokratischen Republik 1969, pp. 35–41

190 Stolper (1960) pp. 266, 273; The low relative productivity is mainly explained by Stolper's data on West Germany. The value of West German production is somewhat high, and the number of employed persons too low.

(1999)[191], where LP = Labour Productivity and S_i = Share of employment in particular branch or industry.

$$LP^{\text{West}} - LP^{\text{East}} = \sum_{i=1}^{n} (LP_i^{\text{West}} - LP_i^{\text{East}}) \frac{1}{2}(S_i^{\text{East}} + S_i^{\text{West}}) + \sum_{i=1}^{n} (S_i^{\text{West}} - S_i^{\text{East}}) \frac{1}{2}(LP_i^{\text{East}} + LP_i^{\text{West}})$$

On the right hand side of the equation differences of labour productivity are decomposed into an "intra branch effect" and a "structure effect". The "intra branch effect", which is the first term, accounts for differences in productivity levels within each branch. The "structure effect" is in the second term and accounts for differences in employment structures.

In 1936 East German labour productivity was merely 9 percentage points below West Germany, in 1954 the gap was at least 35 percentage points. The total gap for all industries is shown in the grey shaded squares and horizontally sums the total of the intra branch effect and the structure effect. A first observation is that intra branch differences are most important. They account for two thirds of the productivity gap in 1936, i.e. 6 percentage points. In 1954 intra branch differences account for even more than the total productivity gap, as the structure of the East German industrial sector proves – albeit a little – favourable in comparison with West Germany. This is primarily explained by a relatively large share in 'food, beverages, tobacco' in East Germany.

Table 4.6. Decomposition of the East German productivity gap in comparison with West Germany in 1936 (9 percentage points) and 1954 (35 percentage points)

	1936			1954		
	Intra branch	Structure	Total	Intra branch	Structure	Total
Mining	1.6	–4.7	–3.2	3.1	–3.3	–0.2
Food, Beverages, Tobacco	–1.0	–1.0	–2.0	–5.6	4.6	–1.0
Textiles, Wearing Apparel	–0.3	7.7	7.4	–1.4	2.2	0.8
Leather Products, Footwear	–0.1	–0.7	–0.8	–1.6	0.2	–1.3
Wood Products, Furniture	–0.2	0.1	–0.1	–1.8	1.1	–0.7
Paper and Printing	–0.5	1.4	0.9	–1.2	–0.8	–2.1
Chemicals, rubber, plastic, oil refining	–1.5	0.4	–1.1	–4.2	1.0	–3.2
Stone, Clay, Glass	–0.7	0.6	–0.1	–1.7	–0.7	–2.4
Metal, Machinery, Transports	–3.1	–6.1	–9.2	–19.2	–3.5	–22.7
Electrical Equipment	–0.1	–1.3	–1.4	–3.2	1.6	–1.6
Optics and Fine Mechanics	0.0	0.7	0.7	–1.0	0.4	–0.6
Total Industries	–6.0	–3.0	–9.0	–37.9	2.8	–35.0

Sources: Annex C

[191] Timmer (1999) pp. 109–112

Vertically the grey shaded squares sum the contribution of the manufacturing branches and mining to the productivity gap. It shows that the productivity difference between the two parts of Germany is largely situated in the branch 'metal, machinery, transports'. This applies both for 1936 and 1954. A closer examination shows that in 1936 the contribution to the productivity gap of this branch mainly concerned a structure effect, whereas in 1954 the intra branch effect was dominant.

The structure effect in 1936 relates to the pattern of regional specialisation where 'basic and fabricated metal' had a larger employment share in West Germany, and 'textiles, wearing apparel' had a larger employment share in East Germany. As a consequence of the division of East Germany and West Germany after the Second World War the previously existing pattern of specialisation disappeared. East German 'basic and fabricated metal' faced difficulties in retrieving the necessary inputs, which were insufficiently produced by its own mining sector. As an alternative, East Germany started using (metal) scrap.[192] To some extent the intra branch effect in this branch in 1954 shows the end of a specialisation pattern between the two parts of Germany: East Germany did not benefit of West German resources anymore.

In turn the branch 'basic and fabricated metal' could not supply the necessary inputs for the branch 'machinery, transports' either. Within the branch 'machinery, transports' there is a high interdependency of parts that are produced in different plants. According to Barthel there were discontinuities in production due to shortages of specific parts.[193] However, not all problems relate to the disintegration of the German division of labour. The Soviet Union dismantled many East German plants of the 'basic and fabricated metal' branch.[194] The branch 'Machinery and Transports' was confronted with a largely obsolete capital stock.[195] Clearly, the branch 'Metal, Machinery, Transports' was a bottleneck sector of the East German economy during the 1950s.

4.3. Regional differences

In 1936 the German empire existed of the East German territories, the West German territories and also some territories east of the Oder-Neisse, now belonging to Poland. There were three major industrial agglomerations in Germany, which were located in Berlin, the Ruhr-area (Rheinprovinz, Westfalen) and *Sachsen (Land)*. Whereas *Sachsen* is the area with the most ancient industrial roots, during the late nineteenth and early twentieth century the Ruhr-area surpassed the importance of *Sachsen*. During the same

192 Mühlfriedel and Wießner (1989) p. 213

193 Barthel (1979) p. 155

194 Eckart (1988)

195 Mühlfriedel and Wießner (1989) p. 245–258; Unger (2000) pp. 147–169

period Berlin realised unprecedented growth in industrial employment, after it had become the centre of large transportation networks, namely the railroads.[196]

Based on the criterion of their labour productivity performance, in 1936 these three industrial agglomerations would be ranked as follows: (1) Ruhr, (2) Berlin, (3) *Sachsen*. *Sachsen* was characterised by a in comparison to other industrial branches – low productive but very large – 'textiles, wearing apparel' branch. Mining and metal industries were largely located in the Ruhr area. Mining depends on the availability of natural resources. Since the metal industries needed coal for heating and iron ores to melt, which are characterised by high transportation costs, these industries tend to locate near the natural resources.[197] The industries of Berlin depended very much on the embedding in a transportation network. Since Berlin did not have its own natural resources, the industries depended on supplies from outside. Therefore the industries of Berlin were primarily 'light industries', since the transportation costs of the raw materials and half products are much higher in the 'heavy industries'.

Most of the supplies needed in Berlin were imported from 'other German areas'. At that time the different parts of Germany formed an integrated economy. Table 4.7. shows trade in agricultural and industrial products in 1936 and the flows of products between German areas and with other countries for East Germany, West Germany, and for Berlin.

Almost 70 percent of West German production was produced for the own territory, versus less than 50 percent in East Germany and less than 25 percent in Berlin. Most of the 'exports' went to other German areas, at that time part of the domestic market. Whereas East Germany and Berlin had a strong focus on the German market, in West Germany exports towards other German areas and other countries were more similar.

The same patterns become visible in the structure of imports. In particular Berlin had a very high amount of imports as a percentage of its own production: 93 percent. Most of these were received from German areas. To a lesser extent this is also true for East

Table 4.7. Markets and imports in per cent of own agricultural and industrial production in East Germany, West Germany and Berlin in 1936

	Markets for Production			Imports in % of own production		
	Own area	Rest of domestic market	Abroad	Domestic market beyond own area	Abroad	Total
East Germany	46%	43%	11%	42%	7%	49%
West Germany	69%	18%	13%	17%	11%	28%
Berlin	22%	67%	11%	78%	15%	93%

Source: Own calculations based on Gleitze (1956) p. 6

[196] Tipton, Jr. (1976)

[197] Pollard ed. (1980)

Germany, that imported almost half of the value of its own production. West Germany did import the least. Moreover, the West German imports from German territories and those from other countries were not so different in size as in East Germany and Berlin.

From the perspective of the separation of Germany after World War II the reliance upon trade with other domestic areas gives some indication of the effects of the division on the economy. In this view a high production in the own area, and low "imports" from other domestic areas indicate a high potential to move independent from other areas. Thus Table 4.7. shows that in 1936 the West German territory was in a far better position to be selfreliant than were Berlin and the East German territory. This is partly a matter of scale: West Germany covers a larger area, with a relatively small 'domestic market beyond its own area'; East Germany covers a smaller area, with a relatively large 'domestic market beyond its own area'.

So far the falling behind of the East German industries relative to West Germany from 1936 to 1954 was examined at the 'national level'. How well do the sub-regions of provinces and *Länder* fit into this pattern?

A ranking based on labour productivity in 1936 and labour productivity in 1954 that includes all provinces and *Länder* of Potsdam-Germany helps to identify regional differences. It shows that in 1936 there is no clear distinction between the regions on the East German territory and the regions on the West German territory. In 1954, however, there is a clear demarcation of what is East and what is West.

In 1936 the East German regions do not deviate in a negative sense from West German regions such as *Württemberg-Hohenzollern*, *Württemberg-Baden*, *Bayern*, *Baden*, and *Hessen*. However, the East German regions are not represented in the highest ranks either. It can thus be concluded that the different level of industrial labour productivity at the 'national level' result from the outstanding performance of some West German regions. Besides some of the smaller regions such as *Bremen* and *Hamburg*, the high productive regions include *Nordrhein-Westfalen* (Ruhr-area), and *Rheinland-Pfalz*, the main location for 'basic and fabricated metal' industries.

In 1950 the regional pattern fits the observed productivity gap between East Germany and West Germany at the national level: all East German regions (and West Berlin) are clearly below the level of industrial labour productivity in the West German regions. Strikingly the level of industrial labour productivity in West Berlin was still at approximately the same level as in East Berlin at that time. West Berlin was in many respects a special case. Geographically it was a West German "island" surrounded by East German territory. This damaged the embedding in the transportation networks that explained the success of Berlin before World War II. Other peculiarities include the political and military events, in particular the Berlin blockade in 1948, and the fact that the Soviet Union occupied Berlin. Between May and July 1945 West Berlin experienced dismantling of its assets by the Soviet Union.[198]

---

198 Karlsch (1993) pp. 60–63

Graph 4.3. Regional levels of industrial labour productivity 1936 (Reichsmarks), 1950 (DM)

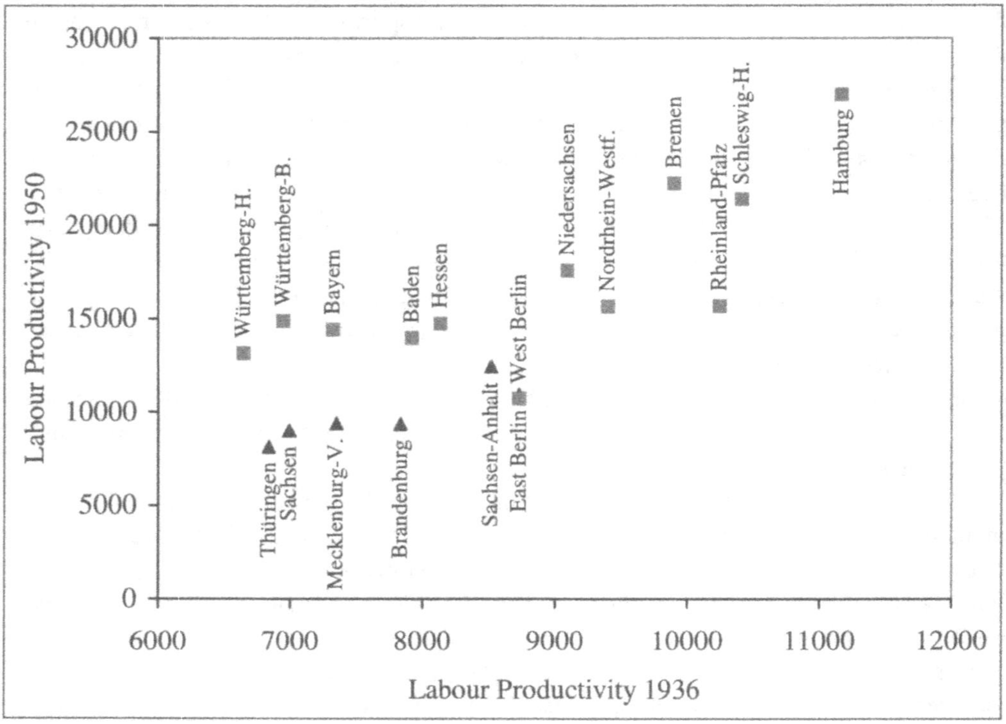

Notes: Triangles refer to East German regions; boxes refer to West German regions
Sources: Annex C

Chapter summary and conclusion

The period from 1936 to 1954 includes the sudden changes of the political, institutional and economic environment that relate to the Second World War, the beginning of the *cold war*, and the division of Germany. This chapter started off with an intertemporal perspective on the East German and West German economy – with a strong focus on the industrial sector – from 1936 to 1954. In 1944–1945 there was a drastic fall of output in both East Germany and West Germany, from which West Germany recovered much better in particular after 1947.

Negative East German industrial output growth from 1936 to 1950 was analysed in a growth accounting framework and it appeared that the main explanation lies in the depletion of its capital inputs. East Germany suffered from war damage, dismantling by the Soviet Union, and also from reparation payments to the Soviet Union. As reparations mainly concerned deliveries out of current production the effect on the East German capital stock was indirect. It is argued that reparations put a heavy burden on national income, so that possibilities for productive investment were sharply reduced. It relates to the low investment in capital stock as found in Chapter 3. Furthermore there was an under-utilisation of the capital stock that relates to the division of Germany, as the economic structure of East Germany was disproportionally endowed.

Whereas the quantity of labour inputs increased – there was an outflow of human capital. In this chapter no adjustment was made for the quality of labour inputs, so that its effects on industrial output growth are accounted for in total factor productivity (TFP) growth. Similarly under-utilisation quantitatively appeared in TFP growth. Moreover negative TFP growth in East Germany includes the effects of the use of less efficient technology in 1950 than in 1936. Between 1936 and 1939 East Germany gained a new industrial centre, that aimed to produce substitutes for all kinds of raw materials that could not be obtained from abroad in the war economy. In comparison to the use of the 'original' raw materials, the use of substitutes had adverse effects on productivity.

The cross country perspective showed that in 1936 there was a division of labour with a somewhat more 'modern' industry structure in West Germany and a minor difference of the level of labour productivity (9 per cent) in the two parts of Germany. In 1954 the labour productivity gap had increased. Based on sales value the gap ranged between 35 to 38 percentage points. It is still problematic to arrive at estimates on value added, however, if one accepts the official statistics on this matter, the input output relationship was similar to 1936.

Using shift share techniques the productivity gap in 1936 and 1954 were decomposed. For both years the 'metal, machinery, transports' branch is of major importance. In 1936 because of a negative structure effect – this high productive branch was much larger in West Germany. In 1954 because of a negative intra branch effect – this branch was far more productive in West Germany than in East Germany. Backgrounds to this productivity difference include the existence of bottlenecks (partly due to the division) and a reduction of the capital stock. Regional data supported the importance of the 'metal, machinery, transports' branch as in 1936 the productivity performance of the Ruhr-area – the major location for this particular branch – was well above the other German regions. After World War II industrial labour productivity in all East German regions were well below the West German regions, the special case West Berlin being the only exception.

Insofar the negative effects of bottlenecks are related to political aims – the ambition of autarky, and the reluctance for international trade – these effects are the result of the political economy rather than of the division of Germany. This chapter argues that the cold war provided rationality to the ambition of autarky. Moreover, the inability of the Soviet Union to deliver the wanted raw materials and heavy industry products – and the lack of hard currency as East Germany was not allowed to participate in the Marshall programme, suggest that the political reluctance to participate in international trade was not all what prevented these bottlenecks from being lifted.

Chapter 5: The industrial sector, 1950–1989

5.1. Two countries, two systems

As I have argued in Chapter 4, the backwardness of the East German economy in comparison with West Germany, as it existed in 1991, largely arose between 1936 and 1950: East Germany suffered from war damage, reparations to the Soviet Union and the disintegration of existing patterns of trade and specialisation. But between 1950 and 1989 the labour productivity gap between East Germany and West Germany widened further, so that the economic performance during the period of socialism also accounts for a considerable part of the East German falling behind.

Despite the different initial conditions between the two countries, the forty years of divided Germany is almost an ideal case for the analysis of the influence of institutions on economic performance. During the term of economics minister Ludwig Erhard West Germany introduced the concepts of the "social market economy" simultaneously with the currency reform in 1948. Prices and competition were supposed to be the primary means to organise the economy. The state was supposed to merely provide a framework to secure competitive practices in open markets without intervening in pricing policies, providing subsidies, or permitting monopolies or cartels.[199] A critical account on the continuity and discontinuity of this period is found in Abelshauser (2004), who observes a re-emergence of the "korporativen Marktwirschaft": the German model that existed before the Second World War.

Between 1947 and 1948 the issue of sovereignty in East Germany was still undecided. Before the Second World War Germany was a federal state with competencies being split between the central government and the *Länder*. After World War II a third authority was added in East Germany, namely: the Soviet Military Administration, as the Soviet Union occupied the territory. Economic plans were made by the Soviet Military Administration, by the predecessor of the central government, and by the *Länder*.

---

[199] Feldenkirchen (1999); At the same time the state should block undue concentrations of power, support the weak, and prevent market excesses, as well as acting as a stabilizer by controlling money supply and implementing social reforms.

Gradually the central government became the main sovereign of East Germany. A first result was the announcement of the two-year plan in 1948.[200]

In 1950 West Germany had established itself as a democracy and a market economy; and East Germany had turned into a communist state with a centrally planned economy. In the East German industrial sector of 1950 state enterprises were already dominant, private enterprises accounted for a mere 23 per cent of total industrial production. Between 1950 and 1960 the importance of 'public' enterprises increased even more, so that in 1960 only 4 per cent of industrial production took place in private enterprises. It illustrates the large influence of the East German government on the economy in general, and on the industrial sector in particular.

How bad was the East German performance in terms of labour productivity? In the industrial sector, which included manufacturing and mining, East German growth rates of value added and labour productivity were well below those of West Germany. Labour productivity is defined as value added per worker.

The relative performance of East Germany in comparison with West Germany differs between decades. During the 1950s both economies realised a high growth of value added and of labour productivity in the industrial sector. Thereafter growth of production and labour productivity declined, but it remained much faster in West Germany during the 1960s. During the 1970s growth of value added was faster in East Germany than in West Germany, but growth of labour productivity remained faster in West Germany. During the 1980s output and productivity growth in East Germany collapsed.

For the interpretation of the growth rates, the actual levels of output and productivity at the beginning of the period are helpful. For instance, the rapid growth of East German labour productivity – and to a lesser extent of value added – during the 1950s may come as a surprise, as at that time West Germany experienced the "supergrowth" which is known as the *Wirtschaftswunder*. However, as was already shown in Chapter 4, there is a major difference between East German and West German growth during this

Table 5.1. Average annual growth rates of real production (value added) and value added per worker in the industrial sector, 1950–1990 (in percent)

	Production (Value Added)		Labour Productivity	
	East Germany	West Germany	East Germany	West Germany
1950–60	7.7	9.6	6.1	6.1
1960–70	2.2	4.8	2.0	4.6
1970–80	2.3	1.6	1.9	2.7
1980–90	0.5	0.9	0.2	1.4
1950–90	3.3	4.3	2.6	3.8

Sources: Calculations from Annex A

200 Nettl (1953)

period. Whereas West German growth mainly concerned an expansion beyond the pre-war levels of production and labour productivity, in East Germany most of the growth was restoration.

Furthermore the size of the population developed differently in the two countries, with a declining East German population and an increasing West German population. (See Chapter 3). As a result the relative size of the pool for labour inputs had a favourable development in West Germany in comparison with East Germany. In the 1950s West Germany realised a higher growth of value added – and a similar growth of labour productivity – marking an increase of the amount of labour inputs in West Germany relative to East Germany.

Although the building of the Berlin Wall in 1961 effectively reduced migration from East Germany to West Germany, and thus reduced the rate of decline of the East German population, in the 1960s the West German pool for labour inputs was still favourable in comparison with East Germany through increases of the size of the West German population.[201] However, contrary to the 1950s performance of labour productivity was very different in the two economies. As was discussed in Chapter 3, labour productivity may improve through substitution of labour by capital, the introduction of new technology, the improvement of human capital, and by factor reallocation.

In the early 1970s West Germany realised a higher growth of industrial labour productivity, whereas industrial value added rose faster in East Germany. It indicates that East Germany increased its labour inputs in industries relative to West Germany. As it was shown in Chapter 3 this is related to factor reallocation: between 1970 and 1989 West German labour share in the industrial sector decreased rapidly.

5. 2 Assumptions on East German value added

Official East German statistics are very much distrusted in the literature. Even though this chapter aims at interpretation – and measurement was discussed elaborately in Chapter 2 – there is not always a clear division between the two. In this study the industrial sector includes mining and eleven manufacturing branches. Estimates of the growth of value added are calculated separately for each of the manufacturing branches and for the sector mining. The series are based on physical quantity indicators that were allocated to a particular branch (or to mining). Doing so, I arrived at a sample of indicators for each branch, which were aggregated to that branch according to their unit value in 1991. To arrive at series for the industrial sector all manufacturing branches and the sector mining were aggregated, extrapolating the value added in 1991. As will be dis-

201 Giersch, Paqué and Schmieding (1994) stated that in West Germany "the period 1960–73 is characterised by a strong influx of foreign labour or *Gastarbeiter*, mainly from Southern Europe"

cussed in more detail in Chapter 2 this method goes back to Bergson and Alton, although their aggregation was based on adjusted factor cost weights.[202]

Problems related to the estimation of growth of value added using physical quantity indicators include the ignorance of improvements of product quality and changes in the input-output relationship. This section first examines the problem with regard to the quality of products. This is best illustrated by looking at passenger cars. Whereas the series count the number of passenger cars that were produced, it is known that in quality there are great differences between the average passenger car in 1950 and in 1989. It is argued that series based on quantity indicators observe that twice as many cars were produced, but overlooks the fact that these cars were of a different quality. What are the effects of improved quality on the *growth* of labour productivity and on the relative *level* of labour productivity?

Adjusting productivity level comparisons for quality differences

To begin with the latter, it is emphasised that quality differences are apparent across countries. To stay at the example of passenger cars: the average passenger car in 1989 was something different in the two German economies. How can these quality differences be accounted for when comparing the relative *level* of labour productivity?

In a benchmark comparison of the East and West German manufacturing labour productivity in 1987, Van Ark included a crude quality adjustment for passenger cars.[203] Without the quality adjustment he estimated the East German labour productivity in total (!) manufacturing at 35.6 per cent of the West German level; after adjusting for quality it was estimated at a mere 32.0 per cent. It shows that a different product quality can have significant effects on the relative level of labour productivity.

Despite the crudeness of the method this adjustment draws attention to the importance of quality differences in international comparisons. It is nevertheless important how such quality differences were measured. Van Ark used the price of a passenger car that was sold in East Germany as well as in West Germany: the Czech skoda. Its West German price was compared to the average price of a new car of West German make; and its East German price was compared to the average price of the East German trabant. Doing so, the skoda was the convertor for East and West German passenger cars.[204]

A main drawback of Van Ark's quality adjustment is the ad hoc character of his method. To begin with the choice for the Czech skoda is arbitrary: why not the Russian

---

202 Bergson (1961); Alton *et al.* (1981)

203 Van Ark (1995)

204 Van Ark extrapolated the results for passenger cars to other products in machinery and transport equipment; after adjusting for quality the average East German car was estimated at 33 percent of the average West German car.

lada? Moreover the result may be biased for institutional reasons. On the one hand East German prices for the Czech skoda might not reflect quality differences very well, as these were the result of political decision-making.[205] On the other hand the Czech skoda was perhaps relatively cheap on the West German market as during the late 1980s Eastern European countries dumped products to obtain 'hard' currencies. Finally the adjustment for passenger cars is too limited to shed light on other industries: were quality differences equally large across the whole range of manufacturing products? Table 5.2. shows the East German product quality relative to West Germany distinguished for branches.

Table 5.2. is based on statistics on commodity trade. Kilogram-prices can be calculated from foreign trade statistics that show the total quantity of a product exported by a country to a particular market and the total revenue thereby achieved. The idea is that products with relatively higher quality will be characterised by relatively higher kilogram prices on third markets. It allows the comparison of an elaborate range of manufacturing products. According to Bentley the Yugoslav market is a good "third market" for the comparison of East and West German products.[206] A main advantage of the Yugoslavian market in comparison with a western market is that the East German kilogram prices were not affected by East German dumping practices in their pursuit of hard currency.

Still, from the Yugoslavian perspective the East German imports are "soft" currency imports, whereas the West German imports are "hard" currency imports. Given the pursuit of hard currency in Yugoslavia this could affect kilogram prices in favour of East Germany for other reasons than quality differences. Therefore these estimates of East German product quality relative to West Germany are an upper-bound.

The first column of Table 5.2. shows that the sample consists of 119 products sold on the Yuguslavian market that were imported from both East Germany and West Germany. For two branches, i.e. "mining" and "leather products, footwear" there were no matches. The number of products in the other branches varied from 3 products in "wood products, furniture" to 29 products in "machinery, transports".

Secondly it shows the relative quality for all matched traded products per branch, based on the unweighted average. The results suggest relatively high quality of East German products in "food, beverages, tobacco", "textiles, wearing apparel", and "stone, clay, glass". In particular the branches "wood products, furniture", "basic, fabricated metal" and "electrical equipment" show higher quality of West German products.

The average branch quality indicator hides the huge underlying inner-branch quality differences. To give an impression how many products had higher quality and how many products had lower quality than the unweighted branch average Table 5.2. in

---

[205] Maier (1997) pp. 247 ff.; Maier suggests that the council of ministers had a particular interest in the prices of passenger cars, as it deliberated on the prices for the Russian Lada and also on the prices for the imported Mazda 323.

[206] Bentley (1992)

Table 5.2. East German branch product quality of traded goods on the Yugoslav market in 1967 (West German quality = 1)

	Matches	Unweighted average	Matches above mean	Matches below mean
Mining	0			
Food, beverages, tobacco	4	1.34	2	2
Textiles, wearing apparel	16	1.16	4	12
Leather products, footwear	0			
Wood products, furniture	3	0.72	1	1
Paper, printing	5	0.98	1	4
Chemicals, rubber, plastic, oil refining	20	0.95	11	9
Stone, clay, glass	8	1.34	3	5
Machinery, transports	29	0.95	10	19
Basic, fabricated metal	15	0.73	8	7
Electrical equipment	13	0.82	4	9
Optics, fine mechanics	6	1.01	3	3
Total	119		47	71

Note: In "Wood products, furniture" there is 1 match at the mean.
Source: OECD Series C, Commodity trade

cluded the final two columns. It shows that in total 47 East German products had a higher quality than their branch average, versus 71 with a lower quality. In "wood products, furniture" one matched product is exactly at the mean. A very uneven distribution between products above and products below average indicates that results may be affected by products with exceptional high (or exceptional low) product quality. This may particularly the case in "textiles, wearing apparel" and "paper, printing".

The example of 'textiles, wearing apparel' clearly shows that product quality of some East German products (mainly synthetic) was relatively good, whereas for most other products the quality was inferior to West German standards. It is my purpose to give an indication of the variety of the quality of East German products relative to West German standards in the late 1960s. It is shown that quality differences were not equally large across the whole range of products.

Some final remarks stand out. Firstly, it is noted that the sample refers to products traded on the Yugoslavian market in 1967. Any extrapolation to the quality of East German production in general needs to deal with the 'soft' currency versus 'hard' currency distinction described above and also with the issue of the representativity of exported goods to the Yugoslavian market for all goods produced in two German economies. Secondly, aggregation from matched products to an average branch quality indicator is hazardous. It hides the huge underlying inner-branch quality differences and therefore requires further research that provides appropriate weights based on the production structure in East and West Germany.

Table 5.3. East German kilogram prices in "Textiles, wearing apparel" in 1967 (West German kilogram price = 1)

Description	SITC	EG/WG
Clothing of text fabric, not knitted crocheted	n841.1	0.21
Clothing accessories of text., not knitted/croch	n841.2	0.57
Clothing and accessories, knitted or crocheted	n841.4	0.37
Yarn and thread of synthetic fibres	n651.6	1.99
Yarn and thread of regenerated fibres	n651.7	0.53
Cotton fabrics, woven, other than grey	n652.2	0.48
Woolen fabrics, woven	n653.2	0.79
Fabrics, woven, of synthetic fibres	n653.5	1.72
Fabrics, woven, of regenerated fibres	n653.6	0.80
Knitted or crochd fabrics not elast nor rubberd	n653.7	5.76
Tulle, lace, embroidery, ribbons, trimmings	n654	0.93
Coated or impregnated textile fabrics & prod.	n655.4	0.68
Tarpaulins, tents, awnings, sails, etc.	n656.2	0.88
Blankets, travelling rugs and coverlets	n656.6	1.50
Made-up articles of textile materials	n656.9	0.49
Linoleum and similar floor coverings	n657.4	0.87

Source: OECD Series C, Commodity trade

Quality differences and the growth of value added

Quality improvements emerged over time presumably in both East Germany and West Germany. This is especially the case in consumer durables and investment goods, and to a lesser extent for basic goods which represent intermediate stages of production.[207] Measurement of East German output growth in this study is based on quantity indicators, such as: liters of beer, tons of steel, tons of yarns, number of passenger cars, etceteras. Growth series of Alton and Bergson, who also used quantity indicators to estimate growth in centrally planned economies, have received criticism for not properly taking into account quality improvements and the introduction of new products.[208] Besides the example of the passenger car that was much better in 1989 than in 1950, the criticism also points at a selection bias. It is argued that a sample of physical quantities is likely to be biased towards traditional items (e.g. tons of steel) rather than toward modern products (e.g. amount of computers), leading to downwardly biased growth rates.

However, the downward effect of the missing new (and improved) products on the growth rates for East Germany presented in this study is easily exaggerated. To begin with the selection bias, it is true that for some branches the sample of physical quantities is larger than in others. Supposed that the available indicators are particularly biased

207 Van Ark (1993) p. 34

208 Marer (1985) p. 175

towards traditional branches – which is not at all obvious from the data as shown in Annex A – would it influence the growth rates? No. This study uses a different sample for each branch, and calculates the growth rates of each branch independently. Insofar the overall sample bias for the industrial sector leads to a different size of the sub-samples for the underlying branches, such a bias does not harm the results.

At worst the selection of the physical indicators could be biased towards the traditional products within the sample of a particular branch. However, modern products and new products *are* in fact accounted for. For instance the sample for electrical equipment includes televisions, vacuum cleaners, and refrigerators along with more traditional products such as light bulbs. Moreover, for some products information on specific types is so detailed that it reflects quality differences. It is for instance possible to distinguish several types of yarns, depending on the material that is was made of.

A final remark regarding the product mix I want to make is that East Germany in fact put a lot of effort in producing traditional products. Chapter 3 already showed the increase of mining, with traditional items such as coals, and ores. A major investment project in the 1950s built up *Eisenhüttenstadt*, where steel was produced. It illustrates that to a large extent the traditional items account for the actual growth of output – as follows the *Tonnenideologie* of the regime.

The second aspect of the quality problem concerns the 'product content', i.e. the improvement of product quality over time. For this purpose the cross country comparison of East Germany and West Germany gives some indication of product quality in East Germany. Assuming comparable product qualities before the two economies were divided, the larger the quality difference – the less East German product quality improved.[209]

Boretsky found that growth rates based on physical quantity indicators were downwardly biased for West Germany and also for the United States, and concluded that this indicates that growth of the Soviet economy might be substantially underestimated.[210] Similarly this also indicates that the use of physical quantity indicators leads to downwardly biased growth rates for East Germany. It is my impression, however, that the downward effect of using physical quantity indicators is much smaller in the East German case – and probably also in the case of the Soviet Union – than it is for West Germany and the United States, as East Germany realised fewer qualitative improvements.

Input output relationships and the growth of value added

Besides quality, also input output relationships differ across countries and may change over time. As shown in Chapter 4, the benchmark comparison for 1954 showed a lower estimate of East German relative labour productivity based on gross output than based

---

209 Minor increase of product qualities in East Germany also relates to the domination of process innovations rather than product innovations (see Chapter 1).

210 Boretsky (1987) pp. 517–542

Table 5.4. Input/output ratios in the East and West German industrial sector 1950–1988 (based on current prices)

	1950	1960	1970	1980	1988
East Germany	0.47	0.47	0.57	0.59	0.66
West Germany	0.51	0.62	0.60	0.64	0.62

Sources: Own calculations from Schwarzer (1999); Statistisches Jahrbuch der Deutschen Demokratischen Republik 1990; Statistisches Jahrbuch für die Bundesrepublik Deutschland, several issues; Statistisches Bundesamt (1991)

on value added. Hence, East Germany used fewer intermediate inputs than West Germany. Changes of the input output relationship are not accounted for in this study's time series based on physical quantity indicators – where the input output relationship of 1991 was assumed for the entire period. Table 5.4. shows the actual input/output ratios based on current prices in the two countries for selected years.

Whereas in 1950 the input output relationship was more or less the same in East and West Germany, in 1960 there was a huge difference between the input output relationship in the two countries. Between 1963 and 1967 East Germany introduced the new economic system (NES) which was accompanied by a price reform. Prices of intermediate inputs increased relative to prices of final products, so that in 1970 the input output relationship in the two countries seems more equal again.

As the input/output ratios above were estimated with current prices of the own country's currency, in real terms the figures need not show that the input output ratio was actually more equal between East Germany and West Germany in 1970 than in 1960. Neither is it necessarily so that East Germany used more inputs relative to outputs in 1970 than in 1960, as it may be fully explained by the relative increase of prices for intermediate inputs during this period. Logically – assuming that prices were an incentive in East Germany – the increase of prices of intermediate inputs relative to final products leads to a decrease of actual use of intermediate inputs. According to Steiner[211] and Maier[212] before the economic reform in the 1960s the prices of raw materials were too low. Prices covered for 71 per cent of costs of black coal, 52 per cent of brown coal, and 81 per cent of iron and steel.

Chapter 2 discussed East German prices in more detail. It is nevertheless clear that there are severe difficulties with the East German data, so that interpretation of the East German input output relationship is hazardous. The information on input output ratios as shown above suggests that the amount of intermediate inputs (energy, raw materials and semi-fabrics) that is used in the production process increased faster than gross production. However, how much is explained by price changes? Although the *regime* did publish series where intermediate inputs and final products were deflated separately –

211 Steiner (1999) p. 189

212 Maier (1997)

i.e. double deflated series – in the case of East Germany there are some serious methodological shortcomings.[213] In East Germany the constant series were based on reported data of enterprises, which included the production in current prices and according to prices of the preceding years. As was explained in Chapter 2 some problems were involved, in particular with modified (new) products.

The use of value added weights for 1991, and assuming the input output relationship of 1991, had the advantage of 'market' prices. At that time the two German economies were already integrated. For East Germany the use of intermediate inputs probably increased faster than gross output. This implies an upward bias of the value added series presented in this study. As a result growth of value added and also of labour productivity may be (a little) too high.

5.3. Defining labour inputs

This study defines labour productivity as value added per worker. Obviously it makes a difference whether someone works for instance 2000 hours or 1700 hours per year. Between 1950 and 1989 the average working hours per employed person per year decreased in West Germany and also in East Germany. Clearly the hours worked is more precise as a measure for the quantity of labour inputs than the number of persons that are employed. At the same time it can be argued that there is some stretch in the meaning of hours worked, as it does not only count for the time spent on the job, but also for time spent on waiting in the queues, coffee-breaks, etceteras. The decreasing working hours per employee was established by reductions of the length of the working day, more vacation, and the introduction of the Saturday as a day off. For the *performance* of labour productivity this means that growth of labour productivity per hour was higher than growth of labour productivity per worker as shown above.

The development of the average yearly working hours per person employed differed in the two German economies. In West Germany the average working hours per year decreased faster than in East Germany. West Germany outperformed East Germany in terms of value added per worker, but in terms of value added per hour worked the gap was even bigger.

Table 5.5. Average yearly working hours per employee in the industrial sector

	1950	1955	1960	1965	1970	1975	1980	1985	1988
East Germany	2090	2050	1915	1970	1880	1741	1711	1704	1714
West Germany	2293	2295	2068	1938	1906	1726	1698	1666	1629

Sources: ICOP; Haustein (1990)

213 See Chapter 2

Graph 5.1. Value added 'per worker' and 'per hour' in the industrial sector Logaritmic scale, (1950 = 100)

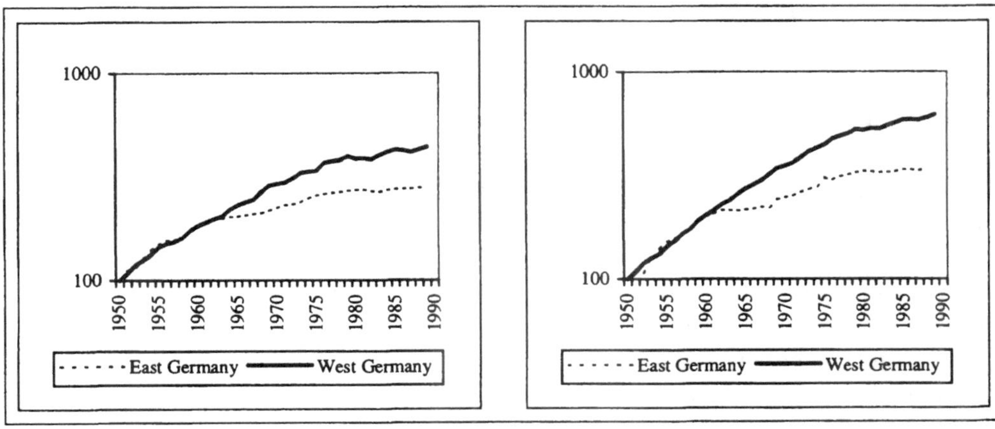

Sources: Annex A

The divergence of the East German and West German growth of labour productivity occurred from the late 1950s/early 1960s onwards (see also Table 5.1.). There is a clear pattern of East German growth with increases of labour productivity during the 1950s and 1970s, and a relatively slow development during the 1960s and 1980s. Especially the series on value added per hour show that East German labour productivity hardly increased between 1962 and 1968, and after 1980.

In the case of East Germany workers increased their incomes not by working hard during regular hours but by overtime; management welcomed the flexibility offered by overtime wages because it provided the means to satisfy the work force. Even means to encourage hard working such as piece rates were (mis)used as a way to satisfy the workers: piece-workers increased their wages through easily overfulfilling weak piece rates.[214]

As an explanatory variable for labour productivity the stretch in the meaning of hours worked can be seen as "working ethics". An attitude of workers towards work, that existed within the context of the centrally planned economy, where workers had to wait for intermediate inputs to arrive, where people had to wait in queues to buy new shoes, and where high labour participation of men and women required some flexibility of employers to establish a work-life balance. Alternatively it can also relate to hidden unemployment, as East German labour market policy aimed at full employment. As a result there were more workers to do the job than there were jobs to be done.

214 Kopstein (1997) pp. 155–172; Kopstein shows the example of VEB Mikromat, an electronics enterprise in Dresden, where in the 1970s piece rates were usually met at a rate of 160 percent.

5.4. Labour productivity growth in industries, 1950–1989

Chapter 3 already examined the effects of factor reallocation between different sectors for the total economy, and for the entire period from 1950 to 1989. Using shift share techniques the annual labour productivity growth was decomposed into intra branch effects, static shift effects, and dynamic shift effects. Intra branch effects account for improvements of the sector productivity levels; static shift effects account for productivity growth caused by a shift of labour towards sectors with a higher productivity level at the beginning of the period; and dynamic shift effects measure shift effects towards more dynamic sectors, i.e. sectors with higher labour productivity growth rates.

For the total economy East Germany showed high dynamic shift effects. This fits the model of a centrally planned economy where the economic structure changes 'top down' rather than 'bottom up' as in a market economy. The East German regime could direct investments in capital and technology, and shifts of labour inputs simultaneously towards priority sectors. As labour moves towards sectors where at the same time the capital stock is renewed and technology is improved, high dynamic shift effects are a probable outcome. At the same time a concentration on priority sectors may have neglected other parts of the economy. This could have resulted in a crowding out of investments in other sectors so that aggregate labour productivity growth was suppressed.

Similarly to Chapter 3 this chapter decomposes the growth of labour productivity into intra branch effects, static shift effects, and dynamic shift effects for the industrial sector. Whereas the total economy was studied for the whole period from 1950 to 1989, the analysis of the industrial sector is divided into four sub-periods. This makes it possible to relate the policy of the East German regime to the developments within industries.

Table 5.6. Decomposition of annual labour productivity growth in the industrial sector, 1950–1989

	East Germany				West Germany			
	1950s	1960s	1970s	1980s	1950s	1960s	1970s	1980s
Labour productivity growth	6.1	2.0	1.9	0.2	6.1	4.6	2.7	1.4
Percentage explained by:								
Intra branch effect	98.3	97.2	93.9	113.8	99.3	97.6	91.6	89.1
Static shift effect	–0.8	3.5	9.4	–11.8	–1.3	2.2	6.7	11.5
Dynamic shift effect	2.5	–0.7	–3.3	–2.0	2.0	0.2	1.7	–0.6
Total	100.0	100.0	100.0	100.0	100.0	100.0	100.0	100.0

Sources: Annex A; Melzer (1980); OECD, *The OECD STAN Database for Industrial Analysis*

In both German economies, and for all four decades, intra branch effects explain most of the labour productivity growth in the industrial sector. It indicates improvements of branch productivity levels, for instance through extra capital inputs, better technology, and/or better human capital. Obviously, a high percentage of labour productivity growth explained by the intra branch effect need not imply that the actual branch productivity growth is also high. This is best illustrated with the 1980s, where the intra branch effect for East Germany is very high: 113.8 per cent. Meanwhile the labour productivity is very low: a mere 0.2 per cent. Here the improvements of branch productivity levels account for more than all growth in labour productivity. However, for this period the dominant story is not so much on extra capital inputs, better technology, and/or improved human capital, as it is on the low labour productivity growth.

For the same reasons the widely different static shift effects in the 1980s are also related to the low East German labour productivity growth at that time. Static shift effects refer to the reallocation of workers from branches with low productivity levels towards branches with high productivity levels. Looking at the benchmark for the industrial sector in 1954 as shown in Chapter 4, static shift effects could be achieved through a shift of employment from 'textiles, wearing apparel' to 'chemicals, rubber, plastic, oil refining'.

In contrast to the findings for the total economy, within the East German industrial sector the dynamic shift effects were not particularly high. On the contrary. During the 1960s, the 1970s and – again related to the low labour productivity growth – the 1980s, dynamic shift effects were negative. This means that workers were directed towards branches where labour productivity growth was lower than in the branches in which they were previously employed. How do these findings relate to ideas on priority branches and processes of crowding out?

One hypothesis is that the low aggregate labour productivity growth in the industrial sector was related to the crowding out of non-priority sectors for investments in capital stock and technology. It is known that the East German regime had a strong focus on the development of particular industries, such as basic and fabricated metal industries during the 1950s. In Chapter 3 it was suggested that as priority branches received most of the investments in capital and technology these branches probably also realised a high growth of labour productivity in comparison to other branches. A shift of labour towards these priority branches could therefore lead to a high dynamic shift effect.

However, another outcome may also be possible. For instance the expectation on a relatively high growth of labour productivity in priority branches may not have hold. In the 1970s and 1980s many investments were directed towards the production of raw materials such as brown coals, at the expense of investment in other branches.[215] Whereas the size of the manufacturing sector decreased between 1970 and 1989, more workers got employed in mining. In this sense, mining can be seen as a priority sector in

215 Baar, Müller and Zschaler (1995) p. 50

these two decades. As it is shown in Chapter 6, however, labour productivity growth in mining was quite low.

Another reason could be that the synchronicity between labour shifts and the investments in capital and technology has (statistically) adverse effects. For example, investment in capital may contribute to labour productivity growth if capital per worker increases. Therefore it is useful to look in more detail at the role of branches in total industrial labour productivity growth in East Germany. In the following this will be analysed for all four decades from 1950 to 1990. It will be related to the different branches that are considered to be important and also with some general outlines of policy.

For this purpose I will use so-called "Harberger diagrams".[216] Originally this diagram visualised the contribution of each branch to the growth of total factor productivity of the whole industrial sector or the whole economy; however, it can also be used to show the branch contribution to the aggregate growth of labour productivity. The diagram ranks branches according to their labour productivity growth over the period. On the x-axis it shows the corresponding cumulation of initial value added; on the y-axis it shows the cumulation of labour productivity growth.[217] For the interpretation of the results Harberger used the appealing metaphor of 'yeast versus mushrooms': yeast causes bread to expand very evenly, like a balloon being filled with air, while mushrooms have the habit of popping up, almost overnight, in a fashion that is not easy to predict. Applied to labour productivity growth in the industrial sector 'yeast' refers to a growth process where many branches contribute to aggregate growth, whereas 'mushrooms' refer to aggregate labour productivity growth that relies on only few branches.

What about East German labour productivity growth? Was it a mushroom process, where only few branches carried all the improvement? Or was it a yeast process, where increases of labour productivity occurred within all branches of the economy?

Yeast versus mushrooms in the 1950s

In the 1950s total labour productivity growth in the industrial sector was high, at 6.3 per cent per year. Branches that contributed most to aggregate labour productivity growth were 'basic and fabricated metal', 'machinery and transports', and 'food, beverages, tobacco'. The priority of the regime was very much directed towards the branch 'basic and fabricated metal' in order to lessen existing bottlenecks that resulted from the division of the two German economies. Moreover, the focus on these industries fits the idea of 'socialist industrialisation'. All Eastern European countries followed the example of the industrialisation pattern of the Soviet Union, with an emphasis on heavy industries.

In Graph 5.2. branches were ranked corresponding to their growth of labour productivity; those branches where labour productivity growth was highest are more to the left

---

216 Harberger (1998)

217 For more details on the calculation see Annex A

on the x-axis, whereas those branches where labour productivity growth was lower are more to the right. The horizontal grey dotted line shows the total labour productivity growth in the industrial sector. For the 1950s it is only after the accumulation of the best eight/nine branches (looking at their growth of labour productivity) that the total labour productivity growth for the entire sector is reached. The first vertical line estimates their share – measured by their initial value added – at about 70 per cent. The remaining 30 per cent Harberger calls 'overshooting'. At this intersect there are some branches that contribute to the total labour productivity growth, but it is offset by other branches with negative labour productivity growth.

During the 1950s aggregate labour productivity growth was clearly a wide process that occurred in most manufacturing branches. With merely two branches having a negative contribution to labour productivity growth the diagram shows much more of a yeast process than could be expected considering the strong indications for a policy focus on heavy industries. Why?

To begin with the contribution to aggregate labour productivity growth of the branches 'basic and fabricated metal' and 'machinery and transports' it is clear that their contribution was much higher than in other sectors. Contribution was more than twice as high as in the branch ranked third: 'food, beverages, tobacco'. This is to some extent

Graph 5.2. Harberger-diagram of East German labour productivity growth in the 1950s

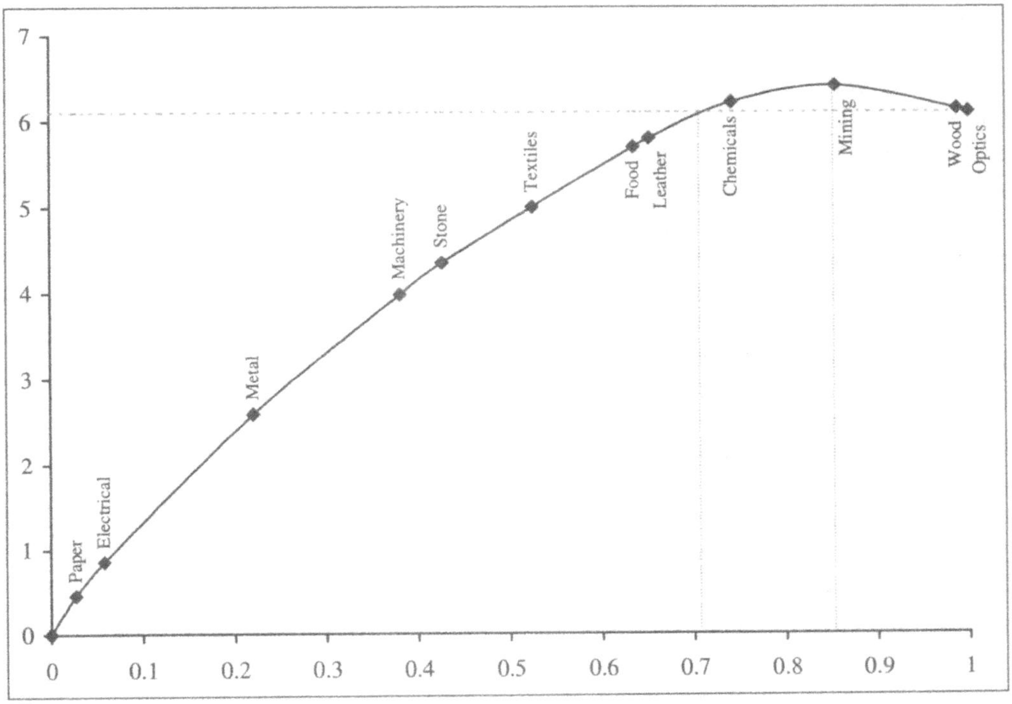

Sources: Calculations from Annex A

related to the low initial level of labour productivity in 'basic and fabricated metal' and 'machinery and transports', which were at the lower levels of East German industrial labour productivity in 1954. (See Table 4.5.).

Furthermore it is stressed that in the early 1950s the East German economy suffered very much from bottlenecks. The lack of particular supplies – particularly those produced by heavy industries – could start a domino of bottlenecks throughout the industrial sector. Similarly, solving this problem that is due to the interdependency within this sector could also accomplish results that reach beyond the boundaries of the heavy industries. It is recalled from Chapter 4 that in the early 1950s East German industries produced below their production possibilities frontier, partly as a result of bottlenecks. When bottlenecks were lifted production – and productivity – could increase easily.

Instead of asking why labour productivity growth was so much a yeast process, it is also legitimate to ask: why not? The expected mushroom process was based on the existence of a priority sector, and the crowding out of non-priority branches that resulted of it. Firstly, the emphasis of the East German regime on heavy industries should not be overestimated. According to estimates of Baar et al. investment in 'basic and fabricated metal' and 'machinery and transports' during the late 1950s was about 16 per cent of all investments in the industrial sector.[218] This is well below its share in value added, which gives nuance to its characterisation as a priority sector. As the emphasis on these particular branches should not be underestimated either it is noted that investment in 'basic and fabricated metal' and 'machinery and transports' accounted for a larger share of all investment in the early 1950s. A similar conclusion is found in Hoffmann, who stated that since 1953 the "Auf- und Ausbau der Schwerindustrie – zwar nicht zurückgenommen wurde, gleichzeitig aber andere, bisher als eher randständige angesehene Wirtschaftsbereiche (z.B. Leicht- und Konsumgüterindustrie) zumindest partiell aufgewertet wurden".

Secondly, it is unlikely that in the 1950s the existence of priority sectors led to a process of crowding out. During these years East Germany was still in the phase of restoration after the Second World War. Industries could easily resume production with only little amounts of money, through repairments on existing capital stock or through the elimination of bottlenecks.

Yeast versus mushrooms in the 1960s

East German labour productivity growth in the industrial sector during the 1960s amounted to 2 per cent, well below the West German growth rate. The branches that contributed most to aggregate growth of labour productivity were 'chemicals, rubber, plastic, oil refining', 'machinery and transports', and 'food, beverages, tobacco', lea-

[218] Baar, Müller and Zschaler (1995)

ving 'basic and fabricated metal' at a fourth position. There are two main events that characterise the policy of the East German government during the 1960s. First the Berlin Wall was built in 1961, which reduced migration to West Germany. Second, East Germany introduced the 'new economic system' between 1963 and 1967. The economic reforms included a comprehensive price reform, executed in several stages, the aim of which was to eliminate a significant part of the price distortions then existing.[219] Furthermore there was a massive organisational restructuring of the economic administration, which is sometimes misconceived as a moving up in the direction of a 'market economy'. Many decisions were passed on to the 'Vereinigung Volkseigener Betriebe' and also to the enterprises. This does not mean that decisionmaking became decentralised as in a market economy, as decentralisation presupposes autonomy. In the East German organisational restructuring autonomy remained at the central authorities; rather than decentralisation of decisionmaking there was delagation of decisionmaking to subordinate institutions such as the 'Vereinigung Volkseigener Betriebe'. Fundamental decisions were made centrally, decisions on details were deconcentrated.[220]

The grey dotted line again shows the total labour productivity growth in industries. For the 1960s the remarkable characteristic is that there was no 'overshooting': all branches contributed to the total growth of labour productivity in the industrial sector. East German labour productivity growth in the 1960s was a yeast process. Why was the growth of labour productivity so much balanced?

It makes sense to relate yeasty labour productivity growth to sources for improvement that are beneficial to all branches. For example through the introduction of new 'general purpose technologies', or through an improvement of 'human capital' in East Germany. As a result of the Berlin Wall that was built in 1961 migration to West Germany – of foremost well educated young East Germans – came to a halt. More than before those who finished their schooling in East Germany also reinforced the East German labour supply, providing it of new (and improved) human capital.

Secondly the yeast process can also relate to the new organisation design of the economic administration. It is likely that deconcentration of planning and decisionmaking smoothed the bureaucratic machinery; enabling a more adequate response to current issues. Not only were the 'Vereinigung Volkseigener Betriebe' better informed on the particular industries they had to decide upon than the central authorities were, also the flexibility of the regime to act quickly increased. This can be seen as a potential source for the improvement of efficiency that was beneficial to all branches.[221]

Finally the evenly expansion of labour productivity growth relates to the absence of 'real' priority-branches in the 1960s, which leaves little reason to expect a crowding out of other branches. In the 1960s there was no economic plan that was executed. Leptin

---

219 Leptin and Melzer (1978) p. 36 ff.

220 Steiner (1999)

221 See: Steiner (1999); Steiner finds that the effects of the reforms on productivity were minimal.

Graph 5.3. Harberger-diagram of East German labour productivity growth in the 1960s

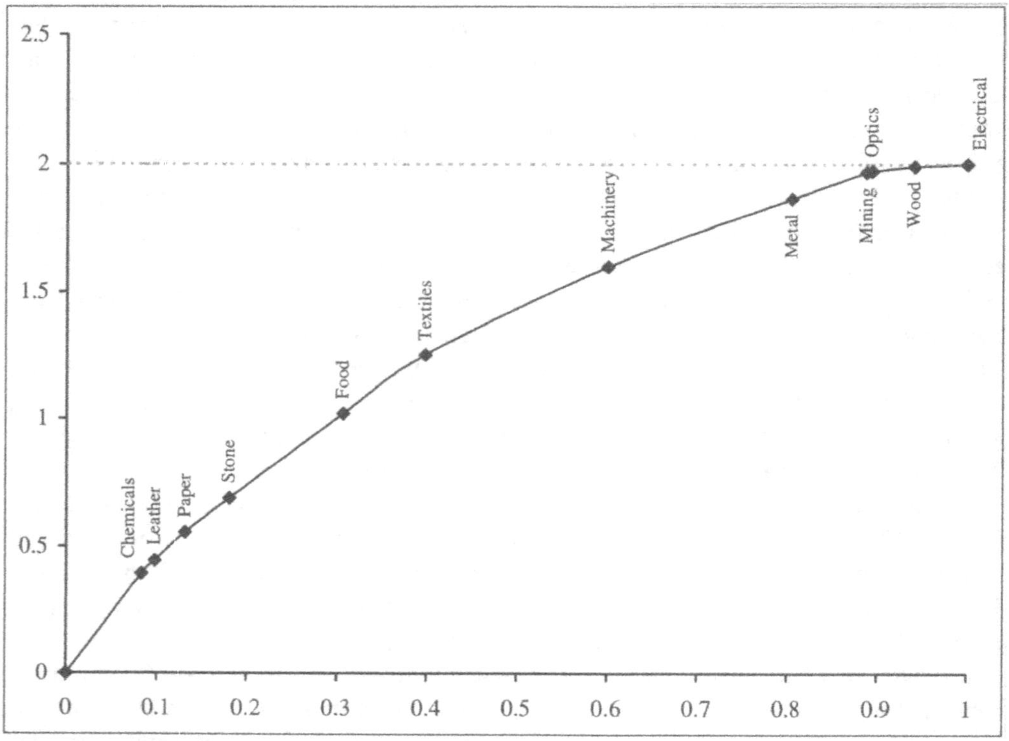

Sources: Calculations from Annex A

and Melzer wrote that "the seven-year plan (1959–65), which had taken the place of the second five-year plan (1956–60) when the latter was terminated in 1959, was in its turn terminated in 1963 (after it had in fact collapsed in 1961) and in 1966–67 the new long-term plan for 1966–70 did not come into being because, owing to the postponement of the third phase of the price reform [...] no uniform standard of valuation for the plan existed".[222] In a sense the East German industries were muddling through rather than planning ahead.

Only in the years from 1968 to 1970 it is possible to recognise a system of priority planning, as part of the 'forcierte Strukturpolitik', i.e. the strategy of 'overtaking without catching up'.[223] It adds to the explanation for the high ranks for 'chemicals, rubber, plastic, oil refining' and to a lesser extent of 'machinery and transports'. However, in 'electrical equipment' – also a branch of core interest – labour productivity hardly increased. According to Leptin and Melzer (1978) and also according to Steiner (2004) the system of priority planning between 1968 and 1970 failed because of bottlenecks in

222 Leptin and Melzer (1978) p. 17

223 See Steiner (1999) pp. 442–502 for an elaborate discussion of this policy

the supply of electricity and as a result of supply industries lagging behind plan targets.[224]

Also the high productivity growth in Chemicals is related to bottlenecks and in particular to the East German position in international trade. Abelshauser (2004) and also Steiner (2004) mention the completion of the oil pipeline "Freundschaft" with the Soviet Union. Access to oil was crucial for the development of the petrochemical industries in East Germany during the 1960s. After gaining access to a larger amount of oil East Germany showed its capability to increase labour productivity in Chemicals through the application of 'new' technologies that had started to diffuse in the West about ten years earlier.

Yeast versus mushrooms in the 1970s

During the 1970s the annual growth of labour productivity in the industrial sector in East Germany amounted to 2 per cent, which is less than one per cent below the West German rate. Branches with the highest contribution to aggregate labour productivity growth were: 'basic and fabricated metal', 'textiles, wearing apparel', and 'chemicals, rubber, plastic, oil refining'. In 1971 Erich Honecker replaced Walter Ulbricht, and the strategy of 'overtaking without catching up' – overtaking the West in chemicals, machine building, and electronics before actually catching up with its economy as a whole – was done away with. In the late 1960s Ulbricht announced the aim to sell computers in the West in 1975; Honecker was more in favour of a social turn, with raised pensions, reduced mandatory hours in the work week, improved systems of day care, child support and maternity leave.[225]

The social policy was very much related to the economic policy. In Honeckers words: "Es kann nur das verteilt werden, was vorher erarbeitet worden ist". Besides the ever-eminent aim to increase production capacity the increase of labour productivity gained the attention of the regime. It was seen as the key to the improvement of the standard of living.[226] The Harberger diagram for the 1970s shows much more the signs of a mushroom pattern of development than the 1950s and the 1960s. There is considerable overshooting and there is a negative contribution to the total industrial labour productivity growth in 'mining' and the relatively large 'machinery and transports' branch.

Meanwhile, the majority of branches contributed to aggregate industrial labour productivity growth. Looking at the branches that added to total labour productivity growth only, it would have reached 2.3 per cent growth at maximum. In 1970 the non-priority supply industries faced bottleneck situations which, like the lagging growth of sectors

---

224 Leptin and Melzer (1978) pp. 73 ff.; Steiner (2004) p. 149 ff.

225 Kopstein (1997)

226 Bundesministerium für innerdeutsche Beziehungen (1987) pp. 23, 24

Graph 5.4. Harberger-diagram of East German labour productivity growth in the 1970s

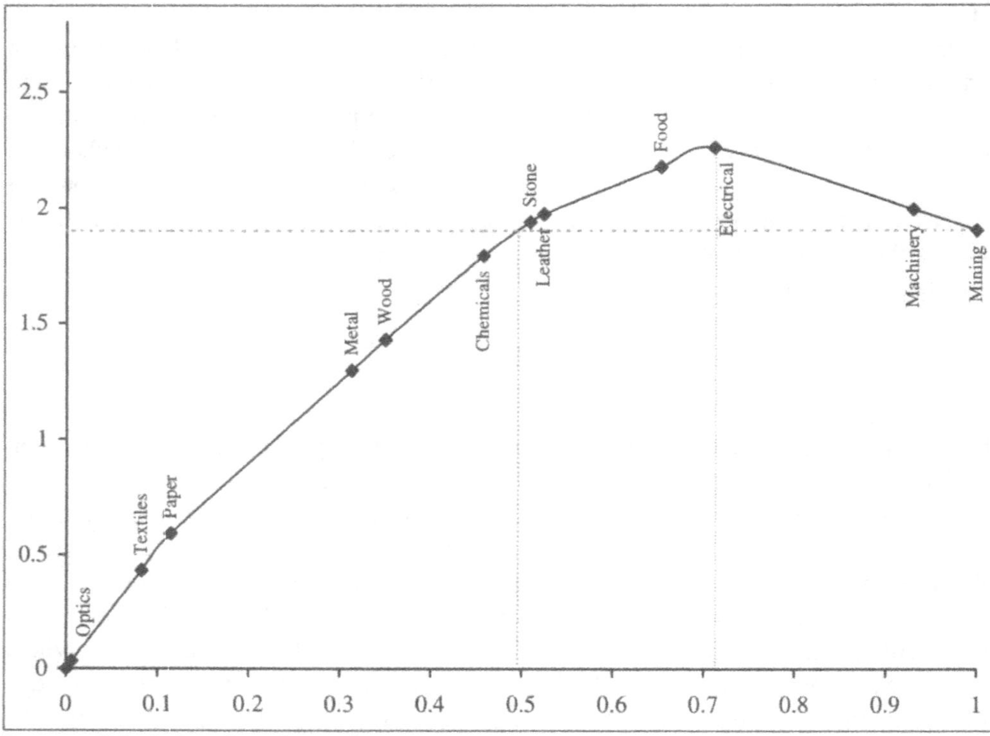

Sources: Calculations from Annex A

of the economy outside industry, in turn affected the priority sectors.[227] Therefore, one of the aims of economic policy must have been to reassure these needed supplies.

There are two ways to obtain the needed goods of the non-priority supply industries. Firstly it is possible to start producing these goods in larger amounts; secondly these goods can be purchased through increased participation in international trade. The 1970s are regarded as a period of increasing integration of the socialist markets, with an increasing division of labour between its members.[228] The degree of economic integration should not be overestimated, though two examples illustrate that there were some signs of specialisation.

The first example refers to the earlier mentioned petrochemical industries that make use of oil and gas as an intermediate input, such as refineries and plastics.[229] In the 1970s new capacities were built in Zeitz, Böhlen, Schwarzheide, Leuna and Buna. The use of oil, mainly imported from the Soviet Union, doubled between 1970 and 1980.

[227] Leptin and Melzer (1978) p. 77

[228] Van Brabant (1987)

[229] The example is based on DIW (1980)

However, during the second half of the 1970s prices for crude oil increased rapidly.[230] The Soviet Union could only supply for 19 million tons of oil per year; finance for supplies from other countries was difficult. Therefore East Germany increasingly used (brown) coals as an intermediate input that replaced the input of oil, as East Germany could produce coals by itself. On the one hand the example indicates the existence of an international division of labour within the COMECON countries. On the other hand it shows its fragility as in the end this led to a renaissance of the East German production of brown coals.

The second example concerns the machine tools industries.[231] Whereas the chemical industries depended very much on imports, machine tools were export oriented and as such a source of income in international trade. In 1970 as much as 80 per cent of the production was exported, most of it to other COMECON countries. However, at the end of the 1970s it was losing much of its markets. Other COMECON countries could produce the less advanced equipment themselves, and had not enough money to purchase specialty machines. In comparison with products in the West at the end of the 1970s the East German products were technologically lagging behind, as they were not automated through the use of microelectronics. Obviously the participation in an international division of labour created a vulnerable spot in the centrally planned economy – as its success is subject to changes of demand and product competitiveness.

No wonder that East Germany expanded its production in some potential bottleneck industries such as brown coals but also metal products.[232] It relieved the economy – and particularly the planning authorities – from the unpredictability of the outside world. Schröter (1999) found that some typical East German innovations in the chemical industries aimed to relax upon the need for foreign currency.[233] As it was argued in Chapter 4 such a pursuit of autarky is negative for productivity growth.

Regarding the production of machine tools, a branch that was very much oriented to exports, it is only sensible not to increase production any further after a loss of market share. East Germany was simply unable to keep up with technological developments of the time. Similar reasoning applies for other products in the branch 'machinery and transports', which explains for a stagnation of value added in this branch. A study of Bauer (1999) on East German passenger cars – the *trabant* and the *wartburg* – describes the 1970s as a transition phase from relative innovativeness to decline. To explain for the transition Bauer mentions general problems of the car industries that relate to the high throughput of materials, some specific problems of East German projects, and also lacking modernisation due to the economic system. Referring to the process of creative

---

230 See also: Ahrens (2000) pp. 331 ff.

231 The example is based on DIW (1982); see also Roesler (1999) pp. 349–390

232 Besides improving its labour productivity 'basic and fabricated metal' also realised an increase of value added.

233 Schröter (1999) p. 312

destruction he concluded that the destruction part of the process was insufficient, so that the implementation of the desired new combination of production factors failed.[234]

During the 1970s the 'textiles, wearing apparel' branch shows high growth rates of labour productivity. Following Heimann (1997) this could be an example of the positive effects of prioritisation on labour productivity growth. Whereas this branch suffered from crowding out effects during the 1950s and the early 1960s, as it had a low priority, from the second half of the 1960s investment rose.[235] Also during the first half of the 1970s Heimann concludes that investment was probably high. Graph 5.3. shows that this branch indeed attained a high rank of labour productivity growth, whereas it attained to a more modest performance in the previous decades.

Although East German production was not isolated from its outside economy, it is safe to assume that labour productivity was to a large extent determined by forces within the East German economy. Unlike the machine tools industries, in most industries value added was earned at the domestic market, where competitors could hardly get access. Departing from a growth accounting framework this would imply that during the 1970s either capital inputs or that total factor productivity increased. The latter for instance through the improvement of human capital, the diffusion of new technologies, and/or the improvement of the organisation design.

Yeast versus mushrooms in the 1980s

Annual labour productivity growth in the 1980s was merely 0.2 per cent. Highest contribution to aggregate labour productivity growth was realised in 'food, beverages, tobacco', 'chemicals, rubber, plastic, oil refining', 'electrical equipment' and 'textiles, wearing apparel'. There was a large overshooting, so that the 1980s are a clear example of a mushroom process.

In the 1980s it was aimed to come to grip with microelectronics, which to some extent made the branch 'electrical equipment' a priority branch. A substantial part of products still consisted of already outdated technology. In 1980 the proportion of colour televisions was 46 per cent of total production, the majority still consisted of black and white sets. At the end of the 1980s the share of colour televisions had moved up to 77 per cent of total.[236] Similarly the replacement of manual typewriters through electronic typewriters was lagging. Above all East Germany did want to develop a computer industry at Robotron.

---

234 Bauer (1999) p. 309 In response to the (hard) production targets the worn off machinery was maintained as a capacity reserve, using up an increasing share of employment.

235 Heimann (1997) p. 204, 258

236 Examples are from Bentley (1992) pp. 47ff.; In West Germany the proportion of colour televisions was already at 94 per cent in 1980.

Graph 5.5. Harberger-diagram of East German labour productivity growth in the 1980s

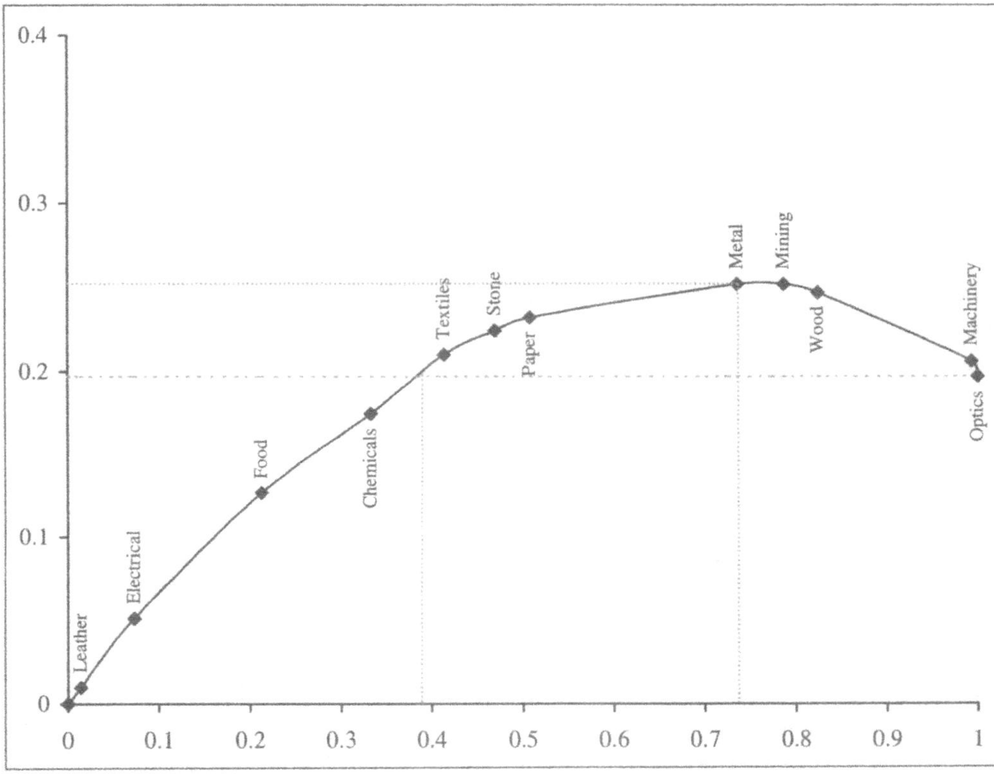

Sources: Calculations from Annex A

However, it is neither the 'boost' of some priority branches nor the negative contribution to industrial labour productivity growth that needs explanation. Aggregate productivity growth was very low, and none of the branches were truly successful. Leaving aside the branches with a negative contribution to the total growth of industrial labour productivity, growth would still remain below 0.3 per cent.

As was the case with the decomposition of labour productivity growth into intra branch effects, static shift effects, and dynamic shift effects, the decomposition of labour productivity growth into different branches is affected by the very low growth rates for the total industrial sector. Sure, the Harberger diagram shows a mushroom, with a decline of labour productivity in 'mining', 'wood products, furniture', 'optics, fine mechanics', and 'machinery and transports'. However, rather than the differences between branches the remarkable development is the stagnating growth of labour productivity through time across the branches.

In the literature the decline of the East German growth of labour productivity is explained by an inadequate substitution of labour by capital. It relates to the extensive growth hypothesis that theorised about a continuous increase of the production capacity.

For the Soviet Union Easterly and Fischer concluded that there was a low elasticity of substitution between capital and labour, which caused diminishing returns to capital to be especially acute.[237] Even though from the 1970s onwards East Germany aimed at intensive growth rather than extensive growth, Haustein indeed observed diminishing returns to capital.[238]

On the one hand this relates to lacking modernisation. Chapter 3 quoted the example of Easterly and Fischer that it is more difficult to substitute more and more drill presses for a labourer than it is to substitute a drill press plus a computerised inventory and distribution system for a labourer. On the other hand the problem is related to the social right to get a job; labour that is set free through the use of more advanced technology was kept in employment. This implies that there was a serious problem of hidden unemployment, or as Haustein put it: "Weniger produzieren mehr, aber genausoviel bleiben beschäftigt!".

Chapter summary and conclusion

This chapter examined the growth of East German labour productivity in the industrial sector from 1950 to 1990. Even though the emphasis is on the interpretation, I started looking at aspects of the measurement of value added (the numerator); and at the definition of labour inputs (the denominator). Thereafter the growth of labour productivity was analysed for decades, through decomposition based on shift share techniques, and in more detail through decomposition to the contribution of the underlying branches.

To begin with the measurement issues on value added, the discussion was confined to the incorporation of quality differences and changes in the input output relationship. Other measurement related issues were discussed in Chapter 2. As the series used in this thesis are based on physical quantity indicators – there is the implicit assumption that quality of each indicator remains constant. In the cross country comparison with West Germany it was shown that product quality can differ substantially. As a result the growth rates are downward biased. Similarly changes of the input output relationship are not accounted for. In East Germany the use of intermediate inputs probably increased faster than gross output. Therefore the assumed fixed input output relationship gives an upward bias to the growth of East German value added and thus also of labour productivity.

Regarding the definition of labour inputs the performance for the total industrial sector was examined looking at value added 'per worker' and at value added 'per hour'. It shows that East German labour productivity growth was higher if based on 'per hour', though the relative falling behind in comparison with West Germany 'per hour' is more

237 Easterly and Fischer (1994)

238 Haustein (1990)

dramatic than 'per worker'. For the further analysis all estimates are based on value added per worker.

The interpretation of the growth of industrial labour productivity first showed a decomposition of the annual labour productivity growth into 'intra branch effects', 'static shift effects' and 'dynamic shift effects'. Most of the labour productivity growth occurred through the intra branch effects, some of it through static shift effects (i.e. the reallocation towards branches with higher levels of labour productivity), and hardly any through dynamic shift effects (i.e. the reallocation towards branches with high productivity growth rates).

Decomposition into the contribution of branches to the total growth of industrial labour productivity in East Germany, using Harberger diagrams, showed that during the 1950s and the 1960s labour productivity expanded very evenly across branches. This may come as a surprise, as in the 1950s there was a clear focus on heavy industries, which might induce to the neglect of other (non-priority) branches. However, other branches were also taken care off and the expansion of 'basic and fabricated metal' could set free other branches that were suffering from bottlenecks. Moreover, the 1950s are very much characterised as restoration, which enabled East Germany to improve its labour productivity through resume production after repairing existing capital stock.

During the 1960s East German industrial labour productivity growth was a very clear yeast process. Still, the branch 'chemicals, rubber, plastic, oil refining' realised an outstanding labour productivity growth. This is explained by the prioritisation of this branch combined with the technological opportunities to develop petrochemical industries (as the West had already done) and also the improved access to the necessary resources (crude oil) as a result of the completed oil pipeline 'Freundschaft'.

In the 1970s labour productivity growth was less balanced, there was a large overshooting with a negative contribution to the total industrial labour productivity growth by 'mining' and 'machinery and transports'. The examples of the imports-dependent chemical industries (crude oil) and the exports-oriented machinery industries showed that these findings are consistent with the changing position of East Germany in the international economic context.

The very low growth of industrial labour productivity in the 1980s troubles the decomposition analysis. Based on findings in the literature it was related to lacking modern technologies which enable to increase labour productivity; and also to existing institutions that prohibited the increase of labour productivity through rationalisation, as everyone had the right to get a job. In a sense this is a mirror image of the extensive growth hypothesis as it proved difficult to substitute labour by capital. However, extensive growth also relates to lacking modernisation, for instance the lagging replacement of manual typewriters through electronic typewriters in the 1980s.

Chapter 6:
The non-industrial sectors

6.1. The non-industrial sectors

This Chapter examines the non-industrial sectors of agriculture, public utilities, construction, and transports and communications. These non-industrial sectors add up to 37 percent of the total East German employment in 1950 and to 25 percent in 1989.[239] How productive were these sectors in comparison with West Germany before the division? And how did these sectors perform thereafter?

The Chapter not only helps to establish a much more complete picture of the East German economy as a whole, it also sheds light on the performance of some sectors that were much more neglected than the prioritized industrial sector. What were the effects on the productivity performance of these sectors?

6.2. Agriculture

The agricultural sector encompasses animal production, crops, forestry and fisheries. The series presented in this study are primarily based on estimates of Alton et al. in the *Research Project on National Income in East Central Europe*.[240] Findings of the *Research Project* were derived from several occasional papers which together cover total crop and animal production from 1950 to 1989. From 1965 to 1989 this source offers data which includes forestry and fisheries. For the period from 1950 to 1965 I made a rough estimation to complete the picture for forestry and fisheries. For details see Annex B.

---

239 See Chapter 3

240 The Alton series are based on quantity indicators. The method is very much inspired by the ideas developed by Bergson for estimating the production potential of the Soviet Union and the estimates of the CIA that aimed to monitor the production capacity in Eastern Europe during the cold war. As such they represent the dominating approach for "western" statistics on centrally planned economies.

Before the division of Germany agriculture in East Germany was far more productive than in West Germany. Using a sample of 17 products of the crops sector and 5 animal products I estimated the East German labour productivity in 1934-1938 at 158 per cent of the West German level.[241] The estimate is based on quantity indicators (i.e. tons of wheat, tons of potatoes, liters of milk, etceteras) weighted at prevailing German prices. The result corresponds to estimates of Grünig, whose estimates for 1936 arrived at an East German agricultural labour productivity of 156 per cent of the West German level.[242]

According to my estimates based on backward extension of comparative levels from 1991 East German labour productivity was already below the West German level in the 1950s. The East German level of labour productivity in agriculture remains at the same distance of West Germany between 1950 and 1960. From 1960 to 1989 the comparative labour productivity diverged to the disadvantage of East Germany, except during a short upheaval in the mid 1960s.

Graph 6.1. East German value added per worker in agriculture, 1936–1989 (West Germany = 100)

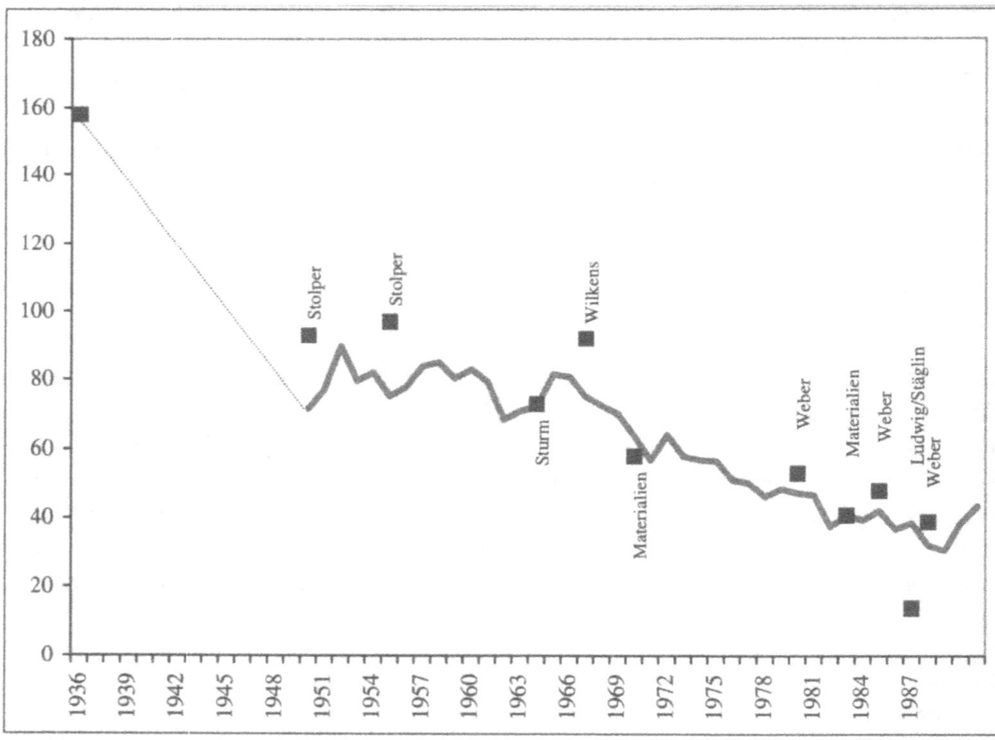

Sources: Annex B, Annex C, Benchmarks (see text)

---

241 Annex C

242 Grünig, (1948)

The benchmark comparisons were put into the graph as a check of the time series. Most of the benchmark comparisons correspond to my estimates based on backward extrapolation from 1991. Particularly the estimates of Sturm for 1964,[243] and those published by the West German government in their *Materialien zum Bericht zur Lage der Nation im geteilten Deutschland.* The most pessimistic estimate is based on the calculations of Ludwig and Stäglin, where the relative level of agricultural labour productivity is estimated at less than 14 per cent of West Germany in 1987.[244] Ludwig and Stäglin showed that the use of intermediate inputs in East German agriculture is a lot higher if valued at *Deutschmark* than if valued at *Ost-Mark*. Based on gross output rather than value added they estimated East German labour productivity in 1987 at 48 per cent of West Germany.

For the 1980s the graph shows three benchmarks of Weber.[245] It is noted that Weber's estimates are for the crops sector, thus animal production and forestry were not included. For 1967 Wilkens arrived at a higher level of East German agricultural labour productivity relative to West Germany than my series based on backward extrapolation.[246] Also estimates for the 1950s of Stolper show a higher relative level of East German labour productivity in the agricultural sector.[247] At that time the East German data on agricultural production lacks comparability with West German data, as East Germany registered biological yields (i.e. before harvesting) rather than barn yields (i.e. after harvesting), which requires an adjustment for in between losses.

Catch-up potential and realisation

From the late nineteenth century onwards technology opened up new ways to increase labour productivity in agriculture through the diffusion of chemicals, internal combustion engines, new machinery, electricity, factory farming techniques, scientific management, and other inputs.[248] Compared to the United States the diffusion of new technologies in Germany was at a slower pace. For instance, during the 1920s and 1930s there was a less intensive use of chemical fertilisers and a slower adoption of the tractor in Germany (in comparison with the United States).

As an example of the slow mechanisation in Europe Svennilson gives three reasons for the much faster diffusion of the tractor in the United States than in Europe. First the early tractor was technically constructed to be used on large farms and was less well adapted to medium-sized and small farms. Second European agriculture had access to a

243 Sturm (1974)
244 Ludwig and Stäglin (1996)
245 Weber (1991)
246 Wilkens (1976)
247 Stolper (1960)
248 O'Brien and Prados de la Escosura (1992)

large supply of labour at a low level of wages: these low wages not only reduced the savings in labour costs that followed the use of tractors, but also made the cost of breeding and feeding horses relatively low. Third the purchase of a tractor involved large cash expenditure, which was difficult given the weak financial position of the farmers.[249]

A very similar reasoning is found in O'Brien and Prados de la Escosura (1992) when discussing a benchmark for 1910. They found a "rational economic interest" for continental Europe to use "their abundant resource, labour, to intensify the cultivation of land and to maximize monetary returns per hectare".[250] They concluded that by 1910 at given levels of technology the potential on the continent for raising output per worker, output per hectare, and incomes of populations dependent on agriculture seems rather limited. Convergence to higher levels could only be realised "by radical shifts in the allocation of labour away from primary production".

Whereas in West Germany the size of the agricultural workforce decreased, in East Germany its size increased from the 1930s to 1950.[251] Figures of Stolper (1957) estimate the employment in East German agriculture at 1.7 million in 1939, in 1950 it amounted to 2.1 million people. One of the causes of employment growth are the Soviet land reforms between 1945 and 1949. During the so-called *Bodenreform* land was expropriated for farms that were larger than 100 hectares, or if the owner had been a member of the NSDAP. These lands were assigned to small farm owners, landless farm workers, and German immigrants from east of the Oder-Neiβe. Vogeler stated that within these five years "the Soviet land reforms fundamentally transformed the regional agricultural structure of eastern Germany", as "huge estates and large-scale family farms gave way to small-sized family farms".[252]

Insofar the argument still holds for the period from 1936 to 1950, that the opportunities to increase labour productivity in agriculture could only be realised by a radical shift in the allocation of labour away from this sector, these reforms contributed to the fall of East German labour productivity relative to West Germany. Furthermore, based on the official estimates in the statistical yearbook, the level of mechanization in this sector was lower in 1949 than in 1939.[253]

---

249 Svennilson (1954) p. 99

250 O'Brien and Prados de la Escosura (1992) pp. 529, 530

251 Stolper (1957) p. 526

252 Vogeler (1996) p.434

253 Statistisches Jahrbuch der Deutschen Demokratischen Republik (1956) p. 199; The yearbook shows the amount of the following machines for 1939 (bracketed) and 1949; Drillmaschinen (197268) 205206; Düngerstreuer (60092) 43711; Mähbinder (119584) 117472; Grasmäher (252049) 207935; Kartoffelroder (137468) 153321; Rübenroder (28861) 15181; Dreschmaschinen mit Kraftantrieb (215822) 206246; Strohpressen mit Garnbindung (91541) 85662; Strohpressen mit Drahtbindung (1673) 664

Graph 6.2. Production and labour productivity in agriculture, 1950–1989 (1950 = 100)

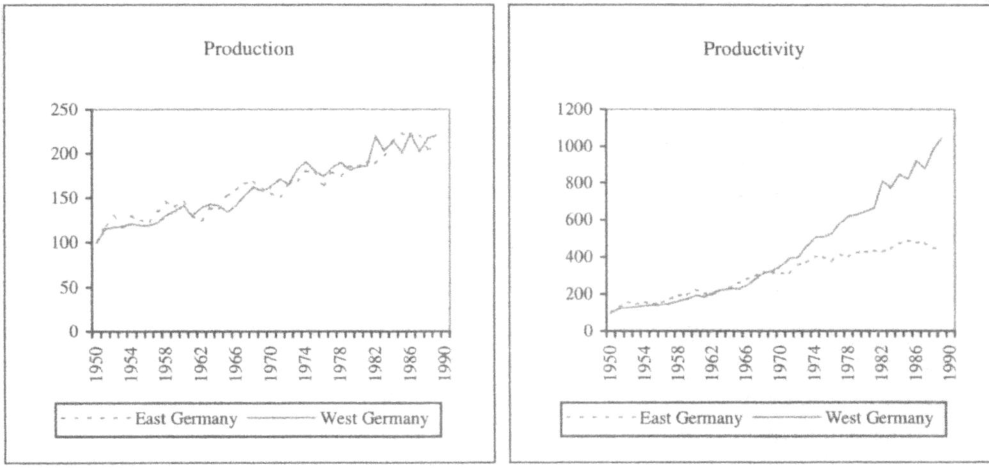

Sources: Annex B

Even though most of the horsepower in the German agricultural sector in the 1930s still came from actual horses, there had been a (slow) diffusion of the tractor. Mechanisation had occurred mainly at some large and medium-sized farms,[254] thus exactly those farms that were expropriated. Besides land the expropriations also encompassed agricultural machinery, which were stored at the *Maschinen-Ausleih-Stationen* (MAS). Farmers who wanted to use machinery could rent it at the MAS, in 1953 transformed into *Maschinen-Traktoren-Stationen* (MTS).[255] The MTS is seen as the driving force for collectivisation in the 1950s, through price discrimination in favour of the *landwirtschaftliche Produktionsgenossenschaft* (LPG).[256]

As it was shown in Chapter 3 between 1950 and 1989 both East and West Germany shifted their labour out of agriculture into industry and services. In East Germany, most of this shift away from agriculture occurred between 1950 and 1970. Thereafter it released agricultural labourers at a much slower pace than in West Germany. Graph 6.1. clearly shows the diverging agricultural labour productivity from 1970 to 1989, that is combined with comparable growth rates of value added in both countries.

Despite modernisation and collectivisation, labour saving in East German agriculture was less effective than in West Germany. West Germany was able to attain higher levels of labour productivity because it was more successful to shift the allocation of labour into other sectors. To illustrate the importance of the argument of redundant labour and underemployment in East German agriculture, Graph 6.3. shows East German value added and East German employment from 1950 to 1997 relative to West Germany.

254 Berthold (1988) pp. 253, 265–267

255 Mahlich (1999) pp. 55–59

256 Leptin (1980) pp. 20–23

Mathematically the series shown in Graph 6. 3 are VA^{EG}/VA^{WG} and L^{EG}/L^{WG}, where VA stands for value added in agriculture, L stands for labour in agriculture, EG stands for East Germany, and WG stands for West Germany. These series do not show the actual increases of value added in East and West Germany as shown in Graph 6.2.; and these series also hide the actual decreases of employment in agriculture throughout the period that is under examination. It pronounces the already observed East German labour surplus in agriculture from 1970 to 1989 compared to West Germany, and also the sharp reduction of employment (accompanied by converging labour productivity) after the unification.

Analogous reasoning as above on continental Europe for 1910 leads us to the question: could there be a rational economic interest for East Germany to use its abundant resource endowment, labour, to intensify the cultivation of land and to maximise returns per hectare? According to Böse and Henrichsmeyer there are many causes for the relatively low East German labour productivity. For the crops sector they mention low fertility of the soil, lack of technology, low quality of agricultural chemicals (fertilizers), organisational problems and a lack of motivation of the workforce. For animal production labour productivity was particularly low in the production of eggs and milk.[257] East Germany lacked the adequate fertilisers, seeds, machines and fodder. A good illustration is the production of milk. An East German cow produced less milk than a West German cow. This was mainly due to shortages of fodder. Moreover, mechanisation was relatively low. In the late 1980s milking machines covered merely 14 per cent of the East German cows.

Graph 6.3. East German value added and employment in agriculture relative to West Germany, 1950–1997 (1950 = 100)

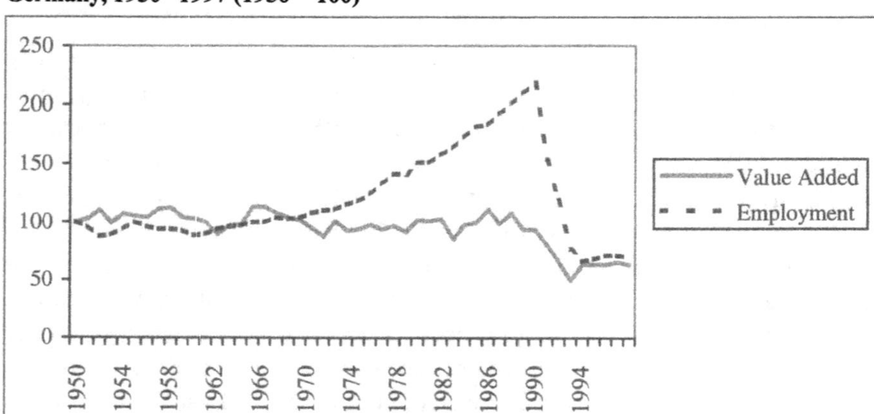

Sources: Annex B

257 Böse and Henrichsmeyer (1991)

6.3. Public Utilities

Before the division of Germany in public utilities the levels of labour productivity were approximately the same in East Germany and West Germany. In 1936 East German labour productivity amounted to 98.8 per cent of the West German level. Public utilities include the supply of gas, water, and electricity. Relative productivity levels differed for each of the underlying components, with a higher East German labour productivity level in electricity and a higher West German level in gas and water. However, in all sectors the level is found to be high in both parts of Germany.

After the Second World War East German labour productivity in public utilities shows a gradual decline relative to West Germany. The existing benchmark estimates of Sturm for 1964 and of Ludwig and Stäglin for 1987 help to determine the appropriateness of the backward extrapolations from 1991. It appears that the series correspond very much to the benchmark estimates of Sturm, though deviate from the estimate of Ludwig and Stäglin. This is partly explained by the higher East German input output ratio that existed as a result of the amount of brown coal used during the 1980s. As it has been argued by Stolper (1958) the use of lignite negatively affects the input output relationship in the production of electricity.

East German series on public utilities are based on physical quantity indicators, i.e. energy and gas, priced at their value added in 1991. Since the unification the use of brown coals has been drastically reduced – though it has remained an important source for energy – so that the input output ratio has become more favourable than it was in the 1980s. This would imply that the series slightly overestimate value added in public utilities for those periods when the use of lignite was highest. A second reason for the difference between the series and the benchmark of Ludwig and Stäglin relates to the employment figure for East Germany. The estimated number of people employed in this sector is somewhat different; as the size of the workforce in this sector is so small the effect on relative levels of labour productivity is high.

Until 1970–71 public utilities experienced a slight decrease relative to the West German level of labour productivity. Thereafter the gap widened faster. Between 1966 and 1970 employment in East German public utilities declined, and labour productivity increased fast. However, there was mass discontent due to shortages in consumer goods and the energy sector.[258] The fact that growth of labour productivity levelled off in 1970–71 coincides with the retreat of Walter Ulbricht and the appointment of Erich Honecker as the leader of the SED, i.e. the East German communist party.

When shortages in the energy sector appeared in 1969–1970, this was mainly a result of higher demand for energy as an intermediate input as well as for consumption purposes. Supply – total production – had increased continuously from 1950 onwards.

---

258 Kopstein (1997) p. 69

Graph 6.4. East German value added per worker in public utilities, 1936–1989 (West Germany = 100)

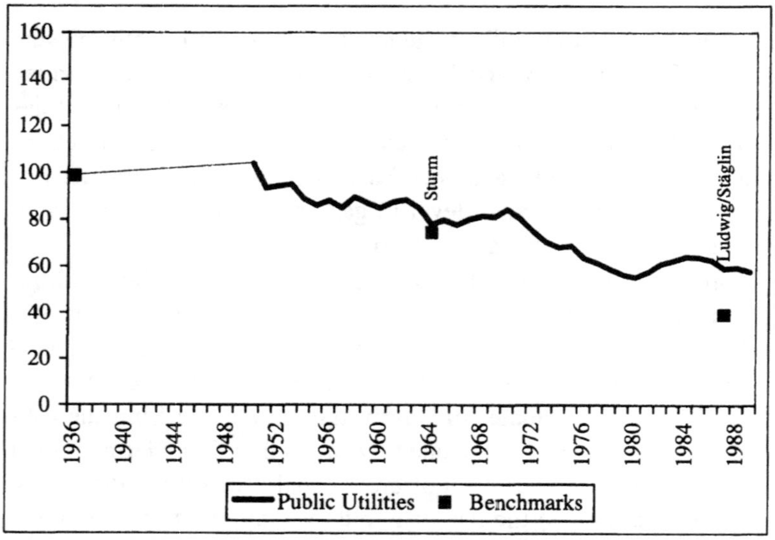

Sources: Annex B; Ludwig and Stäglin (1996); Sturm (1974)

After the emergence of shortages more labour was directed towards public utilities to ensure a higher production.

In comparison with West Germany the economy of East Germany was far less equipped with sufficient infrastructure, and since the unification the energy sector has

Graph 6.5. Production and labour productivity in public utilities, 1950–1989 (1950 = 100)

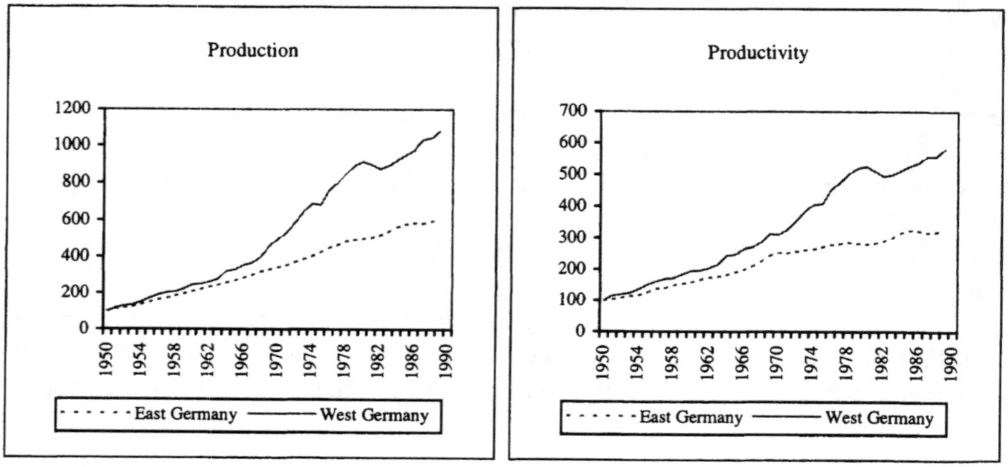

Sources: Annex B

been rapidly modernised. The main explanation of lagging labour productivity in this sector can be found in the size and modernity of the available capital stock.

Focussing on total production West German growth of value added was much faster than in East German public utilities, especially from the late 1960s onwards. In fact it is the expansion in West Germany that explains the divergence. Considering the increasing size of the West German population, in comparison with a declining population in East Germany, the availability of public utilities per head diverged far less than total production. However, as was observed earlier in this section labour productivity did diverge.

Being a major input in the production process, the production of electricity is often used as a proxy for national income. In my view the use of this indicator as a proxy for national income is highly problematic, mainly because increasing efficiency of the use of energy. Indeed, Table 6.1. shows that production of electricity increased more than GDP in both German economies. Among the reasons for such deviations are changes in the input output relationship resulting from changes in the composition of output or from the method of production; and changes in the proportion of electricity use as an intermediate input and for consumption purposes (by households).

Interestingly, the East German production of electricity was much more dependent on solid fuels (extracted from mining) than in West Germany. This explains the increased production in East German mining until the mid-1960s. In West Germany other energy sources, particularly primary oil and waterpower, were much more important.[259]

The reliance on domestic mining in East Germany had a negative effect on overall productivity growth. The extraction of coals, ores and salts became more difficult over time, as the most accessible sources were exploited first. Thus there is a tendency of declining labour productivity.[260] Indeed, East German labour productivity growth in mining was negligible. Furthermore the use of brown coals did bring about high pollution. This had negative environmental consequences.

Table 6.1. East and West German growth rates of GDP and electricity production

	1950–89	1950–60	1960–70	1970–80	1980–89
East Germany					
GDP	3.1	6.7	2.7	2.6	0.3
Electricity	4.6	7.3	5.2	3.8	2.1
West Germany					
GDP	4.3	8.0	4.4	2.8	1.9
Electricity	6.1	9.0	7.0	6.1	1.9

Notes: West German electricity includes other public utilities
Sources: Annex B; ICOP

259 Stolper (1957) p. 541

260 Gales (2002); Abelshauser (2004) p. 382 describes the increasing difficulties for East German brown coals.

6.4. Construction

The labour productivity gap in East German construction in comparison with West Germany amounted to approximately the same relative level throughout the period from 1950 to 1972. Thereafter East German labour productivity converged to the West German level until the early 1980s, a level which it could not sustain. The period of convergence is particularly explained by an impressive increase of East German value added relative to West Germany, which will be discussed below. Between 1936 and 1950 Stolper (1959) already measured a drastic decline of East German production in this sector. Graph 6.6. shows a falling behind of the level of East German labour productivity relative to West Germany.

The estimated level of East German labour productivity relative to West Germany is not the same according to the series and according to the benchmark estimates of Ludwig and Stäglin for 1987 and of Sturm for 1964. In my opinion for the estimates of Sturm (1974) the deviation is clearly related to the data and the estimation procedure. Firstly, the calculations of Sturm depart from an East German employment figure that is too low, leading to a higher estimate of the labour productivity level. Secondly, relative output was estimated using data on newly built living accomodation; labour productivity was derrived assuming that "productivity in residential construction is representative of East German productivity in all construction activities".[261] Importantly,

Graph 6.6. East German value added per worker in construction, 1936 – 1989 (West Germany = 100)

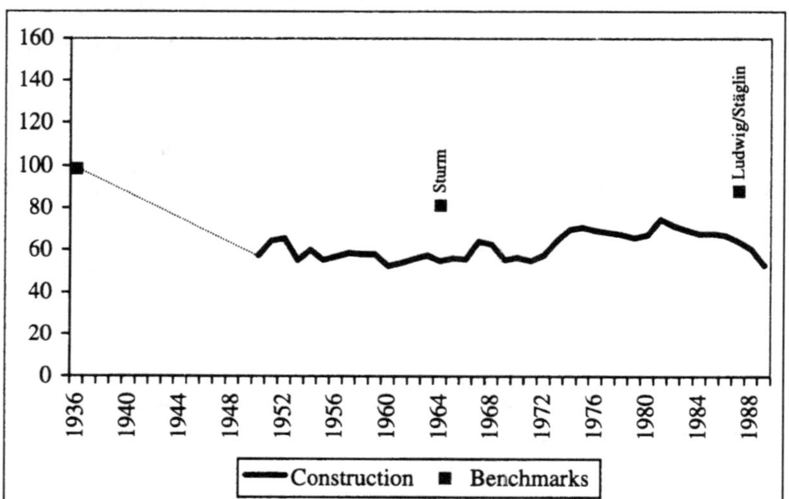

Sources: Annex B; Ludwig and Stäglin (1996); Sturm (1974)

[261] Sturm (1974) p. 90

the quality of East German newly built houses were considered to be the same in East and West Germany. Sturm wrote:

> "Similarity of climate and cultural traditions suggest that quality differentials between residential construction in the two countries should be minor. The fact that multi-story apartment buildings are the predominant type of housing in both countries further supports this argument. In any case, no data on quality differentials exist to permit appropriate adjustment of the quantity data".[262]

Chapter 5 discussed the quality problem in more detail. Contrary to the expectations of Sturm, that quality differentials in construction were minor, there is some evidence that quality differences in this sector were significant. In the 1960s fewer East German than West German houses had the comfort of a toilet inside, a bath, and central heating. Especially in the older buildings East German construction made little effort for improvements.[263] This suggests that assuming a similar quality of East and West German houses resulted in a relative level of East German output that was too high, and thus also a relative level of labour productivity that was too high.

According to the estimates of Ludwig and Stäglin in 1987 value added per worker in East German construction would have amounted to 83.3 per cent of the West German level. As was the case with the benchmark of Sturm, this is much higher than the extrapolated series from 1991. Although this partly results from a different figure for the number of workers, most of the difference relates to the estimated value added for East Germany.[264]

Graph 6.7. shows value added and value added per worker in East and West German construction from 1950 to 1989. Von der Lippe (1995) has been very critical on data for the construction sector from the early 1970s onwards, which overestimate the number of houses that were built.[265] Although the underlying series are based on indicators such as the number of houses built, and also the size of these houses, this does not lead to an overestimation of value added as I used data that were adjusted for this bias.[266] Nevertheless the interpretation of the development of East German value added relative to West Germany is constrained by a data problem. The sample used for estimating East German value added in construction focuses on houses. During the 1950s and the 1960s most of the capacity in this sector was used for non-residential buildings and plants, which is not in the sample. In the early 1970s the *regime* put more emphasis on residen-

262 Sturm (1974) p. 90, footnote 18

263 Bundesministerium für innerdeutsche Beziehungen (1971) pp. 119, 120, 366

264 Ludwig and Stäglin estimate West German employment in this sector at 1859 thousand, whereas the ICOP series that are used in this study estimate West German employment in construction in 1987 at 1814 thousand; Employment for East Germany is 645 thousand in Ludwig and Stäglin, and 638 thousand in this study.

265 Von der Lippe (1995) pp. 2003–2005

266 Annex B; Von der Lippe (1995) pp. 2003–2005

Graph 6.7. Production and labour productivity in construction, 1950 – 1989 (1950 = 100)

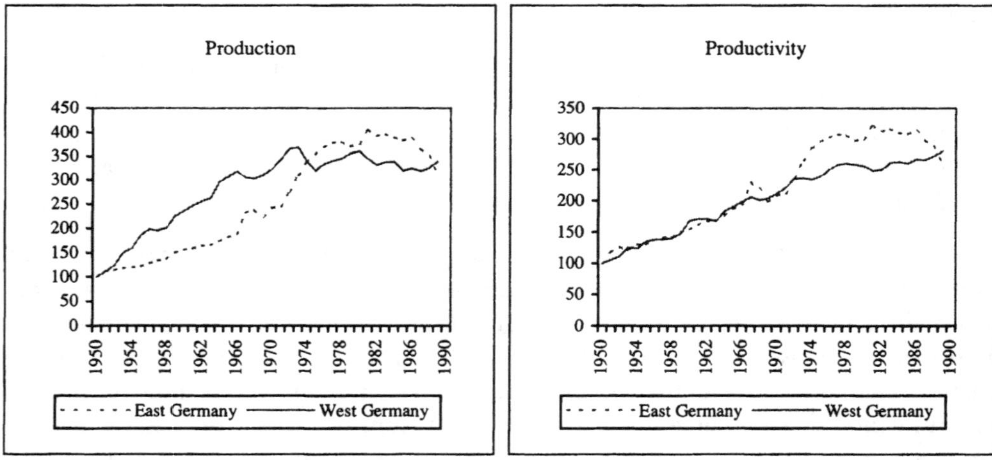

Sources: Annex B

tial buildings, so that part of the increase in East German value added relative to West Germany is related to the inappropriateness of the sample to account for the compositional changes within construction during this period.

It is clear that the East German construction sector performed relatively well. Between 1950 and 1989 there was no falling behind relative to West Germany. Although increases of West German labour productivity in construction were rather low in comparison with the other sectors (except for mining), West German labour productivity was still almost three times higher in 1989 than in 1950. Despite all the criticism it receives nowadays, the East German 'Plattenbau' led to a major improvement of labour productivity in construction. This prefab method of building houses may have reduced variety; it also made the building of houses cheaper and faster.[267]

Still, after the unification East Germany was lagging with regard to (the modernity of) its infrastructure, its industrial constructions, and its housing.[268] To some extent this gives an indication of the efforts of the East German construction sector. After the unification much of the gap was narrowed, as value added at constant prices of 1991 increased from 24.5 billion DM in 1991 to 45.8 billion DM in 1995. In comparison with the period before the unification the composition of the construction sector changed drastically. These changes were marked by a sharp reduction of the newly built houses and increased activity in other types of construction. As a result of the compositional changes within the construction sector the quantity indicator of the newly constructed

---

267 Schretzenmayr (1998)

268 IWH (1999) p. 57 ff.; DIW (1990)

houses, that was used for the period from 1950 to 1989, is not useful as an indicator for value added in construction from 1989 and 1991. Alternatively this study used calculations of the DIW.[269]

6.5. Transports and Communications

Before the Second World War, when East and West Germany were still integrated, Berlin was a major centre of large transportation networks. At that time Berlin had a similar sales value in "trade, communications and transports" as all the other East German territory.[270] Estimates on relative levels of labour productivity of East and West Germany are therefore very sensitive for the way Berlin is taken into account. Moreover, much of the "location bonus" of Berlin in the 1930s had disappeared after Germany (and Berlin) was divided into parts.

Ignoring the problems concerning Berlin, dividing it into two parts of 50 per cent each, East German labour productivity in "Trade, Transports and Communications" would amount to 93 per cent of West Germany. The effects of the division of Germany on the centre-position of Berlin makes interpretation of the meaning of this pre-division benchmark for the period after World War II difficult. On the other hand the direction of the effects of the division are obvious: labour productivity in East Germany worsened in comparison with West Germany.

The backward extrapolated level of labour productivity in transports and communications for the 1950s (here trade was excluded) indeed shows a much lower level for East

Table 6.2. Sales value, employment and labour productivity in trade, communications and transports in the 1930s (Total Germany = 100)

	Sales Value in Mill. RM (1935)	Employment in thousands (1938)	Labour Productivity (Germany = 100)
West Germany	35,807	1,573	100.2
East Germany	10,847	582	82.0
Berlin	10,842	310	153.9
Remaining territory	5,462	305	78.8
Germany (total)	62,958	2,770	100.0

Sources: Länderrat des Amerikanischen Besatzungsgebiets, *Statistisches Handbuch von Deutschland 1928–1944* (München 1949) pp. 37, 38; 479; 576, 577

269 See Annex B

270 In 1935 total sales value in this sector amounted to 10.844 Million *Reichsmark* in Berlin, and 10.847 Million *Reichsmark* in the other provinces and *Länder* that became East Germany; see Länderrat des Amerikanischen Besatzungsgebiets, *Statistisches Handbuch von Deutschland 1928–1944* (München 1949) p. 576

Graph 6.8. East German labour productivity in transports and communication (West Germany = 100)

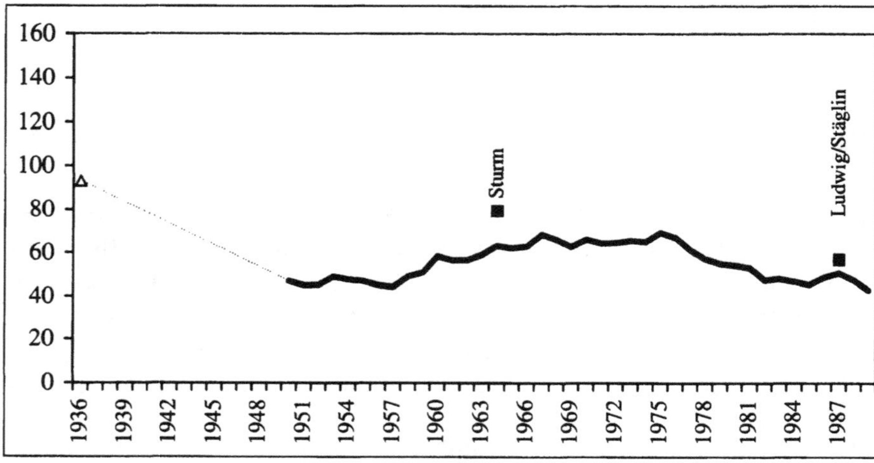

Sources: Annex B; Sturm, (1974); Ludwig and Stäglin (1996)

Germany than in West Germany. Series on the East German transports and communications were based on physical indicators such as passengers (and travel distance), freight tonnage (and distance), and the number of phone calls.

Explanations for the low relative level of labour productivity in the 1950s should include the effects of the division on transportation networks, but also to the reparations to the Soviet Union. According to estimates of the DIW (1972) war damage in transportation was more or less the same in East and West Germany. More recently it has been argued that these estimates need adjustment, damage – and especially reparations towards the Soviet Union – resulted in an unfavourable balance for East Germany in comparison with West Germany.[271]

A study of Kühr (2003) makes up the balance for the reparations and shows that in quantitative terms it involved the dismantling of railroads,[272] and also the transfer of wagons, locomotives, and other facilities. In qualitative terms Kühr finds a more favourable vintage of the capital stock before than after the Second World War.[273] After the initial relative decrease between 1936 and 1950, the labour productivity gap remained at a stable distance from 1950 to 1958. Stability was followed by a period of convergence towards West Germany, and finally by a period of divergence. The comparison of the time series with the benchmark estimates of Sturm and Ludwig and Stäglin

271 Baar, Karlsch and Matschke (1995) pp. 897 ff.

272 See also Fremdling (1997) who stated that reparations involved the dismantling of 6300 kilometers of railroads as double tracks were brought back to single tracks.

273 Kühr (2002) pp. 474–483

Graph 6.9. Production and labour productivity in transports and communication (1950 = 100)

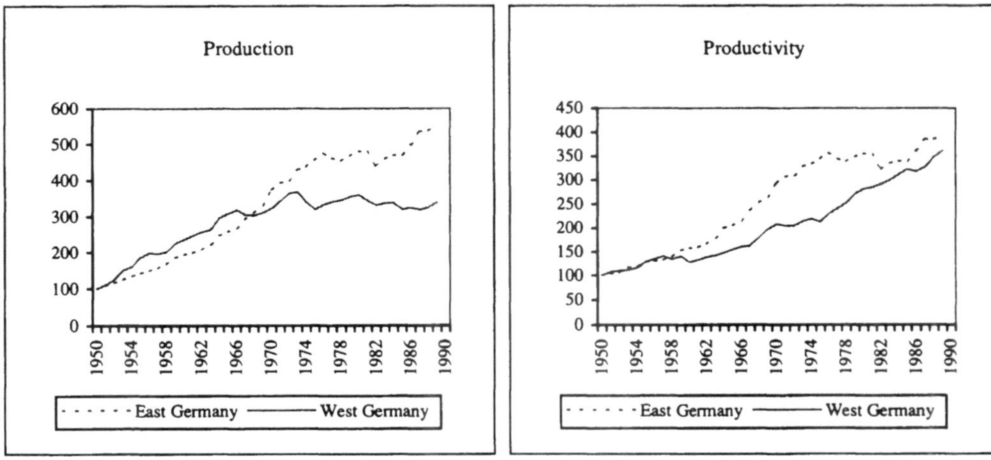

Sources: Annex B

shows that the series are somewhat lower, though not too different from the estimate of Ludwig and Stäglin.

Lower labour productivity in transports and communication was accompanied by relatively low investment in infrastructure. Before the division of Germany roads were in the first place built to travel from East to West and vice versa. East Germany put little effort to improve the infrastructure corresponding to the new status.

From 1950 to 1989 East German production as well as labour productivity increased faster than in West Germany. As the absolute level of East German labour productivity in this sector was well below the West German level, this suggests a process of catching up. Such a process would be the result of the (re)introduction of modern technology. Evidence of Kühr shows a (re)electrification of the East German railroads.[274]

Furthermore productivity gains could be the result of changes in the composition of transports, as transport of freights increased faster than transport of passengers. Importantly, as a sector, transports was characterised by a very low (political) prioritisation in East Germany. Processes of crowding out hindered the restoration. Therefore the East German productivity growth in this sector should be examined in the light of the (very) bad initial conditions and the slow (extended) growth path.[275] Ciesla and Trischler (1999) describe how the "Strategie der intensiven Ausnutzung der vorhandene Kapazitäten" led to the wearing out of the existing capital stock. This explains for the state of East German infrastructure as it was observed after unification; and also for the bad productivity growth performance in East Germany since 1975.

---

274 Kühr (2002) p. 488 shows that electrified railroads doubled between 1936 and 1966.

275 Hascher, Zeilinger (2001) mention the "langen Wiederaufbaus".

Finally, it is stressed that the evidence for a catching up process is scattered and still requires further research. Even though a higher East German growth rate can be conciliated with the worse initial conditions, I should also make a critical point regarding the estimates of this study. As it was discussed in Chapter 4, the extrapolation of East German value added in 1991 using quantity indicators assumes that the input/output relationship remained unchanged. The example of the oil crisis in 1973, within East Germany somewhat later because the 'COMECON-prices' were not immediately affected by the world market,[276] indicates that this assumption might prove particularly problematic for the transports sector. Insofar the ratio of inputs to outputs increased from 1950 to 1990, this study overstates growth of value added.[277]

[276] Schröter (1994)

[277] For the period before the oil crisis Kühr (2002) suggests an improvement of the input output relationship resulting from electrification.

Chapter 7: Unification and transformation

7.1. From plan to market

What began with the persistence of the East German people in their demand for political reforms, ended up with the reform of the political system, of the economy and the unification of East and West Germany in 1990. Inspired by Gorbachev's new policy of 'glasnost' and 'perestroika' in the Soviet Union, and the reforms that already got underway in Poland and Hungary, many East Germans participated in the mass demonstrations that questioned the election results for municipalities on Mai 7th 1989. Other demands from the masses concerned the abolition of travel restrictions. At the fortieth anniversary of the German Democratic Republic in October 1989, Gorbachev made clear that the Soviet Union would not help the East German regime, led by Honecker, through military intervention. Meanwhile demonstrations continued, and many East Germans migrated towards West Germany via Hungary, that had opened its borders with Austria. On October 18th Honecker was replaced by Krenz, who decided to release travel-restrictions towards West Germany on November 9th.[278]

In 1990 East Germany ceased to exist as a nation. Within a short period of time the currency union (July 1990) and the political union (November 1990) of the two German economies were established, and the East German centrally planned economy was transformed into a market economy. Lindblom (2001) defined the market system as "a system of societywide coordination of human activities not by central command but by mutual interactions in the form of transactions".[279] The legal cornerstones of the market system are private autonomy and contractual freedom.

The transition of East Germany from a centrally planned economy to a market economy is a fundamental change of *the rules of the game*, which brings about many practical problems. What is the best means of creating a private sector? The assets to be privatised had been acquired in different ways: expropriation, but also through state investment. Brada (1996) recognises four methods of privatisation: restitution to original

---

278 Oldenburg (1991)

279 Lindblom (2001) p. 4

owners, sale of state property, mass or voucher privatisation and the growth of the private sector "from below" through the formation of new firms.[280] In the case of restitution the kind of dilemmas that are involved are illustrated with two examples that can be found in Brada. The first example concerns the restitution of houses where the demands of the 'original owner' are opposed to the interests of 'current occupants'; the second example concerns restitution of factories where state investments have become commingled with the original property.

Even though the troubled German history of the 1940s may have complicated some of the dilemmas of privatisation – the institutional changes took place rapidly. Regarding the speed of transition from a planned economy to a market economy two strategies stand out. The first strategy implements reforms quickly, the second strategy spreads various reforms over a longer period of time. These strategies are referred to as shock therapy and gradualism, and the East German transition is clearly an example of shock therapy.

It is stressed that East German transition was a special case, as the unification with West Germany solved some of the "fundamental problems of the transition process virtually overnight – monetary stabilisation and the creation of a legal order for the market economy".[281] Moreover, Lindlar and Scheremet (1998) state, in comparison with other transition-economies "unification with the wealthy West Germany promised a much faster and larger inflow of funds for infrastructure and private investment".

During the first years of transition, between 1989 and 1991, East German GDP showed a sharp decline. Unemployment rose and became a major problem. According to Sinn and Sinn "the severity of the depression in East Germany is without parallel in modern economic history. Not even the Great Depression of 1928–1933 was as bad".[282] What explains for the collapse of the East German economy? In this section it is argued that the collapse of the East German economy can be explained by the combined effects of the transformation from a centrally planned economy to a market economy and the integration with the West German economy.

Starting with transformation, it can be observed that a drastic fall of output was common in all countries of transition. Winiecki explains the initial hardship by the elimination of the 'pure socialist production' of the past.[283] No matter whether the transition from the centrally planned economy to a market economy was a gradual process or a shock therapy, within three years all former socialist countries experienced a drastic fall of GDP and even more so of industrial output. The East German crisis fits into a pattern.[284] It results from the distortion of demand in socialist economies: purchases that

---

280 Brada (1996) pp. 68–76

281 Lindlar, Scheremet (1998) p. 15

282 Sinn and Sinn (1992)

283 Winiecki (2002)

284 Winiecki claims that the fall in output links up with the disappearance of 'output that was not' and 'output that existed but should not'. 'Output that was not' refers to biases in the official sta-

Table 7.1. Output levels in industrial branches in 1991 (Percent of 1989)

	East Germany	Hungary	Poland
Food, beverages, tobacco	41	90[a]	72[a]
Textiles, wearing apparel	12	54[b]	63[c]
Paper, printing	41	85[d]	88[d]
Chemicals, rubber, plastic, oil refining	40	71[e]	72[e]
Basic, fabricated metal	38	49[f]	57[f]

Notes: Output levels in Hungary and Poland are levels in 1992 in percent of 1989; [a] only food and beverages; [b] also footwear; [c] only textiles; [d] also wood products; [e] only chemicals; [f] only basic metal
Source: Annex A; Winiecki, (2002)

could only exist because of a lack of alternatives (textiles), excessive purchases in inventories (firms) and also in hoarding of food (consumers) that followed irregular supply. As budget constraints became harder firms reduced the size of inventories. During the inventories liquidation process output fell, which was followed by a structural reallocation.

All branches faced a decline of their industrial output. In comparison with Hungary and Poland the fall of output was more dramatic in East Germany. Does it imply that East Germany had more 'pure socialist production' than Hungary and Poland? I consider the hypothesis of Winiecki as half the story. Besides having to adjust to changes of demand – as there was little need to maintain large inventories and to hoard lots of food – domestic supply was also confronted with new suppliers and buyers, who captured whatever was left of the markets and assets. This was particularly important in East Germany, where two distinct developments occurred simultaneously: transformation and unification. The alternative explanation could, therefore, focus on some of the special characteristics of East German developments.

Winiecki states that the largest part of the otherwise unneeded output consisted of oversized inventories. A study of Görzig and Gornig (1991) compares the inventory to output ratio in the East and West German industrial sector in 1988.[285] They estimated the East German ratio at 170 percent of the West German ratio, which is indeed relatively high. A closer look at the underlying branches shows that inventories were more or less the same in "Food, beverages, tobacco", in "Textiles, wearing apparel", and in paper (but not in printing). Different ratios were calculated for "Chemicals, rubber, plastic, oil refining" and for "Basic, fabricated metal". It is concluded that at the branch level the correlation between the inventory to output ratio and the decline of output is not clear. At the underlying level of analysis of the particular industries within branches the data shows substantial variations.

---

tistics. In Chapter 2 it was argued that for the data used in this study 'output that was not' is an insignificant problem. 'Output that existed but should not'refers to otherwise unneeded output, i.e. output with a negative surplus value.

285 Görzig, Gornig (1991) pp. 38–40

The following sections will discuss the developments of the East German economy since 1991 in more detail. Discussion starts with the unification shock and East German wages. Thereafter the prospects and achievements of convergence of per capita income and of labour productivity will be addressed from a catching up perspective and from the spatial perspective of location and trade. The chapter ends with some remarks on the expectations for the future of the East German economy and the lessons for the enlargement of the European Union.

7.2. Unification and wages

As shown in Chapter 3, 44 percent of the widening gap in GDP per capita and 16 per cent of the labour productivity gap between East German and West Germany since 1936 occurred between 1989 and 1991. The unification with West Germany exposed the East German producers to free trade and competition. Below I will show the negative impact of the unification on the transformation of the East German economy from the perspective of the (existing) East German firms. As an implicit framework the income statement is used, which shows what happened in terms of revenues and costs during this period.

With the currency union flow values, in particular output prices and wages, were converted at a 1 : 1 rate; stock values, in particular corporate debt, were converted by 2 Ost-Mark per D-mark.[286] When the currency union was established in July 1990 East German consumers redirected their demand towards Western commodities. These were more attractive, and also cheaper than East German goods. At that time East German producers were not yet in the position to supply goods and services at conditions prevailing on highly competitive markets.[287] This resulted first in bulging inventories for their products, then in reduced production activity and finally in rising shorttime working and unemployment.[288] As a result the revenues of these firms decreased.

Lower revenues were accompanied by higher costs. There was an enormous increase of wages. Whereas East German wages amounted to 50.8 per cent of West Germany in 1991, in 1995 it had climbed to almost 75 per cent. The story of the high wage increases in East Germany is even more pronounced when 1990 is taken into account; according to Sinn and Sinn (1992) the outcome of the conversion rate meant that the nominal level of East German wages was one-third of that in West Germany.[289]

---

286 Lindlar, Scheremet (1998) p.13

287 Dietz (1991)

288 Schrettl (1991) pp. 1 – 17

289 Sinn, Sinn (1992) p. 62

In an effort to explain for the high wage increases in East Germany Franz and Steiner point at the role of collective bargaining in the wage formation, which in the beginning of the transformation process was a one-sided game.[290] The employer side was represented by either former managers of state owned firms (who knew that their position was highly insecure in the privatisation process) or by representatives of West German firms (who had little incentive to fight for low wages in their prospective competitors). At the end of 1990 about 88 per cent of all managers and supervisors before the 'Wende' were still in position. The old East German trade union, the *Freie Deutsche Gewerkschaftsbund*, was discredited for its collaboration with the communist regime, so that the (West) German trade union, the *Deutsche Gewerkschaftsbund*, easily became the negotiating partner in collective bargaining.

Akerlof *et al.* claim that the superior union organisation, at a time that management was in disarray, and when the owner of the firms – the Treuhandanstalt – remained uninvolved, played an important role in the eventual wage increases.[291] At the same time it is noted that many firms already made losses and were dependent on subsidies from the Treuhandanstalt to continue operations. Even in cases where plant closings were to be expected, workers tried to increase wages, as unemployment benefits were based on terminal wages.

This indicates that the wage increases cannot be understood outside the logic of unification. It is emphasised that the treaty of May 18th 1990 did not only settle the currency union, but also an economic and social union.[292] It means that West German institutions, including regulation on wage negotiations, minimum wages, pensions, etceteras, gained importance in the further development of the East German economy. With regard to the wage negotiations the strict interpretation of the (West) German institutions that ensure the non-interference of government, the *Tarifautonomie*, may have hindered chances for wage moderation. According to Lindlar and Scheremet government could (and should) have bypassed the *Tarifautonomie*. Being the owner of the Treuhandanstalt there was reason for government to participate in the wage negotiations.

Another potential source for higher costs were prices for raw materials and semi-fabrics, i.e. intermediate inputs. Due to transformation and reunification the price structure changed, which led to higher costs in the firms where prices for intermediate inputs increased relative to prices for final products. Similarly in the firms where prices for intermediate inputs decreased relative to prices for final products, this led to lower costs.

To give an indication of the development of the input output relationship during the period from 1989 to 1991, I will show estimates of Ludwig and Stäglin on the input

---

290 Franz and Steiner (1999)

291 Akerlof, Rose, Yellen and Hessenius (1991)

292 Vertrag über die Schaffung einer Währungs-, Wirtschafts- und Sozialunion zwischen der Bundesrepublik Deutschland und der Deutschen Demokratischen Republik (Bonn, Mai 18th 1990)

Table 7.2. Input/output ratios in 1987, based on East and West German currency

	Ost-Mark	D-Mark	Relative (OM/DM)
Agriculture	0.607	0.876	0.693
Public Utilities	0.675	0.507	1.331
Mining	0.442	0.432	1.023
Manufacturing	0.725	0.691	1.049
Construction	0.699	0.530	1.229
Transports	0.601	0.449	1.339
Other sectors	0.552	0.457	1.208

Source: Own calculations from Ludwig and Stäglin (1996)

output relationships in 1987 based on East German currency and also based on West German currency. The input output ratio according to the East German currencies reflects the relationship before the unification, the ratio based on West German D-Mark gives an indication for the input output relationship thereafter, say 1991.

In most sectors share of intermediate inputs relative to gross output was lower if based on the West German currency than it had been in East German currency. This indicates that after unification costs related to the use of intermediate inputs declined, which in general was good news for East German firms. Meanwhile in agriculture the input output relationship worsened and within the industrial sector the effects differed largely across industries.

To sum up the major findings it appears that East German firms received lower revenues through a relocation of demand towards West German products, and to a downward pressure on the product prices. This was accompanied by increasing costs as the institutional setting of the social union led to high wages. East German firms faced a profit squeeze, sometimes alleviated by an improved input output ratio, sometimes worsened by the new input output relationship.

The effects of the rapid increase of wages on East German employment deserve some further attention. In the short run it drove firms to reduce costs through decreasing the number of employees and also through an elaborate use of part-time contracts.[293] Calculations of Lindlar and Scheremet (1998) show a sharp decrease in 1991 of the number of employees and stabilisation since the first quarter of 1992. Also the hours worked per person became more stabilised since the second quarter of 1992. Moreover, their data show that the initial decrease of the hours worked per person was followed by a restoration from the second quarter of 1991 to the second quarter of 1992. At that time the hours worked per person were about the same as they had been at the introduction of the D-Mark.

Besides the short run fluctuations of the East German economy high wages are believed to have contributed to a persistent loss of jobs and competitiveness. The effects

[293] DIW (1991)

of wage costs on East German competitiveness show up in high unit labour costs in comparison with West Germany. Estimates of Franz and Steiner (2000) show that in 1991 East German unit labour costs amounted to 150 per cent of West Germany. Thereafter East German competitiveness improved as the convergence of labour productivity went faster than the ongoing convergence of wages. Their estimates of East German unit labour costs relative to West Germany in 1998 arrives at 124 percent.

7.3. Transformation: convergence and divergence

For the population the effects of the economic integration of the East and West German economies were disappointing. Historical experience with the currency reform in 1948, when West Germany introduced the D-Mark, was of major influence on the expectations of many people. The currency reform of 1948 was very much associated with the West German *Wirtschaftswunder*, in 1989 and 1990 people had hoped for an East German miracle.[294] And so it was promised them by politicians: during his re-election campaign in 1990 Helmut Kohl announced that within five years the new *Länder* (East Germany) would become as prosperous as the rest of Germany.

A miracle did not happen, in 1995 East Germany was not yet as prosperous as the rest of Germany. Meanwhile East German GDP per person employed had strongly recovered from the initial shock and in 1995 was still converging towards West Germany. In a growth accounting framework the growth of value added is based on three sources: labour inputs, capital inputs, and total factor productivity. For a convergence of labour productivity to occur – as labour inputs are in the denominator – East Germany needs improvements of capital intensity (capital per unit of labour) and/or of total factor productivity.

Capital intensity improved rapidly. For the business enterprise sector Klodt (2000) showed that the gross capital stock per worker (at constant prices of 1991) doubled from 1991 to 1998. The improvement of capital intensity was largely achieved by high investment, leading to an increase of capital inputs, but also through a decrease of labour inputs. Using statistics of the *Arbeitskreis "Volkswirtschaftliche Gesamtrechnungen der Länder"* it is possible to decompose East German growth in a growth accounting framework.

It is noted that the use of a growth accounting framework for analysing the East German economy during this period of transformation is rather problematic. Firstly it is difficult to determine the appropriate weights for the contribution of labour and capital. As it was discussed above East German wages rose rapidly. As a result the relative contribution of labour inputs may be too high relative to the contribution of capital

294 Klodt and Stehn et al. (1994) pp. 131–132

Table 7.3. Percentage point contribution to GDP of labour, capital, and TFP, 1991–2000

	1991–1995			1995–2000	
	East Germany		West Germany	East Germany	West Germany
GDP	8.4		1.2	1.9	1.6
Capital inputs	2.7	4.0	1.3	3.1	1.0
Labour inputs	–2.0	–1.5	–0.1	–0.7	0.4
Total Factor Productivity	7.7	5.9	0.0	–0.5	0.2

Notes: See text below. Weights for labour inputs were based on the wage share in value added; weights for capital inputs are complementary. West German labour is weighted at 0.54 for both periods. East German labour was weighted at 0.68 during the first period (left column), and at 0.52 during the second period and the first period (right column).
Source: http://www.statistik-bw.de/Arbeitskreis_VGR/ (20-02-2004)

inputs for the period from 1991 to 1995. Therefore the growth accounts for the period from 1991 to 1995 show two estimates: the left column is based on weights of 1991, the right column is based on weights of 1995. The calculations show the high sensitivity of different weights on the outcomes of growth accounting estimates for this period.

Secondly there is some uncertainty concerning the East German capital stock in 1991. The estimates of the value of the inherited capital stock from its past as a centrally planned economy vary. Early studies of Sinn and Sinn (1992) suggest it was about a third of the book value, i.e. 600 billion DM of 1991. There is also mention of a "junkyard" hypothesis, estimating the stock at zero. The statistics that are used in the present calculations arrive at an East German capital stock of more than 600 billion Euro's of 1995, which is rather high. The size of the East German capital stock is discussed later in this chapter. For the calculations a high valuation of the initial capital stock depresses the effects of the high investment on the growth of the capital stock. This is particularly the case if depreciation of the capital stock is at first rather high. For the growth accounts this has the effect that the contribution of capital inputs may be downward biased.

Setting aside the problems underlying the East German growth accounts for the 1990s, Table 7.3. allows several conclusions. Negative contribution of labour inputs refers to the decrease of employment; quality indicators for education and skills are not accounted for. As it was discussed in Chapter 3, human capital was at a high level in East Germany, although some studies suggest that skill levels should be improved on the job. For the contribution of capital inputs Table 7.3. shows a high contribution for both sub-periods. It reflects the high ratio of investment to GDP throughout the 1990s (see also Table 7.4.).

The development of East German total factor productivity in the 1990s is particularly interesting. Whereas total factor productivity accounted for the lion's share of GDP growth until 1995, it turned negative thereafter. Total factor productivity is mostly associated with technology, and its rapid growth after the unification can be expected from a catching up perspective. A main idea behind the catch up hypothesis is that technologically backward countries can easily adapt or duplicate technologies from more advanced countries. By closing the technology gap, the backward country will converge to the higher level of labour productivity of the advanced country through a higher growth of total factor productivity.

In the case of East Germany transformation created a favourable environment for closing the technology gap. During privatisation West German firms bought many East German firms, which promoted a swift diffusion of modern technology. Growth of GDP and of total factor productivity in the early 1990s was indeed impressive. No wonder that future oriented questions departing from the catching up hypothesis tried to predict the time period of convergence for East Germany to West German productivity and living standards. Estimates on the time needed for East Germany to converge to West German levels varied from 13 to more than 70 years.[295] This corresponds to a year between 2004 and 2066.

At the same time there are authors who questioned whether any further convergence will occur at all. Although East German convergence towards West Germany was impressive in the early 1990s, thereafter it levelled off. The historical example of Mezzogiorno – the southern part of Italy – is a classic case where after a short period of catching up, convergence stopped and labour productivity and per capita income remained well below the more advanced northern part of Italy. Will East Germany become a new Mezzogiorno? An affirmative answer means that there will be no further convergence.[296]

Departing from the catch up paradigm the absence of ongoing East German convergence towards West Germany can result from lacking 'social capability'. The 'social capability' concept is derived from Abramovitz and defines the restrictions to the catch up potential of a country. For the East German convergence towards the level of labour productivity of West Germany this concept indicates that it is important to reduce existing gaps in physical and human capital stocks, and that financial and business services should be made available.

It was already mentioned that East German human capital is considered to be at a high level, and the physical infrastructure improved rapidly. From the unification onwards investment in East German capital stock (and infrastructure) was high, and was stimulated through state subsidies. Table 7.4. shows that the investment to GDP ratio was much higher in East Germany than in the united Germany for all years, although the East German advantage has decreased during the late 1990s. But these investments also include the very large investments in infrastructure, subsidised by the government.

---

295 See Burda and Funke (1995) pp. 327–354

296 Boltho, Carlin and Scaramozzino (1997) pp. 241–264

Table 7.4. Investment to GDP ratio from 1991 to 2000

	1991	1992	1993	1994	1995	1996	1997	1998	1999	2000
East Germany	0.44	0.49	0.49	0.51	0.49	0.45	0.41	0.39	0.36	0.34
Germany	0.24	0.24	0.23	0.23	0.22	0.22	0.21	0.21	0.22	0.22

Source: http://www.statistik-bw.de/Arbeitskreis_VGR/ (20-02-2004)

Sinn distinguishes the investment in buildings and machinery and finds that relative investment in machinery is less impressive.[297] Nevertheless it is found that in manufacturing the plants located in the East were considered to have the appropriate stock of equipment by 1998.[298] I will discuss capital intensity in more detail later in this section. Besides the expansion of the capital infrastructure Boltho, Carlin and Scaramozzino (1997) point at the benefits of the transfer of West Germany's rich institutional framework in the form of the industrial relations and vocational training systems, or of the networks of savings, co-operative, and development banks.[299] Even though it will take time for these institutions to operate as effectively as in the West, I agree with Boltho, Carlin and Scaramozzino that on balance the social capability is favourable.

According to Abelshauser (2004) the comparison of the West German currency reform in 1948 and the introduction of the D-Mark in East Germany in 1990 makes clear that the institutional heritage and a favourable "Konstellation der Produktionsfaktoren" were of the utmost importance in the West German upswing of the late 1940s and the early 1950s. Insofar Abelshauser aims to make clear "dass es falsch war, in der Einführung der Marktwirtschaft allein das Heil zu sehen", he is right to state that the introduction of a market economy by itself did not manufacture a miracle. Lange and Pugh (1998) already concluded that "the outcome of reform depends not only on the prescribed measures but also on the conditions under which they are implemented".[300] Their careful comparative analysis of the West German conditions in 1948 and the East German conditions in 1990 shows why similar reform measures had different outcomes. They conclude that "currency and economic reform in 1948 enabled West Germany's productive potential to be realized in both continued recovery and a qualitatively higher rate of capital accumulation. Monetary and economic Unification in 1990 exposed the East's relative lack of productive potential, while imposing conditions unfavourable to competitiveness, and precipitated a collapse of output". In my view, in the comparison

297 In fact Sinn shows that investment per 'Erwerbsfähigen', i.e. per person in the age-group from 15 to 65 year is about or below the West German level. This is the mirror image of high unemployment in East Germany; on a per worker basis investment would be much more favourable for East Germany. See: Sinn (2000)

298 L. Bellman and M. Brussig, "Productivity Differences between Western and Eastern German Establishments"in: *IAB Labour Market Topics* (1999) 37 as quoted in Barrell and Te Velde (2000)

299 Boltho, Carlin and Scaramozzino (1997) pp. 241–264; pp. 256–259

300 Lange and Pugh (1998) p. 61

of these two reforms, Lange and Pugh do more justice to the East German reform in 1990 than Abelshauser does. Their discussion includes the imposed unfavourable East German conditions such as the high wages that were discussed in Section 7.2. of this thesis, and includes also the effects of market integration that will be discussed in the following section. In comparison, Abelshauser focuses too much on the favourable conditions for the West German reforms of 1948 and ignores the impact of the unification that took place simultaneously with the transformation to a market economy in the East German reforms.

Since 1994 convergence towards West German levels has levelled off. Graph 7.1. shows the persistence of the gap of GDP per worker and of GDP per capita for the East German economy in comparison with West Germany. It also shows that the gap is wider for GDP per capita than GDP per worker, which can be explained by the high unemployment in East Germany. Also the negative total factor productivity contribution since 1995 is disturbing. Growth that is based on mere accumulation of capital, as in East Germany from 1995 to 2000, is unsustainable according to the logic of growth accounting. However, a period of merely five years is probably too short to arrive at conclusions on this matter.

Moreover an alternative hypothesis could be formulated, stating that East Germany climbed the technology ladder too fast. Moving up the technology ladder has some negative effects on productivity due to set-up costs, which are associated with problems

Graph 7.1. Catching up of East German GDP per worker and per capita in comparison with West Germany (Constant prices of 1995)

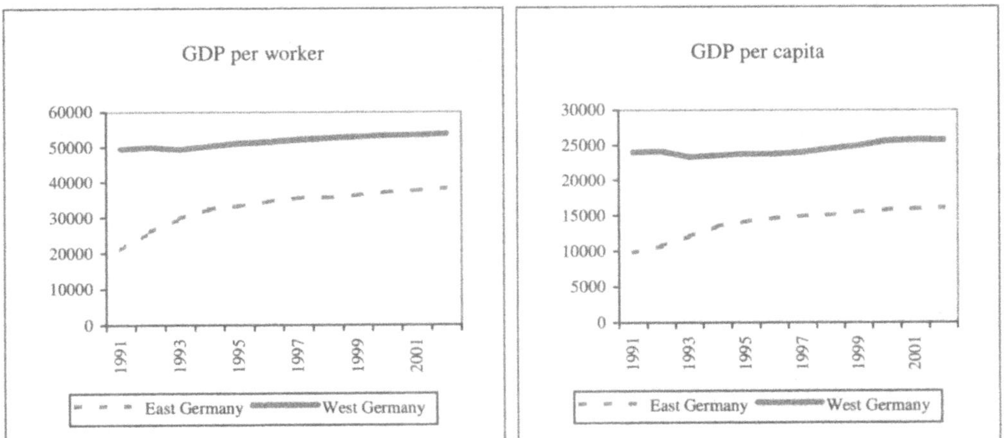

Notes: West Germany refers to the former West Germany including Berlin, East Germany refers to the former East Germany excluding Berlin
Sources: Arbeitskreis "Volkswirtschaftliche Gesamtrechnungen der Länder", http://www.statistik-bw.de/Arbeitskreis_VGR/ (20-02-2004)

of adaptation and adjustment.[301] Timmer (2002) concludes that under a rapid movement up the technology ladder learning periods might be too short in order to fully assimilate new technologies and operate them at full productive potential.[302] This is more likely in cases of leapfrogging than in cases of gradual shifting, and might particularly apply to the rapid introduction of new technology in East Germany.

Following the collapse of the East German economy, East Germany was equipped with a relatively small capital stock and only few machines by 1991.[303] Table 7.4. showed that after unification investment in East Germany was very high. Since 1991 the capital intensity improved rapidly, partly resulting from a massive shake out of labour, and partly explained by a stimulus of government policy through a reduction of the costs of capital inputs.[304]

The underlying estimates of the East German capital stock in Table 7.3. imply a convergence of the East German capital per worker from 39 percent of the West German level in 1991 to 75 per cent in 2000. These estimates excluded East Berlin. Including East Berlin, but confined to the capital intensity in enterprises, the *Institut für Wirtschaftsforschung* estimated East German capital per worker at 46 percent of West Germany in 1991, and at 62 per cent in 1994 (See Table 7.5.). This study notes that the estimates on the East German capital stock, in particular the part of buildings, is probably too high.

Figures of IWH for 1997 are shown for total, and do not separate out capital per worker for machinery and buildings. In that year the East German capital intensity was estimated at 73 per cent of West Germany.

So far catching up was discussed as an economy wide development. However, it makes sense to look at the catching up paradigm for individual sectors. The technology gap, the physical infrastructure and human capital may vary across sectors, so that the prospects for convergence are also different. This is illustrated with the example of the

Table 7.5. Capital per worker in East German enterprises, prices of 1991 (total in 1000 DM, and relative to West Germany)

	1000 DM (Prices of 1991)		West Germany = 100	
	1991	1994	1991	1994
Machinery	29	47	29	44
Buildings	74	101	60	73
Total	103	148	46	62

Source: IWH (1999) p. 19

301 Timmer (2002)
302 Timmer (2002)
303 IWH (1999) p. 19
304 See Sinn (2000)

Table 7.6. Labour productivity in the East German economy (West Germany = 100, current prices)

	1991	1992	1993	1994	1995	1996	1997	1998	1999	2000
Agriculture	42.6	59.7	97.6	88.0	92.1	84.0	90.1	99.0	101.0	102.6
Public Utilities	49.1	53.3	63.3	63.3	68.6	78.8	76.4	74.2		
Mining	54.4	59.6	89.1	99.4	83.8	186.2	183.5	195.5		
Manufacturing	18.0	27.9	39.1	46.3	49.8	54.4	58.2	60.5	62.9	64.9
Construction	49.4	62.5	70.2	79.4	80.0	82.1	79.7	72.7	71.1	68.5
Transports	36.1	38.5	47.7	54.4	53.9	52.8	55.6	57.9		
Other sectors:										
– Trade	45.6	67.0	74.8	75.1	71.5	73.4	70.8	69.8		
– Finance	30.0	40.7	55.4	60.9	63.2	65.8	68.1	69.2	70.0	73.4
– Community	54.3	67.9	76.1	80.0	81.3	82.1	82.9	81.5	81.2	83.1
Total	34.6	48.3	59.5	64.3	65.1	67.1	67.7	67.3	67.5	68.5

Notes: West Germany refers to the former West Germany including Berlin, East Germany refers to the former East Germany excluding Berlin
Source: Ragnitz (2001)

diffusion of technologies in agriculture and in manufacturing. Presumably the implementation of better fertilisers and seeds demands fewer skills than the introduction of computers in the production process, as it mainly requires access to the (new and improved) intermediate inputs.

Table 7.6. shows that patterns of convergence and divergence differ across sectors. Whereas agriculture and mining are currently at a high relative level of labour productivity, in all other sectors the East German level is well below West Germany. Moreover, since 1996 the East German level of labour productivity is falling behind relative to West Germany in public utilities, construction, and trade.

Mining and agriculture are both regarded as capital intensive sectors.[305] Their high labour productivity in comparison with West Germany therefore supports the view that the East German capital stock is sufficiently developed. As in manufacturing the plants were also well equipped with the 'appropriate stock of capital' (see above), the next step looks at other differences between sectors. Differences between sectors could be explained by sector specific skill requirements.

In some respects the catching up hypothesis cannot capture the main changes of the East German economy after 1989 adequately. Firstly increases of total labour productivity until 1994 are to a large extent due to the closing down of low productive plants and a layoff of redundant labour. This only fits the hypothesis if the meaning of 'technology' is stretched so far that it includes the adaptation of new insights of management and organisation. As it relates to the labour market policy and the soft budget

305 ICOP-database, http://www.eco.rug.nl/ggdc/dseries/Data/Sectoral/BV-Germany.xls (07-11-2002)

constraints before unification it makes more sense to look at the decrease of redundant labour as an effect of the transformation of the economic system as it does link up to new 'policy' more than to new 'knowledge'.

Secondly, on a sectoral level, labour productivity in East German mining is much higher than in West Germany. It is unlikely that the difference is explained by a technology gap in which East Germany is the most advanced region. Mining refers to the extraction of iron ores, salts, coals, gas, and etceteras. Labour productivity in mining is highly dependent on the composition of the mining sector, and thus on the region's natural resource endowments. For somewhat different reasons – which will be dealt with more elaborately in Section 7.4. – most probably differences in the composition of the manufacturing sector also explain part of the East-West productivity gap.

Thirdly it is unclear – from the catching up perspective – why some sectors continued to fall behind after 1996. Was technology in West German public utilities, construction and trade advancing, thereby outpacing East Germany? If this were true it would be difficult to explain the divergence of the two parts of Germany in a catching up framework now that East German social capability to diffuse new technologies has improved at such a high pace.

The inadequateness of the catching up paradigm to capture all major developments of the East German economy after 1989 lies in the fact that it focuses on merely one of the two dramatic changes. Due to the integration of East and West German markets the issue is not restricted to the adoption of new technologies and work practices, but also to competitiveness and thus matters of location and trade.

7.4. Unification: location and trade

According to the benchmark comparison for 1936, there existed a pattern of specialisation in the two economies before the two parts of Germany were separated. At that time textile industries were relatively strongly represented in East Germany, versus a relatively large branch 'basic and fabricated metal products' in West Germany. In the 1930s the division of labour was historically determined, in the case of Saxonian textiles; and location advantages, in the case of basic and fabricated metals in the Ruhr-area. As it was shown in Chapter 4, since the division of Germany this specialisation pattern collapsed. East Germany elaborated its production capacity in basic and fabricated metal industries so that in 1954 the industrial sector had a more similar structure in East Germany and West Germany than in 1936.

After the unification of East Germany and West Germany in 1990 the emergence of a new division of labour could be expected. In this section I will compare the structure of the two German economies. What are the patterns of specialisation? What sectors in the economy have become relatively important in size in East Germany, and why? Another question examines the relevance of the distinction between East and West for the explanation of regional differences today. How are firms allocated across regions: will East Germany become the periphery of the united German economy?

A new division of labour?

What are the comparative advantages of East Germany relative to West Germany? And how does the historical legacy of the division of the two parts of Germany influence the structure of the economy after 1991? The employment structure in the two economies in 2002, based on a four sector classification, shows a relatively dominant primary sector (agriculture, forestry and fishing) in East Germany. The industrial sector is larger in West Germany, differences in "Transports and communications" and in the "remaining sectors" account for a larger share in East Germany than in West Germany.

Unemployment is higher in East Germany. Nevertheless the size of the East German primary sector is not only large in terms of a high percentage of employed persons in total East German employment, but also shows a relatively high number of employed persons per 1000 inhabitants. This indicates a pattern of specialisation, where 'agriculture, forestry and fishing' is a remarkably strong sector in East Germany. The weakest developed sector in comparison with West Germany is the industrial sector, in particular manufacturing.

Agricultural products such as vegetables, milk, eggs, meat and fruits are more or less similar regardless of where they are produced, quality differences are not very important. Clearly the agricultural sector had little difficulty to "find" the consumer. Since the unification in 1990 East German agriculture focuses on the production of the crops sector, and particularly the production of fruits. In comparison with West Germany the livestock production is unimportant. Besides specialisation of East German agriculture,

Table 7.7. Employment structure in East and West Germany in 2002

	Relative labour productivity[a, b]	Percent of employed persons[b]		Employed persons per 1000 inhabitants[b]	
	West Germany = 100	East Germany	West Germany	East Germany	West Germany
Agriculture, forestry and fishing	103.6	3.3	2.4	13.8	10.6
Industry and Construction	62.8	29.1	32.5	122.1	145.6
Transports and Communication	58.5	23.4	22.8	98.2	101.9
Remaining sectors	64.4	44.2	42.4	185.4	189.9
Total	63.8	100.0	100.0	419.5	448.0

Note: [a] Relative hourly labour productivity in 2002; [b] Berlin is divided equally between East Germany and West Germany

Source: Statistisches Bundesamt, *Statistisches Jahrbuch 2003*

it can also be observed that East German agriculture is still strongly organised in large enterprises. This results in economies of scale: in comparison with smaller enterprises fewer inputs are needed to achieve the same increase of output.[306] Therefore I conclude that East Germany has developed a strong agricultural sector that is highly competitive.

The aggregate for industry and construction accounts for a higher employment share in West Germany than in East Germany. However, the construction is much larger in East Germany than in West Germany. Since unification construction boomed, it did not have to 'find' demand as demand found the construction sector. Its large size can be seen as a regional effect of the prevailing necessity to improve roads and the state of buildings that had been neglected for many (socialist) years.

In comparison with West Germany the manufacturing sector has become quite small.[307] Based on the total hours worked per head of the population East German manufacturing activity in 2002 is estimated at 61 per cent of West Germany.[308] Contrary to agriculture and construction it has been difficult for East German manufacturing to maintain existing markets and find new consumer markets. Shortly after the Berlin Wall came down East German demand shifted towards Western products.

To illustrate the difficulties in finding new markets: in 1991 16.2 percent of East German manufacturing output was sold on foreign markets. In 2000 this had moved up to 21.6 percent. But still in comparison with West Germany, where in 2000 almost 38 percent was sold at foreign markets, this is a rather low export ratio.[309] East German manufacturing has a relatively small market share, and labour productivity is relatively low.

To explain for the low manufacturing labour productivity it has been argued that in comparison with West Germany the East German economy lacks the beneficial effects of 'economies of scale'. According to estimates of Ragnitz the specific scale structure of enterprises accounts for more than 50 per cent of the productivity gap in manufacturing between East Germany and West Germany.[310] A focus on small- and medium sized firms may simply relate to the firm demography: East German firms are relatively young (and not yet full-grown). Alternatively, it may indicate the emergence into a peripheral region, as within core regions more large size enterprises will occur. Since the unification the factors labour and capital are mobile in Germany, with a relocation of labour and capital. The important question is: where did they go?

---

306 Fiege and Hinners-Tobrägel (2002) pp. 27–34

307 Still there differences between manufacturing branches as well. East German 'food, beverages, tobacco' employs almost as many workers per 1000 inhabitants as in West Germany. See DIW/IfW/IWH, "Gesamtwirtschaftliche und unternehmerische Anpassungsfortschritte in Ostdeutschland: Kurzexpertise" in: IWH (2001) p. 13

308 Own calculations from Statistisches Jahrbuch 2003, pp. 201, 202

309 Loose and Ludwig (2001)

310 Ragnitz (2001)

Core and periphery

Looking at the regional level of GDP per worker and of GDP per capita of the German *Länder* there are no signs of one of the East German *Länder* forging ahead of the others. The economic performance – measured by these indicators – shows much similarity between all East German *Länder*. The differences between the two German economies manifest themselves also on the regional level of the Länder. East German regions attain lower levels of labour productivity and per capita income.

Only Berlin attained a regional labour productivity that surpassed a former West German region: Saarland. All other East German regions are at the lower end of the German regional labour productivity scale. Ten years after the unification what once was "East" is still grouped together. The lack of differences between East German regions becomes even more apparent in per capita income. This is explained by the very high unemployment in all East German regions, resulting in a low labour participation ratio (workers per head of the population).

Graph 7.2. Regional labour productivity in 2000 (1000 Euro)

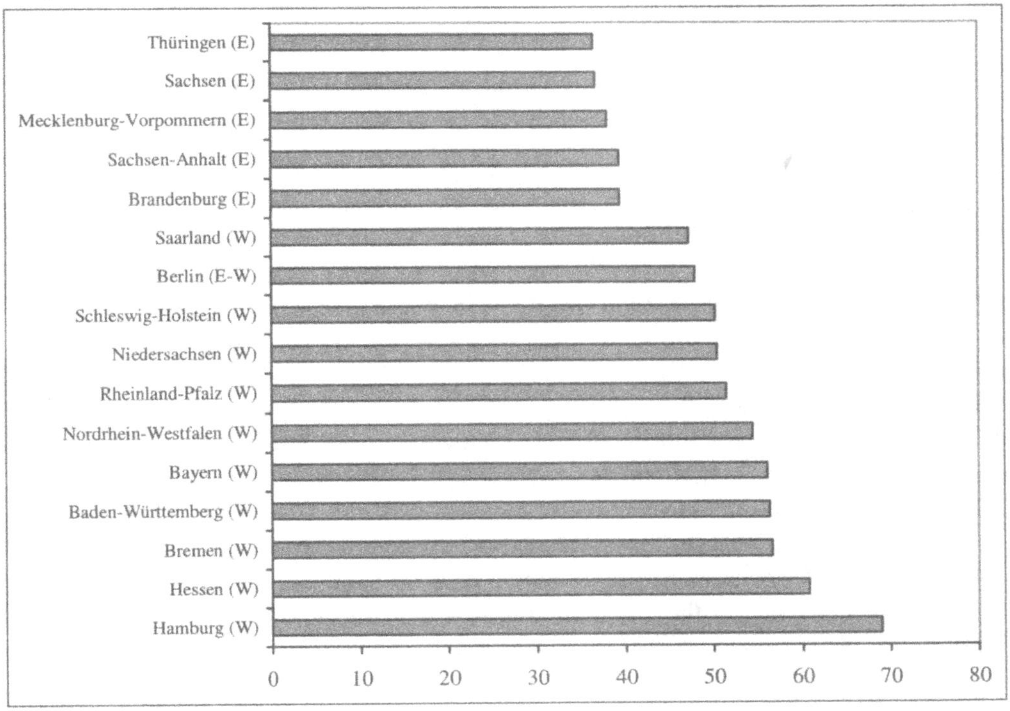

Source: Arbeitskreis "Volkswirtschaftliche Gesamtrechnungen der Länder", http://www.statistik-bw.de/volkspreise/arbeitskreisvgr/bip_95.asp (05-07-2002); http://www.statistik-bw.de/volkswpreise/arbeitskreisvgr/elaender.asp (05-21-2002)

Graph 7.3. Regional GDP per capita in 2000 (1000 Euro)

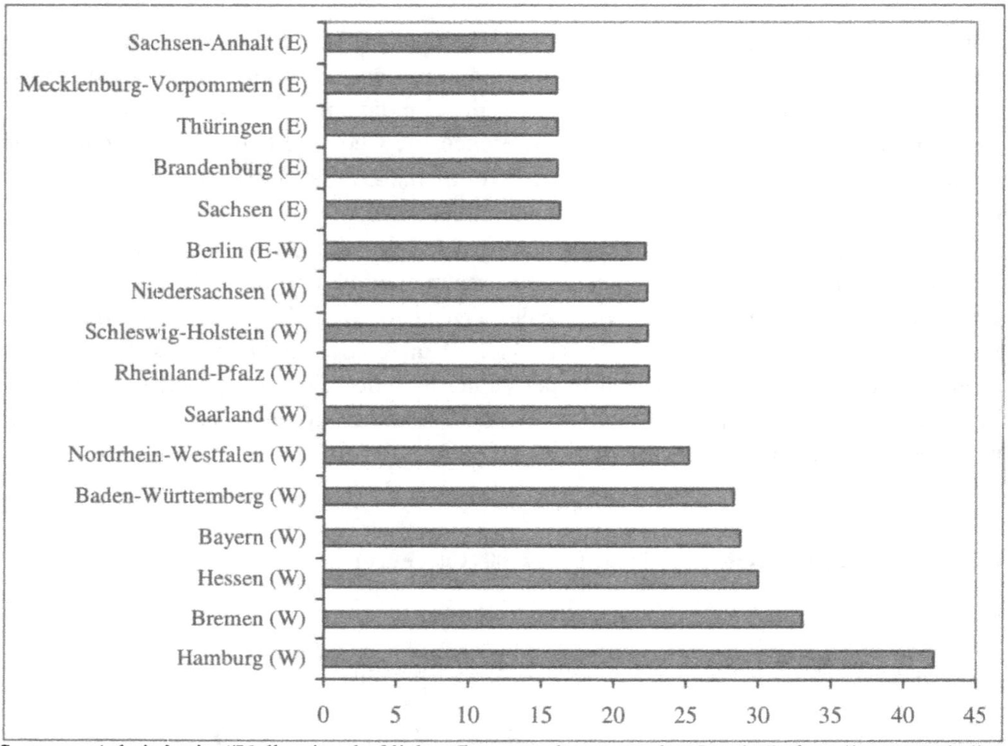

Source: Arbeitskreis "Volkswirtschaftliche Gesamtrechnungen der Länder", http://www.statistik-bw.de/volkspreise/arbeitskreisvgr/bip_95.asp (05-07-2002); http://www.statistik-bw.de/volkswpreise/arbeitskreisvgr/einwohner.asp (05-21-2002)

Krugman describes a 'hypothetical history' which more or less describes the German situation.[311] Initially there were two separate countries, one consisting of four regions, and one of two regions. "We suppose that the two countries initially maintain sufficient barriers to trade and factor mobility that their economic geography evolves independently, with the large country developing a core in region 1 and the small country a smaller core in region 2. Then the two countries [...] merge into a single economic unit. What happens?"

According to Krugman the answer depends on whether the ultimate equilibrium has one core or two.[312] If the integrated economy ends up with one core the region with its head start will attract all the manufacturing away from the smaller core. But if the integrated economy ends up with two cores, manufacturing in the smaller core may

311 Krugman (1991) pp. 84–87

312 This depends on transport costs, economies of scale, and the share of footloose industry in national income.

actually expand at the expense of the larger core, as it gains access to its full natural hinterland.

What characterises a core? The core is a concentration of population and production. Whereas miners live near the minerals, and heavy industries tend to locate near its raw materials to save on transport costs, there are many manufacturing industries and services that are not tied to a particular location for such reasons. These industries and services tend to cluster together. Can such clusters be observed in East Germany?

The full exploration of this issue requires further research, though as a narrative the lacking East German core may provide an explanation for the small manufacturing sector in East Germany. Brakman, Garretsen and Schramm stated that East Germany is becoming a peripheral region. Their evidence looks at several indicators for the German Länder, such as the GDP per square kilometre, average hourly wages, and prices of land per square metre.[313] Krugman defined a core as a concentration of production and population: GDP per square kilometre is a straightforward estimate of the concentration of production. Brakman, Garretsen and Schramm found that GDP per square kilometre is much lower in East German *Länder* than in West German *Länder*.

Average hourly wages are expected to be higher in regions that are part of – or close to – a large market. Thus high wages may indicate a core region, whereas low wages indicate periphery. Brakman *et al.* found the average hourly wages in the manufacturing sector are lower in East German *Länder* than in West German *Länder*.

Finally the authors compared the prices of land per square metre in East German *Länder* and in West German *Länder*. The underlying reasoning departs from the negative feedback of the high concentration of population in the core region: congestion. This, so it is argued by Brakman *et al.* leads to high land prices. Indeed prices of land in the East German *Länder* were below the West German *Länder*, although differences were less convincing as the previous indicators.

Instead of looking at the different *Länder* I will now look at East Germany, West Germany and Berlin. If production is concentrated in core regions, the share of East German GDP in total GDP related to the share of East German population in total population gives also an indication for the existence of a core. This also applies for the share in total employment. In 1998 East German population (including East Berlin) amounted to 18.4 per cent of the total population.

Developments from 1991 and 1995 allowed for optimistic expectations. East Germany was gaining its share in total GDP. From 1996 onwards, however, the East German share in GDP is flat and employment goes down. The declining share of East German employment in the German total is accompanied by actual decreases of employment in all East German regions. Meanwhile all West German regions except Bremen have increased the number of people that were employed. It was already shown that manufacturing production, which is associated with the core, primarily takes place

313 Brakman, Garretsen and Schramm (2002)

Table 7.8. Percentage shares in total GDP and employment, 1991–2003 (East Germany, Berlin, West Germany)

	GDP				Employment			
	1991	1995	2000	2003	1991	1995	2000	2003
East Germany	7.0	11.1	11.1	11.2	17.6	16.2	15.3	14.8
West Germany	88.9	84.6	85.2	85.2	78.1	79.5	80.7	81.3
Berlin	4.1	4.3	3.7	3.7	4.3	4.3	4.0	3.9

Sources: Arbeitskreis "Volkswirtschaftliche Gesamtrechnungen der Länder", http://www.statistik-bw.de/Arbeitskreis_VGR/ (20-02-2004)

in West Germany, whereas agriculture, which is associated with the periphery, is well developed in East Germany. Moreover, despite converging productivity levels neither the East German share in GDP nor the East German share in employment is improving. This also indicates that East Germany is developing into a peripheral economy.

Some remarks on future prospects

Extrapolating the developments since 1991 as shown in Table 7.8. suggests a further decrease of the share of East German employment in total German employment. If the share of East German GDP remains the same, this would imply further convergence of East German labour productivity towards West Germany. As the size of the East German population relative to West Germany declines also, also GDP per capita may further converge to West Germany. It is clear that more sophisticated analysis on the underlying determinants is necessary.

If the core is defined as a concentration of production and population, there are clear signs that East Germany is becoming a peripheral region. Population density decreases and none of the *Länder* produces a relatively high GDP per capita. Only at lower levels of (geographical) aggregation centres of economic activity can be observed, their meaning is a matter of further research. Core regions are associated with highly productive economic structure. Previous sections showed a relatively large manufacturing sector in West Germany, and a relatively large agricultural sector in East Germany. Also within the sectors structural differences are eminent. Moreover, core regions exhibit more large size enterprises, profiting from the beneficial effects of 'economies of scale'. If East Germany has become a peripheral region there are implications on the prospects for further convergence as it probably involves a negative structure effect and lacking benefits of 'economies of scale'.

Therefore it seems unlikely that East Germany will fully converge to West German levels of labour productivity and GDP per capita. Convergence achieved through a rapid transfer of technology and modern management and work organisation practices is restricted by differences of the economic structure. New technologies and new concepts of management help to improve production within similar industries. The maximum possible levels of labour productivity that can be achieved differ for different sectors, branches, and industries. The East German economy has developed a production structure that cannot achieve as high a labour productivity as in West Germany. This does not mean that convergence will come to a complete standstill. Different sectors, branches, and industries did not all reach their maximum possible levels of labour productivity yet. The cause could be the rapid pace of modernisation in East Germany, leading to problems of adaptation and adjustment.

Presently the integration of former centrally planned economies into 'western' markets is happening on a much larger scale with the enlargement of the European Union. It is tempting to analyse the enlargement of European Union as an analogy of the unification of East and West Germany. The obvious similarities are their history as former centrally planned economies, the economic integration with more advanced West European countries, and the currency union. However, in my view East Germany is very much a special case.

Distinctive features that are particularly important are the following. Firstly, the accession countries have transformed their economies into market economies before integration with the European Union; in East Germany there was a simultaneous process of transformation and unification. During the early phase of transformation into a market economy the vulnerability for competition was particularly high. Secondly, within the European Union social policy is largely decided upon on the national level. The effects of the social union on East German wages seriously affected East German competitiveness. Thirdly, the analogy fails on the mobility of factors. Concerning labour mobility countries of the pre-enlargement European Union have set up limitations, and even without such limitations barriers due to language differences are higher than between East and West Germany. Concerning capital mobility accession countries cannot rely on as generous investments as in East Germany.

Chapter 8: Concluding chapter

Institutions, historical events and the development of the East German economy in comparison with West Germany

This study compares the East and West German economies from 1936 to 2002, and in particular the period from 1936 to 1991. During these years the East German economy fell behind the West German level in terms of gross domestic product per capita – and also in terms of labour productivity. When did the once relatively prosperous and high productive East German economy lose track of West Germany? What were the causes?

From 1949 until 1989 the two German economies were separate countries with different *economic systems*: East Germany, the GDR, was a 'centrally planned economy' and West Germany, the FRG, was a 'market economy'. Therefore the influence of institutions on economic performance is a major theme in the comparison of the East and West German economies. Besides the effects of institutional differences the falling behind is also related to the historical events between 1936 and 1950. The economies were harmed by the Second World War and the beginning of the 'cold war' through war damage, dismantling, reparations, migration, and the disintegration of Germany. Finally the historical events between 1989 and 1991, including the fall of the Berlin Wall, East Germany's transformation to a market economy and the integration of the East and West German markets, (at first) contributed to the East German falling behind.

Therefore the analysis distinguishes between three sub-periods of the East German falling behind: (a) from 1936 to 1950, (b) from 1950 to 1989, and (c) from 1989 to 1991. Thereafter East Germany was catching up relative to West Germany.

Falling behind from 1936 to 1950

In 1936 East German gross domestic product per capita was above the West German level, in 1950 it was about 56 per cent of West Germany. Relative levels of labour productivity worsened in agriculture, manufacturing, construction, and in transports and communication. In mining there was no falling behind. Confined to the industrial sector

– which comprises manufacturing and mining – there was a drastic fall of output in the final years of the Second World War. On balance the East German industrial output declined between the benchmark years 1936 and 1950. In West Germany there was still some growth of industrial output in this period.

The East German and West German growth of industrial output were analysed in a growth accounting framework. This framework explains output growth by changes of labour inputs, capital inputs and total factor productivity. It appeared that the main explanation for the decline of industrial output in East Germany lies in capital inputs. East Germany suffered from war damage and dismantling by the Soviet Union. Whereas war damage was more or less the same in the two German economies, dismantling made the East German balance sheet unfavourable in comparison with West Germany.

Furthermore the Soviet Union demanded for reparations. It is argued that reparations, which mainly concerned deliveries out of current production, had indirect effects on the East German capital stock. Reparations put a heavy burden on national income, so that possibilities for investment were sharply reduced. In addition low investment also relates to the institutional change towards a centrally planned economy, which involved expropriations, and thus created a bad investment climate.

Besides a decrease of the capital stock also negative total factor productivity explains for the decline of industrial output in East Germany. After the separation of the two German economies the existing patterns of specialisation were cut loose. Some industries were still dependent on deliveries from West German firms; the division of Germany created bottlenecks in East Germany. Other explanations for the negative total factor productivity include the outflow of human capital towards West Germany and the inferior technology – in terms of efficiency – of the new industrial centre that was built in East Germany during the Second World War. It is noted that labour inputs increased during this period, which relates to the enormous migration towards both East and West Germany from the lost provinces of Pommerania, Silesia, and East Prussia, and of ethnic Germans from all over Eastern Europe.

Before the Second World War labour productivity in the East German industrial sector was already below the West German level, albeit merely 9 per cent. At that time there was a division of labour where the branch 'basic and fabricated metal' was relatively large in West Germany and the branch 'textiles, wearing apparel' was large in East Germany. Looking at the technology regimes during which different industries came into development, this suggests that the West German industry structure was more modern. After the division of Germany the branch 'metal, machinery and transports' explained for most of the difference of East German and West German industrial labour productivity.

Falling behind from 1950 to 1989

From 1950 to 1989 the observed performance based on gross domestic product per capita hides underlying problems of the East German economy that become apparent when looking at gross domestic product per worker. Whereas the East German gross domestic product per capita remained at about 56 per cent of the West German level, the East German labour productivity declined in comparison with West Germany since 1950. This combination is marked by a high participation of labour – defined as the number of workers in per cent of the population – in East Germany.

The relatively low increase of East German labour productivity in comparison with West Germany from 1950 to 1989 is a particularly worrying characteristic as the East German economy also started from a much lower *level* of labour productivity in the early 1950s. From a catch-up perspective the relatively low initial level indicates a great potential to boost labour productivity growth in East Germany through a succesful (re)modernisation of the economy. However, in stead of catching up the East German economy was falling behind even further.

A closer look at the underlying sectors shows a particularly bad comparative performance in East German agriculture. Meanwhile East German construction achieved a similar growth of labour productivity as in West Germany. To explain for these developments several issues are taken into account. Firstly technological improvements – or the lack of them – can explain for labour productivity growth. In East German agriculture this may refer to the few amounts of milking machines, and the low quality of fertilizers; in the construction sector the East German *plattenbau* allowed for very efficient production. Secondly labour productivity may increase through the use of capital instead of labour. Thirdly the composition of what was produced within a sector changed over time and was different between East Germany and West Germany. For instance: agriculture produced crops and livestock products, mining includes black coal, brown coal and iron ores, construction includes housing and industrial structures, etceteras. A shift in the composition of a sector may increase labour productivity.

Similarly the reallocation of factors between sectors can improve labour productivity. In both German economies labour moved out of sectors with a low productivity *level* (e.g. agriculture) and into sectors with a higher productivity level (e.g. manufacturing). This helped to increase the aggregate level of labour productivity. In the case of East Germany it is observed that factor reallocation is dynamic, there is a huge shift of labour inputs towards sectors with higher labour productivity *growth*. This might be related to the system of economic planning where resources for investment in capital and technology – leading to higher productivity growth – and labour inputs are directed into the same sectors of the economy.

Looking in more detail at the industrial sector – where 12 branches are distinguished – one may expect a similar pattern. East Germany focussed on some particular priority sectors, which could easily lead to dynamic shift effects. Moreover, central planning policy might induce crowding out effects of non-priority sectors that received difficulties to get finance for investment and to get employees. However, these patterns were not observed. Decomposition into the contribution of branches to the total growth of industrial labour productivity in East Germany, using Harberger diagrams, showed that during the 1950s and 1960s labour productivity expanded evenly across branches. For the 1950s, when there was a clear focus on heavy industries, this suggests that the expansion of 'basic and fabricated metal' could set free other branches that were suffering from bottlenecks.

From the 1960s onwards the example of the (petro-)chemical industries showed how much the slow progress of East German labour productivity had resulted from its relatively isolated position in international trade. After gaining access to crude oil East Germany built up new industries and realised high growth of labour productivity in the branch "chemicals, rubber, plastic, oil refining". During the 1970s the examples of the imports-dependent chemical industries (crude oil) and the exports-oriented machinery industries showed that these findings are consistent with the changing position of East Germany in the international context. At that time there was a large overshooting with a negative contribution to the total industrial labour productivity growth by 'mining' and 'machinery and transports'.

The very low growth of industrial labour productivity in the 1980s troubles the decomposition analysis. Based on findings in the literature it was related to lacking modern technologies which enable to increase labour productivity; and also to existing institutions that prohibited the increase of labour productivity through rationalisation, as everyone had the right to get a job.

Falling behind from 1989 to 1991

Gross domestic product per capita had remained at a stable distance of West Germany throughout the period from 1950 to 1989, with little falling behind during the 1980s, thereafter the East German gross domestic product per capita collapsed. As a centrally planned economy East Germany could maintain a standard of living at 56 per cent of the West German level through high labour efforts, which were manifested in the participation of women in the workforce and in the hours worked. When the East German economy transformed in a market economy some typical 'socialist production' was no longer continued. This refers to production that could only exist from the distorted demand structure in socialist economies such as purchases that existed because of a lack of alternatives (textiles), excessive purchases in inventories and also the hoarding of food that followed irregular supply. The institutional change led to a drastic fall of output, so that gross domestic product per capita faded.

Labour productivity also declined. Even though the less efficient firms were closed down in general output decreased faster than the amount of labour inputs did. Besides the transformation of the East German economic system it is also recognised that the East German economy integrated with West Germany. Much of the East German demand shifted from domestic products to products of Western origin from the removal of travel restrictions onwards.

The East German firms faced decreasing revenues due to lagging demand and downward pressure on product prices. This was accompanied by increasing costs as the institutional setting of the social union led to high wages. East German firms experienced a profit squeeze, sometimes alleviated by an improved input output ratio, sometimes worsened by the new input output relationship. Besides transformation also the integration of the two economies contributed to the falling behind of the East German economy between 1989 and 1991.

Catching up since 1991

Since East Germany adopted the institutions of a market economy, and it engaged into unification with the technologically advanced economy of West Germany, high growth rates and a convergence to West German levels could be expected. Especially now that investment in East Germany is at a high level. In comparison with other former centrally planned economies in Eastern Europe the convergence of manufacturing labour productivity in East Germany has indeed been impressive.

Meanwhile convergence has levelled off, and is in fact concentrated in an impressive spurt from 1991 to 1994. Increasingly the question arises whether East Germany will converge any further at all. Especially the emergence of a different structure of the economy in the two parts of Germany and the falling behind of East German public utilities, construction, and trade raise doubts.

It is found that the East German economy is relatively strong developed in the agricultural sector whereas the manufacturing sector is remarkably weak developed. This could be explained by the integration of the two German economies – where the spatial issue of core and periphery were newly defined – which supposedly made East Germany a peripheral region within the united German economy.

Therefore it is unlikely that East Germany will attain a level of labour productivity as high as in West Germany. In comparison with West Germany the East German economy has a negative structure effect (some very high productive sectors are located in West Germany) and also lacks the beneficial effects of 'economies of scale'. Within the West German core regions large size enterprises occur, and are able to realise a relatively high labour productivity.

Annex A.: Time series on the industrial sector

Annex A.1. Industrial production from 1936 to 1954

Gross output series for this period are based on several sources. As it was not always possible to separate out developments in East and West Germany, movements from 1936 to 1939 and 1939 to 1944 were based on interpolations. For 1936, 1939, and all years from 1944 onwards there are specific estimates for the two parts of Germany, albeit that the estimate for 1945 merely refers to the last quarter of that year.

	East Germany					West Germany				Strat. Bomb. Survey
		Annex A.3	Abels-hauser	Gleitze	Stolper		Abels-hauser	Gleitze	Stolper	
1936	100	100	100	100	100	100	100	100	100	
1937	112					108				
1938	124					115				
1939	137			137		123		123	123	100
1940	139					124				107
1941	141					126				117
1942	141					126				118
1943	145					129				132
1944	145			145		129		129		133
1945	22		22			21	21			
1946	44	35	44			37	37			
1947	54		54			44	44			
1948	60	49	60			61	61			
1949	68		68			83	83			
1950	75	75			75	113			113	
1951	87	87			88	134			134	
1952	96	96			95	144			144	
1953	106	106			110	157			157	
1954	117	117			120	176			176	

Sources: Annex A.3.; Werner Abelshauser, *Wirtschaftsgeschichte der Bundesrepublik Deutschland 1945–1980* (Frankfurt/M 1983); Bruno Gleitze, *Ostdeutsche Wirtschaft. Industrielle Standorte und volkswirtschaftliche Kapazitäten des ungeteilten Deutschland* (Berlin 1956); Wolfgang F. Stolper, *The Structure of the East German Economy* (Cambridge 1960); Overall Economic Effects Division, *The United States Strategic Bombing Survey: The Effects of Strategic Bombing on the German War Economy* (1945)

From 1936 to 1944 the series for both parts of Germany are based on the estimates of Gleitze (p. 173) for 1936, 1939 and 1944. Interpolation between 1936 and 1939 is linear, and between 1939 and 1944 in proportion to the overall production increase in Germany according to the "Strategic Bombing Survey" (p. 27) as shown in the last column. Series for 1945 to 1949 are from Abelshauser (p. 34). It is noted that the estimate for 1945 is based on the last quarter, and 1949 is based on the first and the second quarter of that year.

West German series from 1950 onwards link up directly to 1936, and were derived from Stolper (p. 242). East German series also link up directly to 1936, and are based on Annex A. 3 in this study, weighted at branch value added weights of 1936. Because the sample of my series is very small in 1946 and 1948, I decided to ignore the results for these specific years.

Annex A.2. Industrial employment and capital stock (1936–1954)

In view of the available data the statistics on employment for the period from 1936 to 1954 can be divided into two sub-periods: from 1936 to 1944, and from 1945 onwards. Data on the first period is based on the absolute number of employed persons in the industrial sectors in each of the countries in 1936 and in 1939. These were obtained from Annex C.1. and from Bruno Gleitze, *Ostdeutsche Wirtschaft. Industrielle Standorte und volkswirtschaftliche Kapazitäten des ungeteilten Deutschland* (Berlin 1956). Ultimately the estimate for 1936 (Annex C.1.) was based on the "industrielle Produktionsstatistik", whereas the estimate for 1939 (Gleitze) is based on the "gewerblichen Betriebszählungen". Different coverage in these two sources harm the continuity of the series between 1938 and 1939. See also: Reichsamt für wehrwirtschaftliche Planung, *Die deutsche Industrie* (Berlin 1939) pp. 56ff. The other years in the sub-period from 1936 to 1944 were estimated from statistics on industrial employment in all Germany according to the frontiers of 1937 as was found in Länderrat des Amerikanischen Besatzungsgebiets, *Statistisches Handbuch von Deutschland 1928–1944* (München 1949) on pp. 480, 481. This makes the estimates for this period very rough; however, I did not use these statistics in the analysis of this thesis otherwise than to give an indication that negative East German TFP between 1936 and 1950 was mainly due to the postwar period. At the end of this Annex a sensitivity test shows that this finding holds.

West German statistics on employment from 1950 onwards were derived from Statistisches Bundesamt, *Volkswirtschaftliche Gesamtrechnungen Fachserie 18, Reihe S. 15 Revidierte Ergebnisse 1950 bis 1990* (Wiesbaden 1991) p. 89. Unfortunately the statistics do not separate out construction and industrial employment for the 1950s. To link up with 1936 it was assumed that 17 percent of the employment in the "Produzierendes

	Employment		Capital Stock	
	East Germany	West Germany	East Germany	West Germany
1936	100	100	100	100
1937	105	105		
1938	108	109		
1939	*135*	*136*		
1940	*128*	*128*		
1941	*130*	*131*		
1942	*128*	*128*		
1943	*135*	*136*		
1944	*134*	*135*	138	136
1945	81			
1946	108			
1947	116			
1948	120	114	69	113
1949	119	115		
1950	118	121	72	122
1951	127	130		
1952	133	134		
1953	137	141		
1954	139	148		

Gewerbe" belonged to construction. Estimates on West German employment in 1948 and 1949 are based on Werner Abelshauser, *Wirtschaftsgeschichte der Bundesrepublik Deutschland 1945–1980* (Frankfurt/M 1983) p. 64. It is noted that these two years were linked to 1950 and based on employment in the third quarter of 1948, 1949 and 1950.

East German statistics on employment from 1950 onwards are described in more detail in Annex A.4. Estimates on East German employment in 1945, 1946, 1947, 1948 and 1949 are based on Bruno Gleitze, *Die Wirtschaftsstruktur der Sowjetzone und ihre gegenwärtigen sozial- und wirtschaftsrechtlichen Tendenzen* (Bonn 1951). Gleitze, who had been the director of the East German statistical office in the 1940s before he migrated to West Germany, gives statistics on total employment from 1945 to 1950 and of the industrial structure (pp. 11, 12). Thus it was possible to get a view on the movement of industrial employment, which was linked to the 1950 estimate in Annex A.4.

The estimates for the industrial capital stock were based on the gross perpetual inventory relation. They refer to machinery, equipment and buildings and the development is estimated looking at the gross capital stock at the beginning of the year plus the gross fixed capital formation during the year minus the retirements during the year. The West German capital stock was completely derived from Rolf Krengel, *Anlagevermögen, Produktion und Beschäftigung der Industrie im Gebiet der Bundesrepublik von 1924 bis 1956* (Berlin 1956). The East German capital stock data primarily relies on Baar, Lothar, Rainer Karlsch, Werner Matschke, "Kriegsschäden, Demontagen und Reparationen" in: Enquete-Kommission 'Aufarbeitung von Geschichte und Folgen der SED-

Diktatur in Deutschland', *Machtstrukturen und Entscheidungsmechanismen im SED-Staat und die Frage der Verantwortung* (Frankfurt/M 1995) p. 915. They estimated the East German capital stock in 1936 and 1948, using material from the archives. The estimate for 1944 is shown in Zank, *Wirtschaft und Arbeit in Ostdeutschland 1945-1949: Probleme des Wiederaufbaus in der Sowjetischen Besatzungszone Deutschlands* (Munich 1987). Finally I estimated the East German capital stock in 1950, extrapolating the above mentioned estimate for 1948 with timeseries of Manfred Melzer, *Anlagevermögen, Produktion und Beschäftigung der Industrie im Gebiet der DDR von 1936 bis 1978 sowie Schätzung des künftigen Angebotspotentials* (Berlin 1980). The timeseries of Melzer are also based on the perpetual inventory method. The estimates for retirements are based on information on the inventory during the 1960s when the new economic system was introduced, and also on West German retirements (average service lives) as were found in the research of Krengel.

Sensitivity of East German TFP from 1936 – 1944 for different developments of labour inputs

"Actual" index number for labour inputs (134) leads to:	TFP:	0.4
Lower index number for labour inputs (108) leads to:	TFP:	1.1
Higher index number for labour inputs (150) leads to:	TFP:	0.1

Annex A.3. Industrial production from 1950 to 1992

Year	Total	(Utilities)	Mining	Food	Textiles	Leather	Wood
1936	205	71	72	133	107	190	
1946		58	78	73	39	57	
1948		72	80	93	55	62	
1950	100	100	100	100	100	100	100
1951	114	111	110	138	123	120	89
1952	124	119	115	162	137	133	77
1953	141	125	125	190	151	145	79
1954	157	136	131	197	166	148	79
1955	167	149	143	207	167	136	76
1956	175	163	146	213	166	125	75
1957	183	170	150	227	173	131	73
1958	189	183	152	234	179	149	75
1959	206	194	153	238	194	171	77
1960	217	207	159	247	203	189	78
1961	221	219	165	251	204	188	76
1962	230	232	170	246	209	188	74
1963	232	243	172	255	208	186	67
1964	238	256	175	263	208	197	62
1965	240	269	171	261	212	207	63
1966	244	284	169	267	213	218	65
1967	247	297	162	277	213	226	67
1968	252	316	163	287	207	225	71
1969	259	328	166	293	207	232	73
1970	270	339	168	316	209	245	75
1971	278	349	166	334	214	257	77
1972	281	367	154	346	217	261	79
1973	289	385	152	360	219	267	82
1974	301	401	153	369	224	273	84
1975	312	422	150	389	229	263	86
1976	322	446	150	397	252	271	89
1977	327	461	152	396	264	273	90
1978	330	482	151	411	267	271	93
1979	337	489	152	426	276	273	96
1980	341	495	155	432	285	276	96
1981	347	501	157	444	288	282	94
1982	342	514	159	442	288	289	97
1983	341	531	160	452	294	292	96
1984	349	559	166	467	298	301	99
1985	356	576	170	477	295	300	97
1986	356	584	170	483	294	300	95
1987	356	580	168	483	295	304	95
1988	360	593	169	487	303	318	97
1989	356	594	161	487	304	317	96
1990	257		129	322	212	199	69
1991	114		*73*	162	37	49	28
1992			55				

Year	Paper	Chem	Stone	Metal	Mach	Electr	Optics
1936	183	77	172	198	582	123	396
1946	63	20	37	34	14		
1948	72	59	60	63	34	8	59
1950	100	100	100	100	100	100	100
1951	111	108	116	120	109	123	86
1952	122	121	126	151	106	127	97
1953	132	131	133	174	139	124	97
1954	137	142	145	190	180	175	116
1955	144	157	163	200	200	201	133
1956	148	166	173	216	216	235	100
1957	154	172	189	231	213	274	97
1958	160	181	198	242	212	310	86
1959	169	187	221	261	259	352	89
1960	174	199	233	272	274	409	92
1961	178	197	235	284	281	412	77
1962	184	207	249	293	312	448	85
1963	185	215	241	288	313	517	87
1964	192	224	260	293	324	523	86
1965	197	256	266	307	300	518	87
1966	201	265	268	312	302	553	88
1967	206	267	282	312	313	536	91
1968	221	280	293	306	340	513	98
1969	228	306	294	316	355	475	118
1970	236	322	303	331	367	510	122
1971	238	329	312	351	365	526	128
1972	246	333	324	370	354	509	117
1973	253	342	338	388	358	519	125
1974	261	369	345	408	380	527	132
1975	271	395	363	427	381	562	143
1976	270	414	379	446	375	597	151
1977	271	416	399	457	378	604	158
1978	276	426	405	463	370	604	158
1979	277	435	412	467	371	636	169
1980	280	452	419	478	360	652	180
1981	278	448	427	483	365	728	175
1982	282	455	409	470	352	715	165
1983	277	459	409	462	349	683	154
1984	289	460	409	474	349	742	146
1985	292	464	408	492	348	836	146
1986	293	465	413	496	345	804	147
1987	295	459	416	501	336	837	139
1988	301	472	431	503	334	835	138
1989	298	478	431	488	337	817	137
1990	167	338	281	359	260	613	93
1991	123	189	114	143	127	321	43
1992							

Sources for industrial production

Backgrounds to the methodology are also discussed in Chapter 2. The estimates for industrial production are based on quantity indicators. For each industrial branch the series link up several sub-periods, which include a different set of quantity indicators. Doing so, the research takes into account as many quantity indicators as the sources allow. Data is derrived from the following sources. Staatlichen Zentralverwaltung für Statistik, *Statistisches Jahrbuch der Deutschen Demokratischen Republik*, various issues; Statistisches Bundesamt, *Sonderreihe mit Beiträgen für das Gebiet der ehemaligen DDR. Produktion ausgewählter Erzeugnisse des Produzierenden Gewerbes 1980 bis 1990* (Wiesbaden 1993); Statistisches Bundesamt, *Produzierendes Gewerbe. Fachserie 4. Reihe 3.1 Produktion im Produzierenden Gewerbe 1992* (Wiesbaden 1993).

The names of some of the branches were abreviated. Time series refer to: "utilities", "mining", "food, beverages and tobacco", "textiles and wearing apparel", "leather products and footwear", "paper and printing", "chemicals, plastics, rubber, and oil refining", "stone, clay, and glass products", "basic and fabricated metal products", "machinery and transports", "electrical equipment", and "optics and fine mechanics".

All products were weighted at their value in 1991. These are unit values calculated from a publication of the Statistisches Bundesamt, *Produzierendes Gewerbe. Fachserie 4. Reihe 3.1 Produktion im Produzierenden Gewerbe 1992* (Wiesbaden 1993). The only exception is in utilities, where I used the shares in total; to arrive at a total for all industries branch gross output values in 1991 were used. The following tables show for each industrial branch the products that were accounted for, the unit of measurement, the weight, and the years of coverage.

Utilities 1950–1992 (3)

Products	Unit	Weight	Coverage
Elektroenergie	Mio kWh	0.33	1936, 1946, 1948, 1950–1990
Elektrizität aus Wärmekraft	GWh		1990, 1992
Gas	Mio m^3	0.67	1936, 1946, 1948, 1950–1989

Weighted at their share in total

Mining 1950–1992 (17)

Products	Unit	Weight	Coverage
Steinkohle	Th t	73.50	1936, 1946, 1948, 1950–1964
Steinkohlenkoks	Th t	229.85	1980–1990
Rohbraunkohle	Th t	22.61	1936, 1946, 1948, 1950–1990, 1992
Braunkohlenbriketts	Th t	128.63	1936, 1946, 1948, 1950–1990, 1992
Braunkohlenkoks	Th t	70.71	1960, 1965, 1970, 1975, 1978–1990, 1992
– Hochtemperatur	Th t	70.71	1955–1980
– Tieftemperatur	Th t	70.71	1950–1980
Braunkohlenstaub	Th t	70.71	1980–1990, 1992
Braunkohlenrohteer	Th t	72.56	1984–1990
Erdöl, roh	Th t	93.77	1980–1990, 1992
Eisenerz	Th t	93.77	1936, 1946, 1948, 1950–1964
Kupfererz	Th t	93.77	1936, 1946, 1948, 1950–1964
Kalisalze	Th t	93.77	1936, 1946, 1948, 1950–1964, 1980–1990, 1992
Stein-, Hüttensalz	Th t	93.77	1980–1990
Salinensalz	Th t	93.77	1980–1990
Schwefelkies	Th t	93.77	1936, 1946, 1948, 1950–1964
Flusspat	Th t	93.77	1980–1990

Weighted at their price per unit in 1991

Food, beverages, tobacco 1950–1980 (36)

Products	Unit	Weight	Coverage
Mehl a.s.	Th t	516.74	1936, 1946, 1948, 1950–1980
Nährmittel a.s.	Th t	881.46	1946, 1948, 1950–1980
Brot, kleingebäck	Th t	1,297.02	1955–1980
Dauerbackwaren	T	4.28	1955–1980
Teigwaren	T	1.56	1955–1980
Fleisch (eigenen Schlachtungen)	T	3.53	1950–1964
Tierische Fette	T	0.57	1950–1964
Fleisch- u. Wurstwaren	Th t	3,531.70	1936, 1946, 1948, 1950–1980
Fleisch- u. Wurstkonserven	T	6.50	1950–1980
Pflanzelöl	Th t	188.90	1950–1980
Margarine	Th t	1,523.59	1936, 1946, 1948, 1950–1980
Butter	Th t	6,289.53	1936, 1946, 1948, 1950–1980
Fettkäse	T	5.81	1950–1964
Käse	Th t	5,809.95	1960, 1965, 1970–1980
Trockenmilch	T	2.47	1955–1980
Dauermilcherzeugnisse	T	2.47	1955–1980
Speisequark	T	5.81	1950–1964
Fischfang	Th t	2,275.78	1946, 1948, 1950–1980
Fischwaren	T	3.67	1950–1955
Fischkonserven	T	3.67	1950–1980

Products	Unit	Weight	Coverage
Weisszucker	Th t	1,265.19	1955–1980
Aus Rüben	T	1.27	1950–1955
Aus Rohzucker	T	1.27	1950–1955
Zuckerwaren	T	3.63	1955–1980
Kakaoerzeugnisse	T	10.65	1960, 1965, 1970–1980
Obstkonserven	Th t	1,806.03	1955, 1960, 1965–1980
Marmeladen	T	2.60	1955–1965, 1970–1980
Sussmost	T	2.60	1955–1980
Spirituosen	Th hl	319.42	1955–1980
Malz	T	0.00	1950–1964
Bier	Th hl	114.99	1936, 1946, 1948, 1950–1980
Alkoholfreie Getränke	Th hl	110.93	1950–1980
Rauchtabak	T	400.00	1936, 1946, 1948, 1950–1964
Zigaretten	Mill. P	30.96	1936, 1946, 1950–1980
Zigarren	Mill. P	176.80	1955–1980
Bohenkaffee	T	4.61	1955, 1960, 1965–1980

Weighted at their price per unit in 1991.

Food, beverages, tobacco 1980–1992 (78)

Product	Unit	Weight	Coverage
Mehl	th t	516.74	1980–1990
Weizenmehl und -schrot	th t	537.92	1980–1992
Teigwaren	th t	1,558.62	1980–1992
Backpulver	t	0.88	1980–1990
Backmittel	t	0.88	1980–1990
Fertigmehl	t	0.88	1980–1990
Kindernahrung auf Obst- und Gemüsebasis	t	3.36	1980–1992
Kindernahrung auf Milchbasis	t	3.36	1980–1990
Trockensuppen und -gerichte	t	0.88	1980–1990
Eierzeugnisse	t	0.88	1980–1990
Stärke und Sago	th t	720.11	1980–1991
Dauerbackwaren (einschl. Müsli-Riegel)	th t	4,283.98	1980–1990
Weißzucker	th t	1,265.19	1980–1992
Melasse	th t	203.26	1980–1992
Zuckerrübenschnitzel	th t	203.26	1980–1990
Obst und Gemüsekonserven	th t		
Obstkonserven	th t	1,806.03	1980–1991
Gemüsekonserven	th t	1,178.76	1980–1991
Tiefgefrorenes Obst	t	1.47	1980–1990
Tiefgefrorenes Gemüse	th t	1,448.93	1980–1990
Marmelade, Konfitüre, Gelee, Pflaumenmus	t	2.6	1980–1990
Sauerkonserven	th t	1,381.32	1980–1992
Fruchtsäfte und -nektare	M l	630.78	1980–1992
Fruchtsirup	M l	630.78	1980–1990

Product	Unit	Weight	Coverage
Obstpektin	t	2.6	1980–1990
Kakaoerzeugnisse	t	10.65	1980–1990
Kakaopulver, ungesüßt	t	10.65	1980–1990
Schokoladenerzeugnisse	th t	10,653.47	1980–1990
Massive Schokoladenerzeugnisse	th t	10,653.47	1980–1992
Zuckerwaren	th t	3,625.32	1980–1990
Karamellen	th t	3,625.32	1980–1990
Kondensmilch und sterilisierte Sahne	th t	2,465.4	1980–1992
Laktose (Milchzucker)	t	2.47	1980–1990
Milchpulver	th t	3,473.36	1980–1991
Kasein	t	6.29	1980–1990
Butter, Butterschmalz und Kräuterbutter	th t	6,289.53	1980–1992
Hart-, Schnitt- und Weichkäse	th t	5,809.95	1980–1990
Schmelzkäse	th t	6,391.75	1980–1992
Frischkäse	th t	2,333.74	1980–1992
Öl- und Preßkuchen	th t	188.9	1980–1991
Rohe Öle für Ernährungszwecke (auch gehärtet)	th t	188.9	1980–1990
Margarine	th t	1,523.59	1980–1992
Tierische Fette, geschmolzen	th t	571.78	1980–1990
Fleisch, frisch und gefroren	th t	3,531.7	1980–1991
Schlachtgeflügel, frisch und gefroren	th t	5,004.1	1980–1990
Wurstwaren (ohne konserven)	t	8.31	1980–1992
Fleisch- und Wurstkonserven	t	6.5	1980–1992
Tiefgefrorene tischfertige Fleisch-soße-Gerichte ohne Beilage	t	5.96	1980–1990
Tiefgefrorene Fischerzeugnisse	t	5.08	1980–1989
Fischdauerkonserven	t	3.67	1980–1991
Röstkaffee	t	4.61	1980–1992
Bier	th hl	114.99	1980–1991
Malz	th t	0.66	1980–1992
Weindestillat	th hl	171.47	1980–1990
Backhefe, frisch und trocken	t	0.01	1980–1990
Spirituosen	M l	3,194.22	1980–1991
Bittere, halbbittere und Kräuterliköre	M l	6,374.39	1980–1992
Fruchtsaft-, Emulsions- und sonstige Liköre	M l	4,429.52	1980–1992
Trauben- und andere Weine	M l	3,403.24	1980–1992
Mineral-, Quell- und Tafelwässer	th hl	44.15	1980–1992
Limonaden, Brausen und Fruchtsaftgetränke	th hl	110.93	1980–1991
Diätistische Erfrischungsgetränke	th hl	70.23	1980–1992
Senfmehl	t	1.69	1980–1990
Senf	t	1.69	1980–1992
Gewürze, Gewürzmischungen und –salze	t	10.64	1980–1990
Trockenkartoffelerzeugnisse (ohne Stärke)	t	2.16	1980–1992
Mayonnaise, Remoulade und Salatmayonnaise	t	3.06	1980–1992
Tiefgefrorene Fertiggerichte	t	5	1980–1992

Product	Unit	Weight	Coverage
Mischfutter (einschl. Eiweißkonzentraten)	th t		
für Heimtiere	th t	594.91	1980–1990
für Kälber	th t	459.8	1980–1992
für Rinder	th t	323.76	1980–1992
für Schweine	th t	387.49	1980–1992
für Nutz- und Mastgeflügel	th t	427.56	1980–1992
Tabakwaren			
Zigaretten	M pieces	30.96	1980–1990
Zigarren und Zigarillos	M pieces	176.8	1980–1990
Rauchtabak	t	400	1980–1990

Weighted at their price per unit in 1991

Textiles, wearing apparel 1950–1980 (42)

Products	Unit	Weight	Coverage
Bastfasern	t	5.72	1950, 1955–1974
Kunstseide	t	5.72	1936, 1946, 1948, 1955–1958
Zellwolle, baumwoll- und wollartig	t	5.72	1936, 1946, 1948, 1955–1958
Perlon	t	5.72	1936, 1946, 1948, 1955–1958
Garne (Erzeugnisse der Spinnereien)	t	7.32	1936, 1946, 1948, 1955–1980
Baumwollgarne (3- und 4-Zylinder)	t	4.58	1950, 1955–1974
Kammgarne	t	7.32	1950, 1955–1974
Kammgarne aus Wolle	t		1950, 1955–1974
Streichgarne	t	7.32	1950, 1955–1974
Gewebe	th qm	1.77	1950–1974, 1976–1980
Baumwoll- und baumwollartige Gewebe	th qm	1.67	1950, 1955–1980
Baumwollgewebe	th qm	1.67	1936, 1950–1980
Kammgarn- und Halbkammgarngewebe	th qm	1.77	1950, 1955–1972
Kammgarn- und Hkg-gewebe (Wolle)	th qm	1.77	1950, 1955–1980
Streichgarngewebe	th qm	1.77	1950, 1955–1974
Streichgarngewebe (Wolle)	th qm	1.77	1950, 1955–1980
Kunstseiden- und Halbkunstseidengewebe	th qm	1.77	1950–1974
Leinengewebe	th qm	1.77	1936, 1950–1974
Sack- und Verpackungsgewebe	th qm	1.77	1950, 1955–1974
Möbelstoffe	th qm	1.88	1950–1980
Dekorationsgewebe	th qm	1.88	1955–1974, 1976–1980
Teppiche und Läufer	th qm	25.97	1950–1980
Tüll und Gardinen	th qm	1.88	1950–1974, 1976–1980
Erntebindegarn	t	8.82	1950–1962
Schlafdecken	th P	32.60	1950, 1955–1974
Strümpfe und Socken	th Pares	1.4	1950–1980
Damenstrümpfe aus Perlon	th Pares		1950–1964
Untertrikotagen	th P	16.30	1950–1980
Untertrikotagen aus Kunstseide, Naturseide und Dederonseide	th P		1955–1974

Products	Unit	Weight	Coverage
Obertrikotagen	th P	3.40	1950–1972, 1976–1980
Säcke aus Geweben	th P	2.33	1950, 1955–1974
Bezüge und Laken (Bettwäsche)	M P	2,329.01	1960, 1963–1980
Wachstuch	th qm	2.17	1950, 1955–1974
Fadenlagen und Polfadenlagennähgewirke aus Wolle und Baumwolle	th qm		1965–1974
Oberbekleidung für Herren und Junioren	th P	16.76	1970–1974
Oberbekleidung für Damen und jugendliche Damen	th P	15.83	1970–1974
Oberbekleidung für Knaben und Mädchen	th P	4.95	1970–1974
Gewirke	th qm	13.02	1976–1980
Baumwollart. Gewirke aus und mit sythet. Fasern	th qm	13.02	1976–1978
Gewirke aus synthetischen Seiden	th qm	13.02	1976–1978
Gestricke	th qm	13.02	1976–1980
Nähwirk-Faden- und Faserverbundstoffe	th qm	17.11	1976–1980

Weighted at their price per unit in 1991

Textiles, wearing apparel 1980–1992 (61)

Product	Unit	Weight	Coverage
Wolle und Tierhaare, bearbeitet	T	5.72	1980–1990
Pflanzenfasern, bearbeitet	T	4.58	1980–1990
Bast- und Hartfasergarn, auch gezwirnt	T	5.72	1980–1990
Polyamidgarne, texturiert	T	6.57	1980–1992
Polyestergarne, texturiert	T	6.01	1980–1992
Näh- u. Stopfmittel, Handstrick- u. Handarbeitsgarn	T	17.11	1980–1992
Näh- und Reihgarn	T	17.11	1980–1990
Stopftwist und -wolle	T	17.11	1980–1990
Handstrickgarn	T	17.11	1980–1990
Handarbeitsgarn	T	17.11	1980–1990
Elastische Binden	T	8.82	1980–1990
Filze, Webfilz und Filzwaren	T	7.86	1980–1992
Gewebe (Meterware)	M m^2	1,766.93	1980–1992
ganz oder überwiegend			
– aus Baumwolle	M m^2	1,672.91	1980–1992
– aus Leinen	M m^2	1,766.93	1980–1990
– aus Wolle	M m^2	1,766.93	1980–1990
Gardinenstoff (Meterware)	M m^2	1,879.03	1980–1992
Teppiche, Läufer, und Bodenbelag	M m^2	25,969.74	1980–1992
Fußbodenbelag auf textiler oder Papierunterlage	th m^2	25.97	1980–1990
Herrenoberbekleidung	th pieces	16.76	1980–1992
Damenoberbekleidung	th pieces	15.83	1980–1992
Kinderoberbekleidung	th pieces	4.95	1980–1992
Herrenwäsche	th pieces	3.33	1980–1992

Product	Unit	Weight	Coverage
Damenwäsche	th pieces	3.46	1980–1992
Kinderwäsche	th pieces	3.09	1980–1992
Damenstrümpfe	M pares	1,401.65	1980–1990
Herrenstrümpfe und -socken	M pares	1,401.65	1980–1990
Kinderstrümpfe	M pares	1,401.65	1980–1990
Oberbekleidung für Herren und Knaben	th pieces	41.12	1980–1992
Anzüge für Herren	th pieces	108	1980–1990
Sakkos und Jacken für Herren und Knaben	th pieces	60.4	1980–1990
Hosen für Herren und Knaben	th pieces	25.31	1980–1990
Mäntel für Herren	th pieces	68.36	1980–1990
Oberbekleidung für Damen und Mädchen	th pieces	21.96	1980–1992
Kostüme (auch Komplets) für Damen	th pieces	55.54	1980–1992
Röcke für Damen und Mädchen	th pieces	18.48	1980–1992
Hosen für Damen und Mädchen	th pieces	15.78	1980–1992
Blusen für Damen und Mädchen	th pieces	26.22	1980–1992
Kleider für Damen und Mädchen	th pieces	49.54	1980–1990
Mäntel für Damen	th pieces	76.62	1980–1990
Arbeits-, Berufs-, Spezialschutzbekleidung und Uniformen (Dienstkleidung)	th pieces	17.43	1980–1990
Arbeits-, Berufs- und Spezialschutzanzüge, einteilig	th pieces	37.19	1980–1992
Arbeits-, Berufs- und Spezialschutzjacken	th pieces	16.72	1983–1991
Arbeits-, Berufs- und Spezialschutzhosen	th pieces	19.1	1983–1992
Uniformen, komplett	th pieces	17.43	1983–1990
Uniformjacken	th pieces	17.43	1983–1990
Uniformhosen	th pieces	17.43	1983–1990
Regenschutzbekleidung	th pieces	14.38	1980–1990
Bademäntel	th pieces	14.38	1980–1990
Ober- und Freizeithemden für Herren	th pieces	14.09	1980–1992
Schirme	th pieces	15.5	1980–1990
Garten-, Markt- und ähnliche Schirme	th pieces	15.5	1980–1990
Segel und Planen	th pieces	50.95	1980–1990
Zelte	Pieces	0.05	1980–1990
Bettfedern und Daunen, aufbereitet	t	6.07	1980–1990
Bettwäsche	th pieces	6.96	1980–1990
Inletts	th pieces	6.96	1980–1990
Hand-, Frottier- und Geschirrtücher	th pieces	1.3	1980–1990
Tischwäsche	th pieces	6.27	1980–1990
Stepp-, Daunen- und Tagesdecken, Kissen, Schlafsäcke	th pieces	6.07	1980–1990
Schlaf- und Reisedecken	th pieces	26.06	1980–1990

Weighted at their price per unit in 1991

Leather products, footwear 1950–1992 (20)

Products	Unit	Weight	Coverage
Hartes Leder	T	3.79	1936, 1946, 1948, 1950–1960, 1963–1965, 1969-1974
Weiches Leder	th qm	37.24	1936, 1946, 1948, 1950–1960, 1963–1965, 1969-1980
Kunstleder auf Basis textiler Flächengebilde	th qm	4.21	1950, 1955–1960, 1963–1965, 1969–1980
Schuhwerk	th Pares	30.34	1936, 1946, 1948, 1950–1980
Schuhwerk aus Leder	th Pares		1936, 1946, 1948, 1950–1972, 1976–
Schuhwerk aus Austauschstoffen	th Pares		1950–1955
Oberleder	th m^2	37.24	1980–1989, 1991, 1992
Futterleder	th m^2	12.88	1980–1983, 1985–1989, 1991, 1992
Bekleidungs- und Handschuhleder	th m^2	19.71	1985–1989
Feinleder für die Lederwaren-herstellung	th m^2	19.71	1985–1989
Hand- und Reisekoffer, Schalen-koffer	Th pieces	28.27	1980–1990
Portomonnaies, Geldschein- und Brieftaschen	Th pieces	6.4	1983–1992
Lederhandschuhe	th pares	25.92	1980–1991
Schuhe (ohne Schuhe ganz aus Kunststoff oder Gummi)	th pares		1980–1991
Arbeits- und Sportschuhe einschl. Stiefeln	th pares	40.94	1980–1992
Straßenschuhe	th pares	31.36	1980–1992
– für Kinder (bis Größe 35)	th pares	20.77	1980–1990
– für Herren (ab Größe 36)	th pares	34.79	1980–1990
– für Damen (ab Größe 36)	th pares	35.79	1980–1990
Hausschuhe	th pares	7.68	1980–1992

Weighted at their price per unit in 1991

Wood products, furniture 1950–1992 (20)

Products	Unit	Weight	Coverage
Schnittholz und Schwellen	th m^3	263.72	1950–1980
Schnittholz aus Nadelholz	th m^3	257.73	1980–1991
Schnittholz aus Laubholz	th m^3	307.55	1980–1991
Imprägnierte Stangen und Masten	th m^3	398.79	1980–1991
Imprägnierte Schwellen	th m^3	398.79	1980–1990
Furniere	th m^3	549.11	1980–1991
Furnierplatten	m^3	1.64	1950–1974
Hartfaserplatten	m^3	0.27	1950–1980
Holzfaserplatten	th m^3	266.50	

Products	Unit	Weight	Coverage
Holzspanplatten	th m^3	266.50	1960, 1963–1991
Schlafzimmermöbel	P	0.15	1955–1964
Wohn-, Speise-, und Arbeitszimmer-möbel	P	0.11	1955–1964
Polstermöbel	P	0.23	1955–1960
Küchen	P	0.10	1955–1964
Pianos und Flügel	Pieces	3.42	1950–1990
Akkordeons und Bandonien, Harmonikas	P	0.06	1950–1978
Streich- und Zupfinstrumente	th pieces	100.00	1980–1990
Blasinstrumente	th pieces	62.17	1980–1991
Ski	th pares		1983–1990
Schlittschuhe (Eislaufkomplets)	th pares		1983–1990

Weighted at their price per unit in 1991

Paper, printing 1950–1991 (21)

Products	Unit	Weight	Coverage
Zellstoff aller Sorten	th t	2,308.67	1936, 1950–1965, 1969–1990
Papier aller Sorten	th t	1,581.10	1936, 1946, 1948, 1950–1991
Zeitungsdruckpapier	th t	1,581.10	1955, 1960, 1963–1974, 1980–1991
Schreib- und Druckpapier und -karton	th t	1,581.10	1955, 1960, 1963–1974, 1980–1991
Kraftpapier	th t	1,802.74	1980–1991
Pack- und Wellpappenpapier	th t	591.97	1980–1990
Karton und Pappe	th t	6,917.57	1936, 1950–1991
Papiersäcke	t/th t	3.56	1950–1974, 1980–1990
Tapeten	t/th roles	4.2	1950–1991 (assumption 1 role weights 1 kilogram)
Echt Pergamentpapier	T	1.38	1955–1974, 1980–1990
Tüten und Beutel	T	3.56	1950–1974
Kartonagen	t/th t	6.92	1950–1991
Wellpappe und -erzeugnisse	T	1.05	1950–1955
Wellpappe	th t	1,054.23	1960, 1965–1974, 1980–1991
Verpackungen aus Wellpappe	th t	1,054.23	1960, 1965–1974
Briefumschläge und Briefpapier-ausstattungen	T	3.37	1955–1974
Briefumschläge	T	3.37	1980–1990
Briefpapierausstattungen	T	3.37	1980–1990
Zeitungen	M P		1955–1980
Holzstoff	th t	2,308.67	1980–1991
Toilettenpapier	th t	1,334.85	1982–1990

Weighted at their weights for 1991.

Note: For the determination of weights for 'tapeten' until 1980, when figures showed the amount in tons, it was assumed that 1 role of tapeten weights 1 kilogram.

Chemicals, rubber, plastic, oil refining 1950–1980 (45)

Product	Unit	Weight	Coverage
Benzin	th t	352.93	1955, 1960, 1965–1980
Dieselkraftstoff	th t	376.63	1955, 1958–1962, 1965–1980
Heizöle	th t	183.79	1955, 1960, 1965–1974
Schmieröle	th t	1,216.91	1955, 1960, 1965–1980
Bitumen	th t	166.51	1955, 1960, 1965–1974
Schwefel	T	3.05	1955–1974
Schwefelkohlenstoff	T	3.05	1955–1978
Schwefelsäure	T	3.05	1936, 1946, 1948, 1950–1980
Natriumhydroxid (Ätznatron)	T	3.05	1936, 1946, 1948, 1950–1980
Natriumsulfat	T	0.44	1955–1978
Kalzinierte Soda	T	3.05	1955–1980
Kaliumhydroxid	T	0.13	1955–1980
Salzsäure	T	0.13	1950–1980
Ammoniak	T	3.05	1936, 1946, 1948, 1950–1980
Kalziumkarbid	th t	3.05	1936, 1946, 1948,1950–1980
Kalzinierte Tonerde	T	3.18	1955–1980
Kalidüngemittel	th t	0.97	1955, 1960, 1965–1980
Stickstoffdünger	T	0.97	1936, 1948, 1950–1980
Phosphordünger	T	0.97	1936, 1946, 1948, 1950–1980
Lithopone	T	3.18	1965, 1970–1980
Borax	T	3.18	1960, 1965–1974, 1978–1980
Methanol	T	3.18	1955–1978
Butanol	T	3.18	1965, 1969–1978
Azeton	T	3.18	1955–1980
Essigsäure	T	3.18	1950–1978
Lösungsmittel	T	3.18	1936, 1948, 1950–1955
Organische Farbstoffe	T	16.19	1950–1980
Rohfilm	th m^2	3.18	1950–1964
Fotopapier	th m^2	3.18	1936, 1948, 1950–1964
Synthetische Gerbstoffe	T	3.18	1936, 1948, 1950–1955
Seifen, berechnet auf 60 %	T	2.8	1936, 1948, 1950–1958, 1960, 1965, 1969–1978
Waschpulver	T	1.82	1950–1958
Lacke und Anstrichmittel	T	3.18	1936, 1946, 1948, 1950–1958, 1960–1964
Kaprolaktam	T	3.18	1955, 1960, 1965–1980
Insulin	M Units	0.04	1950–1978
Penicillin	M Units	35.41	1946, 1948, 1950–1974
Streptomycin	Kg	0.04	1953–1974, 1978–1980
Chloromycetin	Kg	0.04	1952–1974
Synthetischer Kautschuk	T	5.23	1946, 1948, 1950–1974
Kraftfahrzeugdecken	th P	31.52	1948, 1950–1980
Kraftfahrzeugschläuche	th P	15.26	1948, 1950–1964
Fahrraddecken	th P	10.00	1948, 1950–1960, 1965–1974
Fahrradschläuche	th P	5.00	1948, 1950–1960, 1965–1974
Chemische Faserstoffe	T	4.32	1955, 1960, 1965–1980
Zelluloseregeneratfasern	T	4.32	1955, 1960, 1965–1980

Weighted at their prices for 1991.
Notes: Seifen until 1958 "berechnet auf 40 %"; Weights (unit value) for Kraftfahrzeugschläuche is estimated at 50 per cent of Kraftfahrzeugdecken, unit values for Fahrraddecken and Fahrradschläuche are guesstimates.

Chemicals, rubber, plastic, oil refining 1980–1991 (74)

Product	Unit	Weight	Coverage
Vergaserkraftstoff	th t	248.39	1980–1991
Dieselkraftstoff	th t	376.46	1980–1991
Heizöle	th t	183.9	1980–1991
Flüssiggas	th t	183.9	1983–1991
Schmierstoffe	th t	1,216.91	1980–1990
Bitumen	th t	166.51	1980–1991
Chlor	th t	3,046.88	1980–1990
Aktivkohle	t		1983–1990
Ruß	th t	3,046.88	1980–1990
Schwefel in jeder Form	th t	3,046.88	1980–1990
Schwefelsäure eischl. Oleum, ber. Auf SO_3	th t	3,046.88	1980–1991
Syntheseammoniak, ber. Auf N	th t	3,046.88	1980–1991
Natriumhydroxid, ber. Auf NaOH	th t	3,046.88	1980–1991
Kalumhydroxid, ber. Auf KOH	th t	3,046.88	1980–1990
Aluminiumoxid, ber. Auf Al_2O_3	th t	3,046.88	1980–1990
Natriumsulfat, ber. Auf Na_2SO_4	th t	3,046.88	1980–1991
Ethen (Ethylen), ber. Auf 100 %	th t	3,046.88	1980–1990
Propen (Propylen), ber. Auf 100 %	th t	965.59	1980–1991
Reinbenzole	th t	965.59	1980–1990
Styrol	th t		1983–1990
Methanol (Methylalkohol)	th t	965.59	1980–1991
Butanole	th t	965.59	1980–1990
Phenol (Hydroxybenzol)	th t	965.59	1980–1990
Ethylenoxid, ber. Auf 100 %	th t		1983–1990
Propylenoxid	th t	965.59	1980–1990
Methanal (Formaldehyd)	th t	965.59	1980–1990
Phthalsäureanhybrid, ber. Auf 100 %	th t	965.59	1980–1990
Harnstoff (außer für Düngezwecke), ber. Auf N	th t	965.59	1980–1990
Acrylnitril	th t	965.59	1980–1990
Stickstoffhaltige Düngemittel, ber. Auf N	th t	965.59	1980–1991
Kalkammonsalpeter, ber. Auf N	th t	965.59	1980–1990
Harnstoff, ber. Auf N	th t	965.59	1980–1990
Phosphathaltige Düngemittel, ber auf P_2O_5	th t	965.59	1980–1990
Superphosphate, ber. Auf P_2O_5	th t	965.59	1980–1990
Thomasphosphate, ber. Auf P_2O_5	th t	965.59	1980–1990
Pflanzenschutz- und Schädlingsbekämpfungsmittell	th t	5,762.31	1980–1991
Phenolharze	th t	1,157.74	1980–1990
Aminoharze	th t	1,157.74	1980–1990
Polyurethane	th t	1,157.74	1980–1990
Epoxidharze	t	2.53	1980–1990
Alkydharze	th t	2,528.63	1983–1990
Polyamide	t	2.53	1980–1990
Silicone	t	2.53	1980–1990
Polyethylen	th t	2,528.63	1980–1990
Polystyrol	th t	2,528.63	1980–1990

Product	Unit	Weight	Coverage
Polyvinylchlorid	th t	1,239.46	1980–1990
Synthetischer Kautschuk	th t	5,231.67	1980–1991
Cellulosische Spinnfasern und Filamente	th t	5,231.67	1980–1991
Synthetische Spinnfasern und Filamente	th t	3,223.46	1980–1991
Celluloselacke	th t	2,614.36	1980–1991
Lacke u.a. Anstrichstoffe auf der Basis von wasserverdünnbaren Bindemitteln	th t	2,199.29	1980–1991
Druckfarben	t	2.2	1980–1990
Antibiotika	t	35.41	1980–1991
Gelatine	t	35.41	1980–1990
Leime tierischen Ursprungs	t	35.41	1980–1990
Leder- und Pelzhilfsmittel, Gerbstoffe	th t	35.41	1980–1990
Textilhilfsmittel	th t	2,510	1980–1991
Papierhilfsmittel	t	2.13	1980–1991
Bituminöse Dach- und Dichtungsmaterialien	M m^2	1,764.92	1980–1991
Holzschutzmittel	t	1.05	1980–1990
Feuerlöschmittell	t	1.05	1980–1990
Druckplatten	th m^2	4	1980–1990
Filme aller Art	th m^2	4	1980–1990
Seifen	th t	2,797.64	1980–1991
Handreinigungsmittel (ohne Seifen)	t		1980–1990
Waschmittel, -hilfsmittel und Wäschenachbehandlungsmittel	th t	1,818.86	1980–1991
Spül-, Reinigungs- und Putzmittel	th t	1,225.44	1980–1990
Geschirrspülmittel	th t	1,225.44	1980–1990
Schuh- und Lederputz- und -pflegemittel	t	2.17	1980–1991
Fußbodenreinigungs- und -pflegemittel	t	2.17	1980–1990
Möbelpflegemittel	t	2.17	1980–1990
Autopflegemittel	t	2.17	1981–1990
Pulver und Sprengstoffe	th t	1,1626.46	1980–1990
Kerzen aller Art	t	2.49	1980–1990

Weighted at the price per unit in 1991

Stone, clay, glass 1950–1980 (15)

Product	Unit	Weight	Coverage
Gebrannter Kalk	th t	105.45	1936, 1948, 1950–1964
Gebrannter Industriekalk	th t	105.45	1955–1980
Zement	th t	113.17	1936, 1946, 1948, 1950–1980
Ziegelsteine, Normalformat	M P	114.96	1936, 1946, 1948, 1950–1980
Dachziegel, Bibereinheiten	M P	1,149.60	1955–1974
Dachziegel	th P	1.15	1936, 1946, 1948, 1950–1955
Dachpappe	th qm	1.15	1946, 1948, 1950–1955
Betonerzeugnisse	th t	166.27	1950–1980
Schamotteerzeugnisse	th t	166.27	1950–955

Product	Unit	Weight	Coverage
Haushaltporzellan (einschl. Hotelgeschirr)	T	6.43	1950–958, 1968–974
Keramische Röhren und Formstücke aus Steinzeug	T	0.09	1950–974
Fensterglass	th qm	12.47	1936, 1946, 1948, 1950–980
Gips, gebrannt	T	0.08	1955–980
Splitt	th t	52.73	1955–978
Schotter	th t	52.73	1955–980

Weighted at the price per unit in 1991

Note: Weights for Ziegelsteine and Dachpappe are guesstimates.

Stone, clay, glass 1980–1991 (28)

Product	Unit	Weight	Coverage
Kalk- und Dolomitstein, roh und gemahlen	th t	13.36	1980–1990
Gips, roh	th t	22.74	1980–1990
Kreide, roh	th t	22.74	1980–1990
Bausand und –kies	th t	9.78	1980–1991
Form- Kleb-, Quarz- und Glassand	th t	37.38	1980–1990
Kaolin	th t	150.95	1982-1990
Zementklinker (nur Absatz)	th t	108.98	1980–1990
Zement (ohne Zementklinker)	th t	113.17	1980–1991
Branntkalk	th t	105.45	1980–1991
Transportbeton	th t	146.14	1980–1991
Hintermauer- und Vormauerziegel, Klinker	th m^3	186.72	1980–1991
Dachziegel	th m^3	186.72	1980–1990
Rohre und Formstücke aus Steinzeug	th t	92.96	1980–1991
Kalksandsteine	th m^3	104.31	1980–1991
Haushalts und Ziergegenstände aus Porzellan	t	6.43	1980–1991
Haushalts und Hotelporzellan	t	6.43	1980–1990
Haushalts- und Ziergegenstände aus Steingut und Steinzeug	t	3.55	1980–1991
Haushalts- und Ziergegenstände aus Ton	t	5.34	1980–1990
Keramische Installationsgegenstände für sanitäre oder hygienische Zwecke	t	5.34	1980–1990
Isolatoren und Isolierteile	t	6.19	1980–1991
Wand- und Bodenfliesen	th m^2	10.35	1980–1991
Ofenkacheln	t	5.2	1980–1990
Getränkeflaschen ab 150 cm^3 Inhalt	th t	623.78	1980–1990
Konservenglas	th t	623.78	1980–1990
Medizin- und Verpackungsglas	th t	1,884.02	1980–1990
Sicherheitsglas, ein- und mehrschichtig	th m^2	41.76	1980–1990
Isolierglas (Theromoscheiben)	th m^2	45.4	1980–1991
Glasseidengewebe	t	4.33	1980–1990

Weighted at the price per unit in 1991

Basic and fabricated metal products 1950–1980 (21)

Product	Unit	Weight	Coverage
Roheisen	th t	513.07	1936, 1946, 1948, 1950–1980
Rohstahl in Blöcken	th t	513.07	1936, 1946, 1948, 1950–1955
Rohstahl (einschl. Flüssigstahl für Formguss)	th t	513.07	1955, 1960, 1965–1980
Walzstahl, warmgewalzt	th t	513.07	1936, 1946, 1948, 1950–1980
Erzeugnisse der II. Verarbeitungsstufe	th t	565.42	1955, 1960, 1965–1980
Walzsorteneisen	th t	513.07	1950–1955
Walzbleche	th t	565.42	1950–1955
Bandagen	th t	736.26	1950–1955
Walzerzeugnisse aus NE-Metallen	t	11.84	1936, 1946, 1948, 1950–1955
Grau-, Temper- und Stahl-formguss	th t	2,101.23	1936, 1948, 1950–1955
Gusseisen	th t	2,101.23	1955–1980
Temperguss	th t	4,405.18	1955–1980
Stahlguss	th t	4,241.33	1955–1980
Schmiede- und Gesenkstücke aus Stahl	th t	1,470.61	1950–1980
Ketten	T	2.70	1955–1974
Gliederketten	T	2.70	1950–1955
Rohrleitungselemente aus Stahl	th t	1,148.24	1955, 1960–1974
Drahtgeflechte	T	2.02	1950–1955
Schrauben und Muttern	T	3.65	1955, 1960–1974
Blankschrauben	T	3.65	1950–1955
Holzschrauben	T	3.65	1950–1955

Weighted at the price per unit in 1991.

Basic and fabricated metal products 1980–1991 (41)

Product	Unit	Weight	Coverage
Roheisen	th t	513.07	1980–1990
Stahlroheisen	th t	513.07	1980–1990
Gießereiroheisen	th t	513.07	1980–1990
Spiegeleisen	t	513.07	1981, 1982, 1984–1990
Ferromangan	t	1.01	1984–1990
Ferrosilizium	th t	1,008.77	1983–1990
Ferrochrom	th t	1,008.77	1983–1990
Rohstahl (einschl. Flüssigstahl für Stahlguß)	th t	513.07	1980–1991
Schienen	th t	36,668.32	1980–1990
Bandstahl, warmgewalzt	th t	736.26	1980–1990
Verzinktes Blech und Band	th t	736.26	1980–1990
Präzisionsstahlrohre, nahtlos	th t	1,192.00	1980–1990
Präzisionsstahlrohre, geschweißt	th t	1,192.00	1980–1990
Sonstige Stahlrohre, nahtlos und geschweißt	th t	1,047.39	1980–1991
Hüttenaluminium und -legierungen	th t	2,216.25	1980–1990
Umschmelzaluminium und -legierungen	th t	2,216.25	1980–1990

Product	Unit	Weight	Coverage
Raffinade- und Elektrolytkupfer	th t	1,893.06	1980–1991
Kupferlegierungen	th t	1,727.26	1983–1990
Weich-, Fein-, und Hartblei	th t	1,727.26	1980–1990
Hüttenroh- und Feinzink	th t	1,727.26	1980–1990
Umschmelzzink	t	1.73	1980–1990
Zinklegierungen	t	1.73	1982–1990
Zinn	t	1.73	1980–1990
Halbzeug aus Aluminium und -legierungen	th t	4,246.96	1980–1991
Halbzeug aus Zinn und -legierungen	t	2.09	1983–1990
Gußeisen	th t	2,101.23	1980–1991
Stahlguß	th t	4,405.18	1980–1991
Temperguß	th t	4,241.33	1980–1990
Metallformguß aus Aluminium und -legierungen	th t	10,310.86	1980–1990
Metallformguß aus Kupfer	t	7.91	1980–1990
Metallformguß aus Kupferlegierungen	th t	7,908.15	1980–1990
Metallformguß aus Blei und -legierungen	t	7.91	1980–1990
Metallformguß aus Zink und -legierungen	t	7.13	1980–1990
Blankstahl	th t	1,136.46	1980–1990
Bandstahl, kaltgewalzt	th t	1,136.46	1980–1991
Kaltprofile	th t	1,470.61	1980–1990
Draht, kalt gezogen	th t	979	1980–1991
Drahtseile und -litzen aus Stahl	th t	1,905.67	1982–1989
Federn (ohne Uhrfedern)	th t	4,163.05	1980–1991
Ketten	th t	2,700.99	1980–1991
Schrauben, Norm- und Fassondrehteile aus Stahl und NE-Metallen	th t	3,646.47	1980–1991

Weighted at the price per unit in 1991.

Machinery and transports 1950–1980 (63)

Product	Unit	Weight	Coverage
Bagger	P	100.90	1955–1974
Wasserrohr- und Hochdruckkessel über 10t Dampf/h	P	8.00	1950–1955
Warmwasser- und Niederdruckdampfkessel	P	8.00	1950–1955
Schiffsdiesel- und Schiffsgasmotoren	PS	1.00	1950–1955
Stationäre Diesel- und Gasmotoren	P	56.70	1950–1974
Drehmaschinen (ohne Uhrmacherdrehmaschinen)	P	15.43	1955–1978
Revolverdrehmaschinen	P	15.43	1950–1974
Drehautomaten	P	15.43	1950–1974
Karruseldrehmaschinen	P	15.43	1955–1972
Gewindeschneidemaschinen	P	8.29	1955–1978
Zahnradfräsmaschinen	P	1.23	1950–1955
Lehrenbohrwerke	P	15.43	1950–1964
Einspindlige Bohrmaschinen	P	15.43	1950–1974

Product	Unit	Weight	Coverage
Radialbohrmaschinen	P	15.43	1955–1974
Feinbohrmaschinen	P	15.43	1955–1974
Exzenter-, Kurbel- und Kniehebelpressen	P	8.26	1950–1974
Hydraulische Pressen	P	8.26	1950–1974
Scheren	P	8.26	1950–1964, 1966–1974
Langmesserscheren	P	8.26	1955–1974
Walzwerksmaschinen	Th t	12,499.72	1950–1974
Förderer	P	8.26	1950–1964, 1966–1969
Stahlkonstruktionen	Th t	2,611.37	1950–1964
Rohrleitungsbau	t	2.42	1950–1964
Furnier und Sperrholzmaschinen	P	1.75	1950–1955
Traktoren	P	100.90	1955, 1960–1974
Traktorenpflüge	P	100.90	1955–1978
Traktoren, Drill- und Sähmaschinen	P	100.90	1950–1974
Grasmäher	P	100.90	1950–1964
Kartoffelvollerntemaschinen	P	100.90	1955, 1958–1978
Mähhäcksler	P	100.90	1960, 1965–1974
Mähdrescher	P	100.90	1953–1964
Heu- und Strohpressen	P	100.90	1950–1978
Elektrodämpfer	P	8.26	1955–1972
Kippdämpfer	P	8.26	1952–1964
Betonmischer	P	100.90	1950–1974
Dampflokomotiven	P	2,764.79	1950–1960
Elektrolokomotiven	P	2,764.79	1950–1978
Eisenbahn-Personenwagen	P	910.63	1955–1980
Eisenbahn-Güterwagen	P	177.08	1955–1980
Personenkraftwagen	P	8.04	1936, 1946, 1948, 1950–1960, 1963–1980
Lastkraftwagen	P	13.91	1936, 1948, 1950–1980
Kleinkrafträder	P	2.06	1955–1960, 1963–1980
Motorräder	P	2.06	1936, 1946, 1948, 1950–1960, 1963–1980
Autobusse	P	13.91	1955, 1960, 1965–1980
Fahrräder	Th P	212.54	1936, 1946, 1948, 1950–1960, 1963–1980
Radschlepper	P	6.16	1948, 1950–1960
See- und Küstenschiffe	P	6.92	1960, 1965–1980
See- und Küstenfrachtschiffe	P	6.92	1955, 1960, 1965–1974
Fischereifahrzeuge	P	6.92	1955, 1960, 1963–1974
Fischereilogger	P	6.92	1950–1958
Nähmaschinen	P	0.48	1950–1955, 1960, 1965–1974
Fräsmaschinen (ohne Verzahnmaschinen)	P	15.17	1955–1978
Verzahnmaschinen	P	15.17	1955, 1960, 1965–1980
Metallkreissägemaschinen	P	1.44	1955–1964, 1966–1968
Hobelmaschinen	P	1.23	1955, 1960–1974

Product	Unit	Weight	Coverage
Senkrecht-Stossmaschinen	P	11.24	1955–1974
Schleifmaschinen	P	11.24	1955, 1960, 1965–1974
Aussenrundschleifmaschinen	P	11.24	1955–1974
Flachenschleifmaschinen (einschl. Führungs- bahnschleifmaschinen)	P	11.24	1955–1974
Elektrische Brückenkrane	P	39.40	1955, 1960, 1965–1980
Schmiedehämmer	P	11.24	1955–1964, 1966–1968
Spinnmaschinen	P	11.24	1955–1980
Haushaltsnähmaschinen	P	0.48	1955, 1960, 1965–1980

Weigthed at the price per unit in 1991

Machinery and transports 1980–1991 (76)

Product	Unit	Weight	Coverage
Konstruktionen aus Stahl und Leichtmetall	th t	2,611.37	1980–1991
Dampfkessel (Dampferzeuger)	th t	6,395.24	1980–1990
Lokomotiven	pieces	2,764.79	1980–1990
Treibzüge und -wagen für Eisenbahnen	pieces	2,764.79	1980–1990
Personenwagen für Eisenbahnen	pieces	910.63	1980–1991
Standard- und Spezialgüterwagen für Eisenbahnen	pieces	177.08	1980–1990
Bergbau- und Feldbahnwagen	pieces	177.08	1980–1990
Metallbearbeitungsmaschinen	th t		
der spanabhebende Formung	th t	20,060.19	1980–1990
– Numerisch gesteuerte Werkzeugmaschinen	pieces	15.17	1980–1990
– Drehmaschinen	pieces	15.17	1980–1990
– Drehautomaten	pieces	15.17	1980–1990
– Bohr- und Gewindeschneidemaschinen	pieces	15.17	1980–1991
– Fräsmaschinen	pieces	15.17	1980–1990
– Schleifmaschinen	pieces	15.17	1980–1990
– Außenrundschleifmaschinen	pieces	15.17	1980–1990
– Verzahnmaschinen	pieces	15.17	1980–1990
der spanlosen Formung	th t	14,274.70	1980–1990
– Exzenter- und Kurbelpressen	pieces	930.42	1981–1991
– Hydraulische Pressen	pieces	8.29	1980–1990
– Drahtseil- und Kabelmaschinen	pieces	38.37	1980–1991
Hütten- und Walzwerkseinrichtungen	t	12.50	1980–1991
Maschinen und Ausrüstungen für Warmwalzwerke	t	12.50	1980–1990
Holzbe- und -verarbeitungsmaschinen	t	14.44	1980–1991
Dampfturbinen	pieces	2,770.74	1980–1990
Einzelgeräte der Klima-, Luft-, und Entstaubungs- technik	th t	10,390.06	1980–1991
Maschinen für die Bearbeitung von Kautschuk und Kunststoff	t	18.81	1980–1991
Kneter, Mischer, Rührwerke	t	18.81	1980–1990
Kalander	t	18.81	1980–1990

Product	Unit	Weight	Coverage
Extruder	t	45.68	1980–1990
Spritzgießmaschinen	pieces	18.81	1980–1990
Betonmischer für Baustellen und Betonwerke	th pieces	9,114.77	1980–1990
Bagger und andere Erdbewegungsmaschinen	th t	9,114.77	1980–1990
Straßen- und Gleisbaumaschinen	th t	9,114.77	1980–1990
Keramikmaschinen	t	18.47	1980–1990
Glasmaschinen	t	12.84	1980–1990
Pflüge und Kultivatoren (Grubber) mit feststehenden Werkzeugen	pieces	8.26	1980–1990
Maschinen für die Ernte und Nachfolgebehandlung von Halm- und Hackfrüchten	th t	7,049.91	1980–1990
Zubehör, Einzel- und Ersatzteile für Landmaschinen	th t	5,118.26	1980–1990
Ackerschlepper	pieces	8.26	1980–1991
Zubehör, Einzel- und Ersatzteile für Ackerschlepper	th t	3,873.48	1980–1990
Maschinen und Ausrüstungen zur Herstellung von Back- und Teigwaren	t	7.72	1980–1990
Einschlag- und Einwickelmaschinen	t	83.79	1980–1990
Maschinen und Einrichtungen für den Bergbau	th t	9,809.74	1980–1991
Spezialbagger und andere Förder- und Gewinnungsgeräte für den Tagebau	th t	9,809.74	1980–1990
Krane, Verladebrücken	th t	8,241.53	1980–1990
Serienhebezeuge, Flurförderzeuge	th t	6,052.13	1980–1991
Gabelstapler (ohne Schub-, Schwenk-, und Seitengabelstapler)	pieces	21.48	1980–1990
Stetigförderer, Gleis- und Drahtseilförderer	th t	10,475.36	1980–1991
Aufzüge	pieces	21.48	1980–1990
Papierverarbeitungsmaschinen	t	30.88	1980–1990
Druckmaschinen sowie Maschinen und Geräte für die Satz- und Reproduktionstechnik	th t	30,880.38	1980–1990
Textilmaschinen	th t	13,808.26	1980–1991
Maschinen für die herstellung textiler Flächen	th t	13,808.26	1980–1990
Textilveredlungsmaschinen	th t	13,808.26	1980–1990
Zubehörteile für Textilmaschinen	th t	30.40	1980–1991
Haushaltnähmaschinen	th pieces	475.86	1980–1990
Industrie- und andere Nähmaschinen, Nähautomaten	t	31.21	1980–1990
Maschinen für die Leder- Schuh- und Lederwarenherstellung	t	12.60	1980–1991
Feuerwehrgeräte	t	16.42	1980–1991
Armaturen	th t	26,048.80	1980–1991
Getriebe	th t	15,397.61	1980–1991
Landmaschinengetriebe	th t	11,092.70	1980–1990
Wälzlager	th t	11,092.70	1980–1990
Kupplungen und Gleitlager	th t	17,902.59	1980–1991
Personenkraftwagen	th pieces	8,041.11	1980–1991
Liefer- und Lastkraftwagen	pieces	13.91	1980–1991
Omnibusse und Obusse	pieces	13.91	1980–1990

Product	Unit	Weight	Coverage
Kraftwagenanhänger	th pieces	9,483.80	1980–1990
Motorisierte Zweiradfahrzeuge	th pieces	2,063.41	1980–1990
Fahrräder	th pieces	212.54	1980–1991
Kinderwagen und Kindersportwagen	th pieces	106.27	1980–1990
Binnenschiffe	pieces	6.92	1980–1990
Binnenfahrgastschiffe	pieces		1980–1990
Fischereischiffe	pieces	6.92	1980–1990

Weighted at the price per unit in 1991

Electrical equipment 1950–1980 (15)

Product	Unit	Weight	Coverage
Wechselstrommotoren	P	2.74	1948, 1950–1964
Leistungstransformatoren	P	12.19	1948, 1950–1980
Grossglühlampen	th P	6.25	1936, 1948, 1950–1974
Kleinglühlampen	th P	0.11	1948, 1950–1974
Radioempfänger	P	0.25	1936, 1950–1960, 1963–1980
Fernsehempfänger	P	1.75	1953–1960, 1963–1980
Magnettongeräte	P	2.51	1955, 1960, 1963–1969
Staubsauger	P	0.38	1955, 1960, 1963–1980
Elektrische Haushaltsherde	P	0.38	1955, 1960, 1963–1980
Durchlauferhitzer und Heisswasserspeicher, elektrisch und gasbeheizt	P	0.03	1955, 1960, 1963–1980
Elektrische Haushaltswaschmaschinen	P	1.75	1955, 1960, 1963–1980
Haushaltskühlschranke	P	0.38	1955, 1960, 1965–1980
Empfängröhren	th P	62.50	1965–1974
Bildröhren	th P	437.50	1955–1980
Widerstandsschweissmaschinen	P	12.68	1955–1964

Weighted at the price per unit in 1991.

Electrical equipment 1980–1990 (31)

Product	Unit	Weight	Coverage
Elektromotoren und-generatoren	th t	25,020.58	1980–1990
Transformatoren	th pieces	31.76	1980–1990
Neßwandler	th pieces	31.76	1980–1990
Einkristallgleichrichterelemente (Gleichrichterdioden)	M pieces	8,775.28	1980–1990
Elektrische Akkumulatoren, Primärelemente und -batterien	th t	8,775.28	1980–1990
Isolierte Drähte und Leitungen	th t	8,775.28	1980–1990
Wickeldrähte	th t	8,775.28	1980–1990
Schiffskabel	t	4.30	1980–1990
Sonstige Starkstromkabel	th t	4,301.29	1980–1991
Elektrovoll- und -einbauherde	th pieces	379.82	1980–1991

Product	Unit	Weight	Coverage
Elektrogrillgeräte	th pieces	28.70	1980–1990
Elektrische Heißwasserbereiter	th pieces	28.70	1980–1990
Elektrobügeleisen	th pieces	1.03	1980–1990
Speicherheizgeräte	pieces	0.00	1983–1990
Mix- und Rührgeräte	th pieces	69.53	1980–1990
Elektrische Haushaltstaubzauger	th pieces	332.51	1980–1990
Haushaltkühlschränke, -gefrierschränke und -truhen	th pieces	315.79	1980–1990
Waschmaschinen für den Haushalt	th pieces	1,023.97	1980–1990
Elektrische Leuchten	th pieces	17.51	1980–1990
Wohnraum- und Repräsentativleuchten	th pieces	19.79	1980–1991
Elektrische Glühlampen	M pieces	17.51	1980–1990
Entladungslampen	th pieces	17.51	1980–1990
Sprachengeräte	th pieces	38.23	1980–1990
Rundfunkempfangsgeräte	th pieces	250.57	1980–1990
Fernsehempfangsgeräte	th pieces	1,754.00	1980–1990
Plattenspieler	th pieces	250.57	1980–1990
Spulen- und Kassettentonbandgeräte	th pieces	2,505.72	1980–1990
Schallplatten	th pieces	2.02	1980–1990
Foto- und optoelektronische Halbleiterbauelemente	th pieces	2.02	1980–1990
Kondensatoren	M pieces	128.73	1980–1990
Elektrische Ausrüstungen für Fahrräder, Kraftfahrzeuge und Verbrennungsmotoren	t	19.14	1980–1991

Weighted at the price per unit in 1991

Optics and fine mechanics 1950–1991 (17)

Products	Unit	Weight	Coverage
Schreibmaschinen (ohne Rechenwerk)	th P	190.63	1980–1991
Großschreibmaschinen	P	0.19	1955–1960, 1963–1974
Klein- und Reiseschreibmaschinen	P	0.19	1948, 1950–1974
Buchungsmaschinen	P	3.54	1950–1960
Rechen- und Fakturiermaschinen	P	3.54	1955–1960, 1963–1980
Maschinen für das Bankwesen (Geldsortiermaschinen)	P	3.54	1985–1990
Uhren mit Kleinuhrwerk	th P	681.85	1982–1990
Armbanduhren	th P	681.85	1950–1978
Taschenuhren	P	0.68	1950–1955
Wecker	P	0.68	1950–1980
Fotoapparate	P	15.82	1936, 1950–1990
Spiegelreflexkameras	P	15.82	1948, 1950–1955
Sonstige Kameras	P	15.82	1950–1955
Ferngläser	P	0.70	1955–1990
Kontaktlinsen und Brillengläser	th P	28.35	1985–1990
Brillenfassungen	th P	30.00	1984–1990
Drucker und Plotter	th P	453.95	1983–1990

Weighted at the price per unit in 1991.

Annex A.4. Industrial employment from 1950 to 1989 (thousands)

Year	Total	(Utilities)	Mining	Food	Textiles	Leather	Wood
1950	2,721.5	78.5	149.0	208.0	466.8	85.8	241.3
1951	2,924.2	84.9	158.8	237.1	511.7	92.7	243.6
1952	3,070.9	86.2	163.6	263.5	509.5	93.8	238.3
1953	3,163.7	87.2	170.2	280.5	524.0	96.9	240.3
1954	3,215.5	92.4	184.3	280.3	534.8	99.0	235.3
1955	3,213.3	94.1	186.8	272.8	542.4	95.6	235.0
1956	3,195.9	93.5	188.9	271.3	521.8	90.4	232.0
1957	3,308.0	96.4	195.0	279.8	535.7	91.5	232.7
1958	3,378.6	97.3	198.7	288.9	540.3	93.9	236.6
1959	3,466.9	99.4	202.0	294.8	549.9	96.7	242.7
1960	3,475.6	103.0	199.1	299.7	546.0	96.2	242.5
1961	3,471.9	104.5	198.7	299.7	532.1	93.8	243.3
1962	3,454.2	105.6	199.2	293.0	521.8	92.3	241.4
1963	3,442.6	108.5	201.1	291.7	501.4	90.1	236.3
1964	3,468.6	110.9	203.5	289.1	489.8	91.1	229.8
1965	3,482.1	111.5	201.6	285.9	477.9	91.9	226.7
1966	3,515.2	113.0	202.4	286.7	469.7	92.1	226.1
1967	3,553.4	112.0	196.1	291.3	465.3	92.5	226.9
1968	3,549.2	110.7	195.4	291.5	461.1	92.9	225.8
1969	3,558.9	106.2	186.8	298.4	455.2	92.9	226.6
1970	3,560.1	105.4	185.8	299.8	443.5	91.6	224.2
1971	3,573.3	108.9	187.4	303.6	438.5	91.1	222.3
1972	3,586.5	112.3	189.0	307.3	433.6	90.7	220.3
1973	3,599.7	115.8	190.6	311.1	428.6	90.2	218.4
1974	3,612.9	119.2	192.2	314.8	423.7	89.8	216.4
1975	3,626.1	122.7	193.8	318.6	418.7	89.3	214.5
1976	3,653.7	125.9	194.5	325.6	413.9	88.4	213.8
1977	3,681.3	129.2	195.2	332.7	409.1	87.4	213.1
1978	3,708.8	132.4	195.8	339.7	404.4	86.5	212.3
1979	3,736.4	135.7	196.5	346.8	399.6	85.5	211.6
1980	3,764.0	138.9	197.2	353.8	394.8	84.6	210.9
1981	3,773.9	139.0	199.4	353.7	391.5	83.7	213.4
1982	3,783.8	139.1	201.7	353.5	388.1	82.7	215.8
1983	3,793.8	139.3	203.9	353.4	384.8	81.8	218.3
1984	3,803.7	139.4	206.2	353.2	381.4	80.8	220.7
1985	3,813.6	139.5	208.4	353.1	378.1	79.9	223.2
1986	3,809.6	141.6	208.3	352.1	379.8	80.6	222.1
1987	3,805.7	143.7	208.1	351.0	381.6	81.3	221.0
1988	3,801.7	145.8	208.0	350.0	383.3	82.0	219.9
1989	3,757.2	144.6	205.0	347.6	378.3	80.8	217.8

Sources: Statistisches Bundesamt, *Sonderreihe mit Beiträgen für das Gebiet der ehemaligen DDR. Heft 14. Erwerbstätige 1950 bis 1989* (Wiesbaden 1994); Manfred Melzer, Anlagevermögen, *Produktion und Beschäftigung der Industrie im Gebiet der DDR von 1936 bis 1978 sowie Schätzung des künftigen Angebotspotentials* (Berlin 1980); Several issues of Staatlichen Zentralverwaltung für Statistik, *Statistisches Jahrbuch der Deutschen Demokratischen Republik* (Berlin-Ost)

Notes: See following page

Year	Paper	Chem	Stone	Metal	Mach	Electr	Optics
1950	119.6	221.9	140.1	292.3	434.3	203.5	80.2
1951	118.0	232.5	147.1	319.0	475.1	216.7	87.0
1952	119.9	243.8	149.5	336.0	518.8	257.2	90.8
1953	114.8	257.5	147.4	321.7	539.0	289.2	94.8
1954	112.6	267.4	153.7	330.9	538.4	287.1	99.3
1955	108.7	269.8	157.7	330.1	536.2	283.7	100.2
1956	108.4	270.9	160.4	332.4	537.1	288.7	100.1
1957	109.4	278.1	164.0	345.1	568.8	308.4	103.2
1958	110.2	282.3	166.9	355.5	578.7	322.6	106.7
1959	112.5	288.8	169.6	362.4	601.8	336.7	109.5
1960	111.3	292.1	170.1	361.4	604.1	341.0	109.2
1961	110.0	290.6	167.0	360.8	618.9	344.1	108.4
1962	108.3	292.7	164.2	361.1	612.8	353.9	107.9
1963	106.2	294.1	162.8	354.3	625.7	361.1	109.3
1964	105.0	299.2	165.5	362.9	635.9	372.4	113.4
1965	103.3	306.0	164.1	371.9	645.7	376.6	119.1
1966	103.0	309.8	165.2	378.5	660.3	385.9	122.6
1967	102.1	314.4	166.3	385.7	675.1	396.9	128.7
1968	102.0	316.1	167.6	387.7	669.2	400.0	129.1
1969	96.1	317.1	168.7	385.6	679.4	413.0	133.0
1970	100.4	314.0	171.8	386.3	684.3	418.4	134.6
1971	99.9	314.6	173.2	388.5	688.3	423.3	133.7
1972	99.5	315.2	174.6	390.7	692.3	428.2	132.9
1973	99.0	315.8	175.9	392.8	696.4	433.0	132.0
1974	98.6	316.4	177.3	395.0	700.4	437.9	131.2
1975	98.1	317.0	178.7	397.2	704.4	442.8	130.3
1976	98.0	319.3	179.9	400.1	716.7	447.9	129.7
1977	97.9	321.6	181.1	403.0	728.9	453.0	129.1
1978	97.7	324.0	182.3	405.8	741.2	458.1	128.6
1979	97.6	326.3	183.5	408.7	753.4	463.2	128.0
1980	97.5	328.6	184.7	411.6	765.7	468.3	127.4
1981	97.4	327.8	184.4	412.8	769.4	473.7	127.9
1982	97.3	327.0	184.0	414.1	773.0	479.0	128.4
1983	97.1	326.3	183.7	415.3	776.7	484.4	128.9
1984	97.0	325.5	183.3	416.6	780.3	489.7	129.4
1985	96.9	324.7	183.0	417.8	784.0	495.1	129.9
1986	96.4	322.5	182.0	417.3	781.6	496.7	128.7
1987	95.8	320.2	181.1	416.8	779.3	498.2	127.5
1988	95.3	318.0	180.1	416.3	776.9	499.8	126.3
1989	93.8	313.5	177.9	410.7	767.7	495.1	124.4

Sources: see previous page

Notes: The names of some of the branches were abreviated. Time series refer to: "utilities", "mining", "food, beverages and tobacco", "textiles and wearing apparel", "leather products and footwear", "paper and printing", "chemicals, plastics, rubber, and oil refining", "stone, clay, and glass products", "basic and fabricated metal products", "machinery and transports", "electrical equipment", and "optics and fine mechanics".

Annex A.5. Average annual hours per employee

Year	East Germany	West Germany	Year	East Germany	West Germany
1950	2,090	2,293	1970	1,880	1,906
1951	2,100	2,275	1971	1,905	1,862
1952	2,260	2,281	1972	1,855	1,843
1953	2,090	2,279	1973	1,837	1,834
1954	2,085	2,299	1974	1,850	1,782
1955	2,050	2,295	1975	1,741	1,726
1956	2,065	2,243	1976	1,805	1,783
1957	2,005	2,124	1977	1,764	1,755
1958	1,920	2,087	1978	1,748	1,730
1959	1,910	2,075	1979	1,736	1,723
1960	1,915	2,068	1980	1,711	1,698
1961	1,900	2,026	1981	1,729	1,670
1962	1,910	1,976	1982	1,726	1,660
1963	1,930	1,946	1983	1,709	1,672
1964	1,980	1,956	1984	1,718	1,678
1965	1,970	1,938	1985	1,704	1,666
1966	1,970	1,907	1986	1,715	1,650
1967	1,945	1,868	1987	1,732	1,627
1968	1,975	1,911	1988	1,714	1,629
1969	1,875	1,915	1989		1,615

Sources: West Germany derived from ICOP-database; East Germany derived from Heinz-Dieter Haustein, "Die notwendige Beschleunigung des Wachstumstempos der industriellen Arbeitsproduktivität und die Bewertung der lebendigen Arbeit" in: *Wirtschaftswissenschaft* 38 (1990) 2

Annex B.:
Time series on the total economy

Annex B.1. East German GDP from 1950 to 1991

	Total	Agricult.	Public Ut.	Mining	Manufact.	Construct	Transp.	Other
1950	100	100	100	100	100	100	100	100
1951	113	119	111	110	114	112	108	113
1952	122	129	119	115	125	114	116	122
1953	133	117	125	125	143	118	124	133
1954	145	129	136	131	160	120	133	145
1955	153	125	149	143	170	122	142	153
1956	160	124	163	146	179	128	148	160
1957	167	135	170	150	187	134	155	168
1958	174	145	183	152	194	137	166	174
1959	187	140	194	153	212	150	184	187
1960	196	145	207	159	224	156	193	196
1961	199	129	219	165	228	158	198	199
1962	206	125	232	170	238	164	207	206
1963	210	138	243	172	240	165	222	210
1964	216	138	256	175	246	173	246	216
1965	220	152	269	171	248	182	256	220
1966	225	159	284	169	253	188	268	225
1967	235	166	297	162	257	232	292	235
1968	241	169	316	163	263	238	309	241
1969	244	161	328	166	271	223	331	245
1970	256	155	339	168	283	241	375	256
1971	262	151	349	166	292	245	393	262
1972	270	166	367	154	297	275	400	270
1973	282	169	385	152	306	310	429	282
1974	295	180	401	153	320	337	438	295
1975	305	178	422	150	332	353	455	305
1976	314	164	446	150	344	368	476	314
1977	320	179	461	152	349	378	462	320
1978	323	175	482	151	353	380	454	323
1979	327	185	489	152	360	370	468	327
1980	332	186	495	155	365	376	480	332

	Total	Agricult.	Public Ut.	Mining	Manufact.	Construct	Transp.	Other
1981	340	191	501	157	371	406	478	340
1982	334	189	514	159	366	392	439	334
1983	336	198	531	160	364	396	460	336
1984	343	214	559	166	372	389	469	343
1985	349	223	576	170	380	383	471	349
1986	351	220	584	170	380	386	498	351
1987	349	220	580	168	380	365	536	349
1988	348	205	593	169	384	351	538	348
1989	341	207	594	161	381	312	549	341
1990	311	188	653	129	273	303	481	369
1991	231	141	588	73	120	318	252	331

Sources for agriculture

The agricultural sector encompases animal production, crops, forestry and fisheries. For the series presented above the estimates are primarily based on estimates of the *Research Project on National Income in East Central Europe*. Their findings were derived from several occasional papers which together cover total crop and animal production, i.e. agriculture except forestry and fisheries, from 1950 to 1989. From 1965 to 1989 this source offers data which includes forestry and fisheries.

Until 1970 the series are based on indexes for various physical products, which were weighted at East German prices for 1965.[314] To arrive at the *Research Project* subtracted the main inputs. It distinguished between "intermediate products" and "current operating expenses". Intermediate products are those products that are utilised on farms in further production, i.e. seed, feed, and manure. Current operating expenses are defined as the total value of all goods and services bought by the agricultural sector from all nonagricultural sectors, including the foreign sector, and used up in agricultural production.

For the period from 1950 to 1965 a rough estimation completes the picture for forestry and fisheries. It was assumed that input output relationship in these sectors did not change during this period. The indices that were used are "Holzeinschlag" (timber) for forestry and "Fangergebnis" (total catch) for fisheries as can be found in the statistical yearbook.[315] The timeseries of the production of these two physical indicators were weighted at the value for timber and total catch in 1964 (West German prices), as can be found in Sturm.[316] The same source has been used for weighting the series for

---

314 Gregor Lazarcik, *East German Agricultural Production, Expenses, Gross and Net Product, and Productivity, 1934–38 and 1950–1970* (New York 1972) OP-36

315 Staatliche Zentralverwaltung für Statistik, *Statistisches Jahrbuch 1969 der Deutschen Demokratischen Republik* (Berlin-Ost 1969)

316 Peter Hans Sturm, *A Comparison of Aggregate Production Relationships in East and West Germany* (Yale 1974) p. 206 It means that fisheries is weighted at 115 Mill. DM, forestry at 387 Mill. DM, and agriculture at 9157 Mill. DM.

agriculture and for forestry/fisheries. This results in the following series for value added.

	Agriculture	Forestry	Fisheries	Total
1950	76.01	120.04		77.79
1951	91.81	122.67	70.44	92.79
1952	100.12	101.60	87.54	100.03
1953	90.08	106.47	99.21	90.85
1954	100.00	100.00	100.00	100.00
1955	97.69	91.22	109.19	97.57
1956	96.89	81.42	119.16	96.53
1957	105.54	79.53	153.64	105.07
1958	113.49	77.01	148.42	112.45
1959	109.46	70.39	168.02	108.59
1960	113.26	72.30	182.03	112.44
1961	100.00	68.54	207.09	100.01
1962	96.31	67.42	238.97	96.85
1963	107.15	61.73	294.15	107.56
1964	106.69	57.05	347.07	107.56
1965	117.76	56.32	365.08	118.25

After 1965 the *Research Project* included forestry and fisheries in their series. Thus it was not necessary to make additional estimates for these sectors. From 1970 onwards the *Research Project* used the official net material product as the shortcut basis of their estimates. It is stated that as a consequence of the economic reforms in the 1960s more methodological information on the statistics became available, which allowed the conclusion that the official measures of net material product originating in agriculture are calculated by methods closely resembling those used in the West for calculating the net product of agriculture. To approximate the gross value added (rather than net value added) the value of depreciation was added to the value of net material product.[317] The linkage from 1989 to 1991 is based on calculations of Müller-Krumholz.

Sources for Public Utilities, Mining, and Manufacturing

Backgrounds to the series on mining, manufacturing, and public utilities are described in great detail in Annex A. Linkage from 1989 to 1991 for mining and manufacturing was based on quantity indicators as shown in Annex A. Public Utilities was derived from calculations of the *DIW*, provided to me by Andreas Cors. These data included

317 Thad P. Alton, et al., *Statistics on East European Economic Structure and Growth* (New York 1975) OP-48; Thad P. Alton, et al., *Economic Growth in Eastern Europe 1965–1979* (New York 1980) OP-59; Thad P. Alton, et al., *Economic Growth in Eastern Europe 1975–1989* (New York 1990) OP-110

public utilities and mining. To arrive at an estimate for public utilities I used the earlier mentioned estimates for mining and I assumed the relative size of the two sectors in 1991 (mining 46 percent, public utilities 54 percent).

Sources on Construction

For the period from 1950 to 1989 the series for the construction sector are based on two indicators: "Gebaute Wohnungen" and "Geschaffene Wohnfläche". The two physical indicators were weighted at 50 percent each. For the period between 1950 and 1967 the results based on these indicators show enormous fluctuation. Therefore the in between years were based on intrapolations using official statistics on production in this sector as was found in Staatlichen Zentralverwaltung für Statistik, *Statistisches Jahrbuch 1968 Der Deutschen Demokratischen Republik* (Berlin 1968), p. 25.

Although the indicators "Gebaute Wohnungen" and "Geschaffene Wohnfläche" are also available for 1990 and 1991, I prefer calculations of the DIW, provided to me by Andreas Cors. In my opinion the two indicators are inadequate for a linkage of the period before and after reunification. During this period the emphasis in the construction sector was replaced from building new houses towards building infrastructure and restoring old houses. Would the linkage have been based on "Gebaute Wohnungen" and "Geschaffene Wohnfläche", than production in 1991 would have amounted less than than in 1950. Such a result is clearly not satisfactory, considering the fact that after the unification East German construction is seen as the most succesful sector.

Sources on Transports and Communication

For the period from 1950 to 1989 the series for the sector "transports and communication" were based on four indicators: ton-kilometers, person-kilometers, short distance calls, long distance calls. Linkage of 1989 to 1991 was also based on quantity indicators, though here the sample was based on indicators for transports only.

Weights

To arrive at total GDP the series for sectors were weighted at their value added in 1991; 'other sectors' are implicit for the period from 1950 to 1989 as they are assumed to show the same development as GDP. For the linkage from 1989 to 1991 the performance in other sectors was based on Müller Krumholz and for these three years the changes in 'other sectors' were accounted for in the development of the total economy.

Annex B.2. East German employment (thousands) from 1950 to 1992

	Total	Agricult.	Public Ut.	Mining	Manufact.	Construct	Transp.	Other
1950	8,331	2,122	78	149	2,496	521	472	2,493
1951	8,331	1,950	84	159	2,683	497	492	2,466
1952	8,331	1,746	86	164	2,823	470	519	2,523
1953	8,331	1,723	87	170	2,908	510	500	2,433
1954	8,414	1,749	92	184	2,940	481	533	2,435
1955	8,414	1,821	93	187	2,935	488	520	2,371
1956	8,414	1,708	93	189	2,915	488	538	2,484
1957	8,414	1,653	96	195	3,020	495	551	2,404
1958	8,414	1,596	97	199	3,085	505	559	2,374
1959	8,414	1,513	99	202	3,167	521	568	2,344
1960	8,414	1,379	102	199	3,175	527	575	2,457
1961	8,414	1,352	104	199	3,172	511	584	2,493
1962	8,414	1,354	105	199	3,152	512	588	2,504
1963	8,414	1,328	108	201	3,135	513	585	2,544
1964	8,498	1,271	110	203	3,157	513	581	2,661
1965	8,498	1,248	111	201	3,172	510	588	2,667
1966	8,498	1,214	112	202	3,202	508	586	2,672
1967	8,581	1,190	111	196	3,247	525	581	2,730
1968	8,664	1,131	110	195	3,245	563	576	2,844
1969	8,748	1,086	105	187	3,270	588	590	2,920
1970	8,748	1,055	105	186	3,272	603	603	2,925
1971	8,748	1,031	108	187	3,280	601	604	2,937
1972	8,831	991	112	189	3,287	607	611	3,033
1973	8,914	972	115	191	3,297	610	617	3,113
1974	8,997	955	118	192	3,305	617	620	3,190
1975	8,997	946	122	194	3,312	624	624	3,176
1976	9,081	929	125	194	3,337	634	628	3,233
1977	9,247	925	128	195	3,360	641	632	3,366
1978	9,331	927	132	196	3,385	647	634	3,411
1979	9,414	927	135	197	3,407	650	634	3,465
1980	9,497	929	138	197	3,430	653	636	3,514
1981	9,497	936	138	199	3,439	654	637	3,493
1982	9,581	940	138	202	3,447	655	643	3,555
1983	9,664	953	138	204	3,454	653	649	3,613
1984	9,747	968	138	206	3,462	653	650	3,669
1985	9,747	976	139	208	3,469	648	654	3,653
1986	9,747	980	141	208	3,462	643	650	3,663
1987	9,747	982	143	208	3,457	638	657	3,663
1988	9,831	982	145	208	3,449	635	660	3,751
1989	9,747	976	144	205	3,410	627	663	3,723
1990	8,664	651	126	180	2,998	653	598	3,458
1991	7,321	454	115	118	2,049	705	539	3,341
1992	6,387	282	98	78	1,306	800	481	3,342

Sources: Statistisches Bundesamt, *Sonderreihe mit Beiträgen für das Gebiet der ehemaligen DDR. Heft 14. Erwerbstätige 1950 bis 1989* (Wiesbaden 1994); Staatlichen Zentralverwaltung für Statistik, *Statistisches Jahrbuch der Deutschen Demokratischen Republik*, various issues (Berlin-Ost); Wolfgang Fritz, "Historie der amtlichen Statistiken der Erwerbstätigkeit in Deutschland. Ein fragmentarischer Abriß: Darstellungen, Quellen, Daten, Definitionen, Chronik" in: *Historical Social Research Supplement 13* (Köln 2001) pp. 199 juncto 219.

Annex C.: Benchmark comparison

Annex C.1. East German and West German industries in 1936

This annex shows the industrial classification that is used in this paper. It resembles the international standard of industrial classifications of the United Nations.[318] The table below shows the categories of this research (left) and the categories of the industrial census to which it responds (right).

Table of Industrial Classification

This Research	**Industrial Census**
Mining	Bergbau (I, Mining)
Food, Beverages, Tobacco	Industrie der Öle und Fette, Futtermittel und tierischen Leime (XXVI, Mnf. Fats); Spiritusindustrie (XXVII, Mnf. Spirits); Nahrungs- und Genussmittelindustrie (XXVIII, Mnf. Food)
Textiles, Wearing Apparel	Textilindustrie (XXIV, Mnf. Textiles); Bekleidungsindustrie (XXV, Mnf. Wearing Apparel)
Leather Products, Footwear	Lederindustrie (XXIII, Leather industry)
Wood Products, Furniture	Sägeindustrie (XVI, Mnf. Timber); Holzverarbeitende Industrie (XVII, Mnf. Wood Products)
Paper and Printing	Papier-, Pappen-, Zellstoff- und Holzstoffindustrie (XXI, Mnf. Paper); Druck und Papierverarbeitung (XXII, Paper and Printing)
Chemicals, Rubber, Plastic and Oil Refining	Kraftstoffindustrie (II, Fuel industries); Chemische Industrie (XVIII, Chemical industry); Chemisch-technische Industrie (XIX); Kautschuk- u. Asbestindustrie (XX, Mnf. Rubber)
Stone, Clay, Glass	Industrie der Steine und Erden (XIII, Stone, Clay); Keramische Industrie (XIV, Ceramics); Glasindustrie (XV, Glass)
Basic and Fabricated Metal Products	Eisenschaffende Industrie (III, Basic iron and steel); Nichteisenmetallindustrie (IV, Basic non-ferrous metals); Giessereiindustrie (V, Casting of metals); Eisen- u. Stahlwarenindustrie (VI, Mnf.

318 *United Nations*, International Standard Industrial Classification of all Economic Activities, New York 1990 Series M/No. 4, Rev. 3.

This Research	Industrial Census
	Fabricated metal products); Stahl- und Eisenbau (VIII, Mnf. Structural metal products)
Machinery and Transport	Maschinenbau (VII, Machinery); Fahrzeugindustrie (IX, Mnf. Vehicles); [einschliesslich Luftfahrtindustrie]
Electrical Equipment	Elektroindustrie (X, Electrical equipment)
Optics and Fine Mechanics	Metallwarenindustrie u. verwandte Gewerbe (XII, Mnf. Metal products); Feinmechanische und Optische Industrie (XI, Optics and Fine Mechanics)
Utilities	Elektrizitäts- und Gasversorgung (XXIX, Utilities); [Wasserversorgung]

The source of the industrial census is BArch R 3102/3309

Annex C Industrial Census 1936	Sales Value			Value Added	
	East Germany	West Germany	$F(x)$	East Germany	West Germany
Mining					
Eisenerzbergbau	1,706	51,848	0.784	1,338	40,649
Metallerzbergbau	11,947	9,650	0.574	6,858	5,539
Stein- und Kalisalzbergbau	108,921	78,667	0.793	86,374	62,383
Salinen	8,682	16,244	0.593	5,148	9,633
Steinkohlenbergbau	54,871	1338,016	0.776	42,580	1038,300
Kokereien	8,692	678,939	0.217	1,886	147,330
Presssteinkohlenfabriken	4,919	85,373	0.221	1,087	18,867
Braunkohlenbergbau	226,030	140,203	0.877	198,228	122,958
Braunkohlenfabriken	239,212	116,641	0.319	76,309	37,208
Erdölgewinnung	120	47,230	0.827	99	39,059
Graphitbergbau u. Graphitaufbereitung	0	1,700	0.519	0	882
Flussspatbergbau und Flussspataufbereitung	1,920	1,027	0.772	1,482	793
Food, Beverages, Tobacco					
Ölmühlen	32,405	300,571	0.310	10,046	93,177
Ölveredelungsindustrie	14,713	258,955	0.306	4,502	79,240
Talgschmelzen	7,461	20,671	0.206	1,537	4,258
Schmalzsiedereien	13,810	12,870	0.128	1,768	1,647
Margarine- und Speisefettfabriken	36,498	303,985	0.352	12,847	107,003
Abdeckereien	2,499	3,407	0.776	1,939	2,644
Knochenverwertungsindustrie	7,670	9,130	0.372	2,853	3,396
Fischmehl- und Tranfabriken	78	14,686	0.409	32	6,007
Herstellung von Haut- und Lederleim, Gelatine und Kunstdärmen	7,310	34,673	0.566	4,137	19,625
Futtermittelindustrie	37,864	174,309	0.177	6,702	30,853
Landwirtschaftliche Kartoffelbrennereien	36,569	9,118	0.246	8,996	2,243
Melassebrennereien	2,115	1,366	0.336	711	459
Hefelüftungsbrennereien	8,173	35,767	0.647	5,288	23,141
Spiritusreinigungsanstalten Spiritusvergällung in Monopollägern	71,088	80,948	0.198	14,075	16,028
Kornbrennereien	694	15,487	0.278	193	4,305
Weinbrennereien	884	6,381	0.322	285	2,055
Herstellung von Trinkbranntweinen aller Art	55,565	229,181	0.277	15,391	63,483
Getreidemüllerei	361,559	965,552	0.210	75,927	202,766
Schälmühlen	7,400	62,417	0.222	1,643	13,857
Brotindustrie und Bäckereien	65,080	179,257	0.340	22,127	60,947
Fleischwarenindustrie	144,111	393,004	0.249	35,884	97,858
Fischindustrie	6,523	123,854	0.350	2,283	43,349
Zuckerindustrie	321,539	293,109	0.292	93,889	85,588
Süsswarenindustrie	241,752	385,130	0.437	105,646	168,302
Obst- und Gemüsekonservenindustrie	73,527	125,872	0.329	24,190	41,412
Herstellung von Rheinischkraut	0	6,602	0.368	0	2,430
Obstsaft- und Fruchtweinindustrie	12,040	21,140	0.349	4,202	7,378
Dauermilchindustrie	10,202	67,303	0.372	3,795	25,037
Schmelzkäseindustrie	170	31,821	0.295	50	9,387
Teigwarenindustrie	10,141	61,019	0.344	3,488	20,991
Kartoffeltrocknerei	6,619	657	0.347	2,297	228
Stärke- und Stärkeveredelungsindustrie	64,903	19,200	0.491	31,867	9,427
Nährmittelindustrie	10,726	156,528	0.562	6,028	87,969
Kaffeeersatz-Industrie	34,275	58,517	0.420	14,396	24,577
Malzindustrie	46,386	61,564	0.191	8,860	11,759
Brauindustrie (einschl. Braumälzerei)	226,285	735,568	0.700	158,399	514,898
Traubenschaumweinindustrie	809	27,359	0.577	467	15,786
Essigindustrie	6,140	24,726	0.547	3,359	13,525
Senfindustrie	3,818	7,592	0.557	2,127	4,229

Annex C Industrial Census 1936	Employment		Labour Productivity		
	East Germany	West Germany	East Germany	West Germany	Average Germany
Mining					
Eisenerzbergbau	413	14,369	3,239	2,829	1,637
Metallerzbergbau	8,614	7,574	796	731	1,742
Stein- und Kalisalzbergbau	9,745	7,646	8,863	8,159	2,375
Salinen	1,216	1,980	4,234	4,865	2,151
Steinkohlenbergbau	16,216	318,215	2,626	3,263	2,117
Kokereien	346	19,779	5,451	7,449	2,298
Presssteinkohlenfabriken	182	1,889	5,973	9,988	1,959
Braunkohlenbergbau	30,767	17,688	6,443	6,951	2,118
Braunkohlenfabriken	20,774	9,775	3,673	3,806	2,173
Erdölgewinnung	41	3,664	2,420	10,660	2,049
Graphitbergbau u. Graphitaufbereitung	0	373		2,365	1,383
Flussspatbergbau und Flussspataufbereitung	480	386	3,088	2,054	1,334
Food, Beverages, Tobacco					
Ölmühlen	1,133	7,723	8,866	12,065	2,351
Ölveredelungsindustrie	219	2,887	20,558	27,447	2,622
Talgschmelzen	181	533	8,492	7,989	2,028
Schmalzsiedereien	237	230	7,459	7,162	1,984
Margarine- und Speisefettfabriken	1,098	8,691	11,701	12,312	2,513
Abdeckereien	572	669	3,390	3,952	1,009
Knochenverwertungsindustrie	585	751	4,877	4,522	1,653
Fischmehl- und Tranfabriken	13	733	2,454	8,195	2,201
Herstellung von Haut- und Lederleim, Gelatine und Kunstdärmen	829	3,301	4,991	5,945	1,775
Futtermittelindustrie	1,289	4,420	5,199	6,980	1,928
Landwirtschaftliche Kartoffelbrennereien	2,862	524	3,143	4,282	1,760
Melassebrennereien	137	66	5,187	6,954	2,429
Hefelüftungsbrennereien	349	2,019	15,152	11,462	2,660
Spiritusreinigungsanstalten Spiritusvergällung in Monopollägern	788	756	17,867	21,195	2,616
Kornbrennereien	58	1,096	3,326	3,928	1,485
Weinbrennereien	44	275	6,411	7,482	2,213
Herstellung von Trinkbranntweinen aller Art	2,620	8,665	5,874	7,327	1,360
Getreidemüllerei	8,337	18,377	9,108	11,034	1,948
Schälmühlen	247	1,771	6,640	7,826	2,319
Brotindustrie und Bäckereien	4,080	11,401	5,423	5,346	2,124
Fleischwarenindustrie	5,390	12,651	6,657	7,735	1,727
Fischindustrie	708	16,496	3,227	2,628	1,122
Zuckerindustrie	32,511	24,202	2,888	3,536	1,259
Süsswarenindustrie	24,234	35,381	4,359	4,757	1,511
Obst- und Gemüsekonservenindustrie	11,002	20,860	2,199	1,985	1,109
Herstellung von Rheinischkraut	0	1,040		2,336	932
Obstsaft- und Fruchtweinindustrie	1,051	1,966	4,000	3,752	1,233
Dauermilchindustrie	508	1,700	7,470	14,728	1,717
Schmelzkäseindustrie	14	1,731	3,654	5,422	1,432
Teigwarenindustrie	914	4,427	3,817	4,741	1,482
Kartoffeltrocknerei	1,174	231	1,956	987	872
Stärke- und Stärkeveredelungsindustrie	3,461	1,346	9,208	7,004	1,481
Nährmittelindustrie	708	10,190	8,513	8,633	2,468
Kaffeeersatz-Industrie	1,561	3,703	9,222	6,637	2,424
Malzindustrie	1,711	2,371	5,178	4,959	2,104
Brauindustrie (einschl. Braumälzerei)	18,819	49,220	8,417	10,461	2,753
Traubenschaumweinindustrie	88	1,776	5,311	8,888	1,687
Essigindustrie	498	1,801	6,746	7,509	1,628
Senfindustrie	375	739	5,667	5,724	1,580

Annex C Industrial Census 1936	Sales Value			Value Added	
Cont. Food, Beverages, Tobacco	East Germany	West Germany	$F(x)$	East Germany	West Germany
Gewürzindustrie	3,360	18,131	0.320	1,075	5,802
Tabakindustrie	365,368	771,087	0.609	222,509	469,592
Textiles, Wearing Apparel					
Kunstseiden- und Zellwollindustrie	88,652	189,278	0.604	53,546	114,324
Wollwäscherei	1,046	122	0.117	122	14
Wollwäscherei und Wollkämmerei	6,309	21,883	0.130	820	2,845
Kammgarn- und Ramiespinnerei und -zwirnerei	255,833	162,245	0.371	94,914	60,193
Reissereien	16,638	27,088	0.442	7,354	11,973
Streichgarnspinnerei und -zwirnerei	151,177	105,851	0.257	38,852	27,204
Baumwollspinnerei und -zwirnerei	172,675	554,384	0.385	66,480	213,438
Flachs- und Hanfrösterei	4,014	5,136	0.435	1,746	2,234
Flachsspinnerei und -zwirnerei	12,434	18,900	0.420	5,222	7,938
Hanf- und Hartfaserspinnerei und -zwirnerei	6,466	63,851	0.404	2,612	25,796
Jutespinnerei und -zwirnerei	20,152	44,360	0.440	8,867	19,518
Seidenweberei	30,423	302,493	0.434	13,203	131,282
Bekleidungsstoffweberei	506,023	283,691	0.519	262,626	147,235
Allgemeine Weberei	432,928	1020,576	0.424	183,562	432,724
Wirk- u. Strickwarenindustrie	518,500	266,958	0.498	258,213	132,945
Nähfäden-, Stopf-, Stick- und Handarbeitsgarnherstellung	20,410	73,660	0.466	9,511	34,325
Herstellung von Band- und Flechtartikeln, Posamenten usw.	42,497	111,758	0.569	24,181	63,590
Herstellung von Stickereien, Spitzen usw.	53,385	17,127	0.547	29,202	9,368
Herstellung von Zelten, Planen, Säcken	30,462	51,990	0.329	10,022	17,105
Filzherstellung	11,827	16,757	0.411	4,861	6,887
Industriewatteherstellung	4,727	7,954	0.656	3,101	5,218
Verbandwatteherstellung	4,041	3,485	0.399	1,612	1,391
Herstellung von Verbandmitteln	7,573	17,221	0.373	2,825	6,424
Rosshaarspinnerei und Stepperei	1,788	10,027	0.410	733	4,111
Netzindustrie	3,982	3,379	0.537	2,138	1,815
Textilausrüstungs- und Veredelungsindustrie	149,144	279,510	0.493	73,528	137,798
Bekleidungsindustrie	676,812	720,617	0.482	326,223	347,338
Pelzveredelung	16,758	302	0.782	13,105	236
Pelzverarbeitung	19,133	17,368	0.445	8,514	7,729
Leather Products, Footwear					
Lederfabriken und Gerbereien	138,139	444,934	0.444	61,334	197,551
Lederzurichtereien	2,022	10,945	0.593	1,199	6,491
Schuhindustrie	145,489	477,698	0.435	63,288	207,799
Ledertreibriemenindustrie (einschl. Herstellung technischer Lederartikel)	12,219	27,464	0.341	4,167	9,365
Leder- und Sattlerwarenindustrie	50,981	179,449	0.450	22,941	80,752
Lederhandschuhindustrie	18,877	11,761	0.431	8,136	5,069
Wood Products, Furniture					
Sägewerke (einschl. Schwellen- und Mastenfabriken)	154,673	344,494	0.429	66,355	147,788
Hobelwerke	12,191	59,863	0.289	3,523	17,300
Furnierwerke	13,433	25,501	0.566	7,603	14,434
Holzimprägnieranstalten	8,569	24,700	0.779	6,675	19,241
Sperrholzindustrie	2,362	77,765	0.498	1,176	38,727
Möbel- und Bauteileindustrie	191,200	428,505	0.557	106,498	238,677
Klavier-, Harmonium- und Orgelbau	7,210	10,138	0.593	4,276	6,012
Holzwarenindustrie	61,051	102,657	0.611	37,302	62,724

Annex C Industrial Census 1936	Employment		Labour Productivity		
Cont. Food, Beverages, Tobacco	East Germany	West Germany	East Germany	West Germany	Average wages
Gewürzindustrie	175	881	6,131	6,588	1,531
Tabakindustrie	29,785	119,110	7,471	3,942	989
Textiles, Wearing Apparel					
Kunstseiden- und Zellwollindustrie	12,313	20,449	4,349	5,591	1,772
Wollwäscherei	282	37	434	386	1,417
Wollwäscherei und Wollkämmerei	2,129	6,189	385	460	1,842
Kammgarn- und Ramiespinnerei und -zwirnerei	27,702	19,545	3,426	3,080	1,309
Reissereien	1,375	2,189	5,349	5,469	1,260
Streichgarnspinnerei und -zwirnerei	18,032	11,578	2,155	2,350	1,205
Baumwollspinnerei und -zwirnerei	30,524	77,171	2,178	2,766	1,229
Flachs- und Hanfrösterei	1,122	1,659	1,556	1,347	961
Flachsspinnerei und -zwirnerei	2,197	3,547	2,377	2,238	1,068
Hanf- und Hartfaserspinnerei und -zwirnerei	919	7,471	2,842	3,453	1,324
Jutespinnerei und -zwirnerei	3,653	7,584	2,427	2,574	1,135
Seidenweberei	4,143	41,592	3,187	3,156	1,519
Bekleidungsstoffweberei	50,950	29,720	5,155	4,954	1,393
Allgemeine Weberei	64,909	127,255	2,828	3,400	1,366
Wirk- u. Strickwarenindustrie	94,571	50,924	2,730	2,611	3,200
Nähfäden-, Stopf-, Stick- und Handarbeitsgarnherstellung	3,004	10,073	3,166	3,408	1,387
Herstellung von Band- und Flechtartikeln, Posamenten usw.	7,263	18,986	3,329	3,349	1,287
Herstellung von Stickereien, Spitzen usw.	9,158	2,999	3,189	3,124	1,003
Herstellung von Zelten, Planen, Säcken	1,923	4,650	5,211	3,679	1,360
Filzherstellung	1,156	2,365	4,204	2,913	1,652
Industriewatteherstellung	613	1,018	5,060	5,125	1,334
Verbandwatteherstellung	415	685	3,885	2,030	1,295
Herstellung von Verbandmitteln	821	2,055	3,439	3,126	1,200
Rosshaarspinnerei und Stepperei	132	958	5,536	4,293	1,444
Netzindustrie	764	748	2,799	2,426	1,109
Textilausrüstungs- und Veredelungsindustrie	27,450	33,073	2,679	4,166	1,653
Bekleidungsindustrie	93,189	110,020	3,501	3,157	1,271
Pelzveredelung	3,845	64	3,409	3,665	1,532
Pelzverarbeitung	2,032	2,420	4,191	3,193	1,275
Leather Products, Footwear					
Lederfabriken und Gerbereien	9,627	34,206	6,371	5,775	1,802
Lederzurichtereien	357	1,322	3,360	4,909	1,459
Schuhindustrie	23,963	75,113	2,641	2,766	1,406
Ledertreibriemenindustrie (einschl. Herstellung technischer Lederartikel)	1,043	2,426	3,995	3,860	1,630
Leder- und Sattlerwarenindustrie	8,835	26,256	2,597	3,076	1,351
Lederhandschuhindustrie	3,512	2,012	2,317	2,519	1,286
Wood Products, Furniture					
Sägewerke (einschl. Schwellen- und Mastenfabriken)	23,666	47,224	2,804	3,130	1,248
Hobelwerke	678	4,956	5,196	3,491	1,966
Furnierwerke	1,216	3,095	6,253	4,664	1,630
Holzimprägnieranstalten	828	1,924	8,062	10,001	1,903
Sperrholzindustrie	351	10,374	3,351	3,733	1,421
Möbel- und Bauteileindustrie	39,258	87,885	2,713	2,716	1,461
Klavier-, Harmonium- und Orgelbau	1,713	2,452	2,496	2,452	1,723
Holzwarenindustrie	13,844	23,542	2,694	2,664	1,253

Annex C Industrial Census 1936	Sales Value			Value Added	
Cont. Wood Products, Furniture	East Germany	West Germany	$F(x)$	East Germany	West Germany
Holzmehlindustrie	1,067	1,475	0.632	674	932
Fassholzsägerei und Fassindustrie	4,951	22,404	0.396	1,961	8,872
Kistenindustrie	24,697	38,712	0.444	10,965	17,188
Holzwolleindustrie	1,339	4,592	0.481	644	2,209
Stuhlrohrfabriken	0	4,909	0.605	0	2,970
Korbwaren- und Korbmöbelindustrie	1,939	17,877	0.698	1,353	12,478
Herstellung von Schilfrohr- und Strohgeweben, Flaschenhülsen und Trinkhalmen	1,218	4,150	0.504	614	2,091
Korkindustrie	2,286	8,104	0.637	1,456	5,163
Borsten- Faserstoff- und Haarzurichtereien	1,130	3,550	0.474	535	1,683
Bürsten- und Pinselindustrie	19,784	40,042	0.528	10,446	21,142
Herstellung von Waren aller Art aus chemischen Kunststoffen sowie aus natürlichen Schnitz- und Formerstoffen	35,287	50,023	0.581	20,502	29,063
Paper and Printing					
Holzschleifereien	39,933	32,622	0.357	14,256	11,646
Zellstoffindustrie	45,024	110,815	0.461	20,756	51,086
Papier- und Pappenfabriken	276,918	401,418	0.385	106,613	154,546
Papierveredelungsindustrie	45,999	74,503	0.368	16,927	27,417
Druckgewerbe	311,092	655,096	0.642	199,721	420,571
Chemigraphisches Gewerbe	4,102	16,465	0.894	3,667	14,720
Buchbindereien	27,709	53,646	0.714	19,784	38,303
Papierwarenindustrie	64,179	169,259	0.465	29,843	78,706
Pappen verarbeitende Industrie	92,793	103,321	0.498	46,211	51,454
Tapetenindustrie	3,089	23,501	0.576	1,779	13,536
Chemicals, Rubber, Plastic and Oil Refining					
Steinkohlenschwelereien	0	111	0.281	0	31
Braunkohlenschwelereien	43,273	5,520	0.208	9,001	1,148
Herstellung von Montanwachs	8,741	0	0.795	6,949	0
Steinkohlenteerdestillation (einschl. H.v. Dachpappe)	32,905	129,445	0.273	8,983	35,338
Benzolreinigungsanstalten	9,805	120,811	0.221	2,167	26,699
Gewinnung von Benzin u. anderen Mineralölderivaten	158,796	151,133	0.301	47,798	45,491
Herstellung von mineralischen Schmierölen und -fetten	6,053	98,918	0.397	2,403	39,270
Herstellung von tierischen Ölen und Fetten	3,070	15,825	0.402	1,234	6,362
Schwefelsäureindustrie	13,871	48,471	0.577	8,003	27,968
Sulfat- und Salzsäureindustrien	2,927	11,778	0.420	1,229	4,947
Sodaindustrien	29,656	42,855	0.463	13,731	19,842
Alkalielektrolyse-Industrien	58,096	41,191	0.578	33,579	23,808
Herstellung von Wasserstoffsuperoxyd, Natriumperborat, u.a. Perverbindungen	1,586	20,589	0.659	1,045	13,568
Herstellung von Schwefel, Schwefelkohlenstoff u. Rhodanverbindungen	3,633	4,322	0.510	1,853	2,204
Herstellung von Cyan- u. Eisencyanverbindungen	4,315	10,961	0.438	1,890	4,801
Wasserglas- und Bleicheindustrie	3,097	14,835	0.629	1,948	9,331
Herstellung von Metallsalzen u. anderen Chemikalien	50,347	87,277	0.439	22,102	38,315
Stickstoffindustrien	154,406	130,164	0.446	68,865	58,053
Phosphorindustrien	32,895	61,478	0.298	9,803	18,320
Karbid- und Kalkstickstoffindustrien	35,828	92,214	0.282	10,103	26,004

Annex C Industrial Census 1936	Employment		Labour Productivity		
Cont. Wood Products, Furniture	East Germany	West Germany	East Germany	West Germany	Average wages
Holzmehlindustrie	110	173	6,130	5,388	1,440
Fassholzsägerei und Fassindustrie	1,117	4,479	1,755	1,981	1,376
Kistenindustrie	4,451	6,354	2,464	2,705	1,292
Holzwolleindustrie	258	891	2,497	2,479	958
Stuhlrohrfabriken	0	1,017		2,920	1,762
Korbwaren- und Korbmöbelindustrie	990	4,023	1,367	3,102	765
Herstellung von Schilfrohr- und Strohgeweben, Flaschenhülsen und Trinkhalmen	398	1,024	1,543	2,042	784
Korkindustrie	445	1,865	3,272	2,768	1,002
Borsten- Faserstoff- und Haarzurichtereien	166	450	3,225	3,740	1,016
Bürsten- und Pinselindustrie	4,179	7,649	2,500	2,764	1,144
Herstellung von Waren aller Art aus chemischen Kunststoffen sowie aus natürlichen Schnitz- und Formerstoffen	8,616	11,268	2,380	2,579	1,231
Paper and Printing					
Holzschleifereien	2,536	2,371	5,621	4,912	1,687
Zellstoffindustrie	3,113	6,988	6,668	7,310	2,032
Papier- und Pappenfabriken	27,374	36,587	3,895	4,224	1,749
Papierveredelungsindustrie	4,026	5,400	4,205	5,077	1,749
Druckgewerbe	58,159	111,171	3,434	3,783	2,116
Chemigraphisches Gewerbe	905	3,076	4,052	4,785	2,419
Buchbindereien	5,109	9,702	3,872	3,948	1,635
Papierwarenindustrie	10,968	21,077	2,721	3,734	1,324
Pappen verarbeitende Industrie	17,022	19,427	2,715	2,649	1,186
Tapetenindustrie	288	2,465	6,179	5,491	1,908
Chemicals, Rubber, Plastic and Oil Refining					
Steinkohlenschwelereien	0	9		3,466	2,409
Braunkohlenschwelereien	2,656	818	3,389	1,404	2,021
Herstellung von Montanwachs	368	0	18,883		2,528
Steinkohlenteerdestillation (einschl. H.v. Dachpappe)	2,106	6,145	4,266	5,751	2,259
Benzolreinigungsanstalten	154	858	14,071	31,118	2,682
Gewinnung von Benzin u. anderen Mineralölderivaten	10,790	3,433	4,430	13,251	2,474
Herstellung von mineralischen Schmierölen und -fetten	344	4,168	6,988	9,422	*2,582*
Herstellung von tierischen Ölen und Fetten	212	839	5,812	7,582	2,038
Schwefelsäureindustrie	1,261	3,457	6,347	8,090	2,630
Sulfat- und Salzsäureindustrien	343	1,027	3,584	4,817	2,530
Sodaindustrien	2,499	2,708	5,494	7,327	2,663
Alkalielektrolyse-Industrien	3,681	1,876	9,122	12,691	2,699
Herstellung von Wasserstoffsuperoxyd, Natriumperborat, u.a. Perverbindungen	85	924	12,294	14,684	3,090
Herstellung von Schwefel, Schwefelkohlenstoff u. Rhodanverbindungen	223	291	8,309	7,575	2,393
Herstellung von Cyan- u. Eisencyanverbindungen	267	510	7,079	9,413	2,673
Wasserglas- und Bleicheindustrie	230	735	8,471	12,695	2,357
Herstellung von Metallsalzen u. anderen Chemikalien	3,304	5,539	6,690	6,917	2,491
Stickstoffindustrien	8,908	10,988	7,731	5,283	2,781
Phosphorindustrien	1,184	2,431	8,279	7,536	2,552
Karbid- und Kalkstickstoffindustrien	1,990	3,664	5,077	7,097	2,547

Annex C Industrial Census 1936	Sales Value			Value Added	
Cont. Chemicals, Rubber, Plastic and Oil Refining	East Germany	West Germany	$F(x)$	East Germany	West Germany
Thomasschlackenmühlen	0	67,179	0.094	0	6,315
Holzverkohlungsindustrien	7,846	15,842	0.423	3,319	6,701
Herstellung von Essigsäuren aus Acetylen	436	52,148	0.179	78	9,334
Lösungsmittelindustrie	38,132	37,780	0.430	16,397	16,245
Industrie der organischen Säuren und ihrer Salze	16,469	18,128	0.473	7,790	8,574
Industrie der organischen Zwischenprodukte	12,613	141,982	–0.305	–3,847	–43,305
Teerfarbenindustrie	17,385	232,439	0.937	16,290	217,795
Pharmazeutische Industrie	10,346	193,245	0.769	7,956	148,605
Bearbeitung von Drogen	43,706	121,473	0.704	30,769	85,517
Industrie der ätherischen Öle und Riechstoffe	24,234	11,417	0.532	12,892	6,074
Herstellung von Gerb- und Farbstoffextrakten	1,160	8,579	0.497	577	4,264
Herstellung von Nitrozellulose und davon abgeleiteten Produkten	59,372	27,768	0.485	28,795	13,468
Herstellung von Ozetylzellulose, Viskosefolien, u.anderen Zelluloseprodukten	6,649	48,857	0.601	3,996	29,363
Photographische Industrie	63,804	48,345	0.521	33,242	25,188
Kunststoffindustrie	19,498	67,660	0.431	8,404	29,161
Sprengstoffindustrie	99,596	75,864	0.422	42,030	32,015
Herstellung von Zündstoffen und Sprengkapseln	9,941	17,001	0.523	5,199	8,892
Lithopone, Blancfix und Titanweissindustrie	3,183	29,976	0.544	1,732	16,307
Herstellung von Bleiweiss, Bleiglätte und Bleimennige	1,700	15,254	0.386	656	5,888
Buntfarbenindustrie	6,857	23,897	0.460	3,154	10,993
Herstellung von Zinkweiss	0	8,308	0.402	0	3,340
Erdfarbenindustrie	995	4,042	0.522	519	2,110
Russ- und Schwärzindustrie	616	5,827	0.510	314	2,972
Herstellung von verdichteten Gasen	10,550	42,327	0.758	7,997	32,084
Aktivkohleindustrie	2,872	4,158	0.743	2,134	3,089
Pyrotechnische und Zündwarenindustrie	10,015	6,456	0.590	5,909	3,809
Zündholzindustrie	4,887	17,520	0.815	3,983	14,279
Herstellung von Glühstrümpfen	3,497	372	0.753	2,633	280
Herstellung von Naturharzprodukten	4,840	9,184	0.441	2,134	4,050
Herstellung von Klebstoffen	12,679	31,568	0.481	6,099	15,184
Lack- und Anstrichmittelindustrie	51,816	171,413	0.510	26,426	87,421
Herstellung von Druckfarben und Druckwalzenmasse	24,672	19,732	0.615	15,173	12,135
Farbwarenindustrie	4,047	29,164	0.593	2,400	17,294
Bleistiftindustrie	0	18,633	0.610	0	11,366
Herstellung von Linoleum, Wachstuch, Kunstleder und verwandten Erzeugnissen	24,054	78,106	0.513	12,339	40,069
Wachsveredelungsindustrie	995	8,758	0.353	351	3,091
Herstellung von Kerzen und Wachserzeugnissen	24,374	84,943	0.579	14,113	49,182
Stearinindustrie	0	10,311	0.453	0	4,671
Seifen-, Waschmittel- und Glyzerinindustrie	99,638	277,452	0.551	54,901	152,876
Kosmetische Industrie	27,362	91,610	0.693	18,962	63,486
Herstellung von Hilfsmitteln für die Textil- und Lederindustrie	23,272	39,158	0.596	13,870	23,338
Herstellung von Atemschutz- und Frischluftgeräten	21,737	9,142	0.620	13,477	5,668
Herstellung von Kautschukwaren (ausgenommen Bereifungen und Gummischuhe)	48,946	171,698	0.638	31,228	109,543
Bereifungsindustrie	10,463	182,309	0.503	5,263	91,701

Annex C Industrial Census 1936	Employment		Labour Productivity		
Cont. Chemicals, Rubber, Plastic and Oil Refining	East Germany	West Germany	East Germany	West Germany	Average wages
Thomasschlackenmühlen	0	1,333		4,737	2,287
Holzverkohlungsindustrien	206	1,387	16,111	4,831	1,824
Herstellung von Essigsäuren aus Acetylen	42	1,908	1,858	4,892	2,865
Lösungsmittelindustrie	2,448	1,415	6,698	11,481	2,428
Industrie der organischen Säuren und ihrer Salze	907	1,698	8,589	5,050	2,433
Industrie der organischen Zwischenprodukte	1,029	7,177	–3,739	–6,034	2,989
Teerfarbenindustrie	700	8,406	23,271	25,910	3,166
Pharmazeutische Industrie	1,195	13,326	6,658	11,152	2,665
Bearbeitung von Drogen	4,066	10,171	7,567	8,408	1,880
Industrie der ätherischen Öle und Riechstoffe	1,876	809	6,872	7,508	2,614
Herstellung von Gerb- und Farbstoffextrakten	103	555	5,597	7,682	2,678
Herstellung von Nitrozellulose und davon abgeleiteten Produkten	3,726	2,379	7,728	5,661	2,096
Herstellung von Ozetylzellulose, Viskosefolien, u.anderen Zelluloseprodukten	324	3,173	12,334	9,254	2,244
Photographische Industrie	5,256	4,298	6,325	5,860	2,246
Kunststoffindustrie	1,071	4,004	7,847	7,283	2,554
Sprengstoffindustrie	8,838	5,252	4,756	6,096	2,126
Herstellung von Zündstoffen und Sprengkapseln	2,019	2,872	2,575	3,096	1,507
Lithopone, Blancfix und Titanweissindustrie	370	2,363	4,680	6,901	2,567
Herstellung von Bleiweiss, Bleiglätte und Bleimennige	96	651	6,835	9,045	2,611
Buntfarbenindustrie	759	2,049	4,155	5,365	2,138
Herstellung von Zinkweiss	0	323		10,340	2,645
Erdfarbenindustrie	147	775	3,533	2,722	1,754
Russ- und Schwärzindustrie	47	626	6,687	4,747	2,334
Herstellung von verdichteten Gasen	668	2,764	11,971	11,608	2,826
Aktivkohleindustrie	301	314	7,089	9,839	2,505
Pyrotechnische und Zündwarenindustrie	1,685	807	3,507	4,720	1,298
Zündholzindustrie	565	2,119	7,049	6,738	1,388
Herstellung von Glühstrümpfen	784	68	3,359	4,121	1,393
Herstellung von Naturharzprodukten	216	585	9,882	6,923	2,377
Herstellung von Klebstoffen	980	2,213	6,223	6,861	1,968
Lack- und Anstrichmittelindustrie	3,009	9,985	8,782	8,755	2,235
Herstellung von Druckfarben und Druckwalzenmasse	1,618	1,411	9,378	8,601	2,697
Farbwarenindustrie	500	3,603	4,800	4,800	1,675
Bleistiftindustrie	0	3,482		3,264	1,875
Herstellung von Linoleum, Wachstuch, Kunstleder und verwandten Erzeugnissen	2,104	5,365	5,865	7,469	2,225
Wachsveredelungsindustrie	89	341	3,948	9,066	2,089
Herstellung von Kerzen und Wachserzeugnissen	2,083	8,509	6,775	5,780	1,656
Stearinindustrie	0	552		8,462	2,292
Seifen-, Waschmittel- und Glyzerinindustrie	4,473	13,197	12,274	11,584	2,067
Kosmetische Industrie	2,074	6,524	9,143	9,731	1,829
Herstellung von Hilfsmitteln für die Textil- und Lederindustrie	1,463	1,483	9,480	15,737	2,628
Herstellung von Atemschutz- und Frischluftgeräten	2,540	623	5,306	9,098	1,848
Herstellung von Kautschukwaren (ausgenommen Bereifungen und Gummischuhe)	7,299	24,349	4,278	4,499	2,029
Bereifungsindustrie	513	14,062	10,259	6,521	2,341

Annex C Industrial Census 1936	Sales Value			Value Added	
Cont. Chemicals, Rubber, Plastic and Oil Refining	East Germany	West Germany	$F(x)$	East Germany	West Germany
Gummischuhindustrie	2,609	19,967	0.633	1,651	12,639
Herstellung von Regeneratoren, Kautschuk-Plastikaten und -Präparaten	1,229	8,243	0.520	639	4,286
Herstellung von Guttapercha- und Balatawaren	539	3,716	0.565	305	2,100
Asbestindustrie	19,769	17,681	0.708	13,996	12,518
Stone, Clay, Glass					
Steinbruchindustrie und Naturstein-bearbeitung	74,865	170,973	0.875	65,507	149,602
Schieferindustrie	5,347	6,720	0.865	4,625	5,813
Gewinnung von Findlingsquarziten und sonstigen Quarzitgestein	193	2,854	0.922	178	2,631
Gewinnung und Aufbereitung von Natur-asphaltgestein	116	5,505	0.534	62	2,940
Mineralmühlen- u. Aufbereitungs-betriebe	1,026	8,234	0.463	475	3,812
Baukies und Bausandgruben und Baggereien	14,748	42,475	0.914	13,480	38,822
Glassand, Formsand, Klebsand und sonstige Quarzsandgruben	3,888	9,722	0.925	3,596	8,993
Kieselgurgruben	53	1,608	0.913	48	1,468
Gewinnung und Bearbeitung von Torf	0	13,996	0.808	0	11,309
Gewinnung und Aufbereitung von Kreide	0	1,798	0.794	0	1,428
Farberdegruben	5	436	0.891	4	388
Kieselkreidegruben	0	1,083	0.874	0	947
Schwerspatgruben	104	5,916	0.697	72	4,123
Speckstein und Talkumgruben	0	385	0.864	0	333
Feldspatgruben und -werke	1	517	0.919	1	475
Rohton und Bleicherdegruben	4,461	12,694	0.922	4,113	11,704
Kaolingruben (einschl. Aufbereitungs-anlagen)	4,126	3,475	0.878	3,623	3,051
Kalkindustrie	25,249	89,903	0.698	17,624	62,752
Magnesitgruben und -werke	0	0	0.765		
Zementindustrie	39,150	191,667	0.571	22,355	109,442
Gipsindustrie	6,089	7,019	0.686	4,177	4,815
Mörtelwerke	3,504	5,771	0.576	2,019	3,324
Edelputzwerke	1,189	2,543	0.543	645	1,381
Ziegelindustrie	109,795	219,005	0.811	89,044	177,613
Kalksandsteinindustrie	8,858	20,984	0.629	5,572	13,199
Bimsbaustoffindustrie	11	30,011	0.594	7	17,827
Schlackenindustrie	8,822	18,877	0.553	4,878	10,439
Betonwaren und Betonwerksteinindustrie	22,519	46,262	0.609	13,714	28,174
Asbestzementindustrie	1,124	12,454	0.704	791	8,768
Leichtbauplattenindustrie	1,042	16,852	0.562	585	9,471
Steinholzindustrie	2,331	9,764	0.675	1,574	6,590
Herstellung von Korkstein- u. Kieselgur-waren und sonstigen Erzeugnissen für Temperatur- und Schallschutz	3,172	16,276	0.548	1,738	8,919
Industrie feuer- und säurefester Erzeugnisse	12,623	90,790	0.586	7,397	53,203
Steinzeugindustrie	6,438	20,842	0.774	4,983	16,132
Feinkeramische Industrie	109,624	146,944	0.768	84,191	112,853
Schleifmittelindustrie	12,825	45,189	0.639	8,195	28,876
Glashüttenindustrie	92,510	133,481	0.708	65,497	94,505
Hohlglas veredelnde und Glas verarbeitende Industrie	32,579	5,330	0.678	22,089	3,614
Flachglas veredelnde Industrie	9,662	23,400	0.559	5,401	13,081

Annex C Industrial Census 1936	Employment		Labour Productivity		
Cont. Chemicals, Rubber, Plastic and Oil Refining	East Germany	West Germany	East Germany	West Germany	Average wages
Gummischuhindustrie	657	3,850	2,514	3,283	1,415
Herstellung von Regeneratoren, Kautschuk-Plastikaten und -Präparaten	109	863	5,865	4,967	1,960
Herstellung von Guttapercha- und Balatawaren	34	235	8,957	8,934	2,473
Asbestindustrie	2,382	2,381	5,876	5,258	1,805
Stone, Clay, Glass					
Steinbruchindustrie und Naturstein-bearbeitung	24,960	61,418	2,624	2,436	1,442
Schieferindustrie	2,579	2,455	1,793	2,368	1,238
Gewinnung von Findlingsquarziten und sonstigen Quarzitgestein	71	1,263	2,506	2,083	*1,365*
Gewinnung und Aufbereitung von Natur-asphaltgestein	16	858	3,863	3,426	1,582
Mineralmühlen- u. Aufbereitungs-betriebe	123	517	3,863	7,374	1,823
Baukies und Bausandgruben und Baggereien	4,077	8,125	3,306	4,778	1,589
Glassand, Formsand, Klebsand und sonstige Quarzsandgruben	1,163	1,789	3,092	5,027	1,569
Kieselgurgruben	41	739	1,180	1,987	1,408
Gewinnung und Bearbeitung von Torf	0	8,103		1,396	1,239
Gewinnung und Aufbereitung von Kreide	0	301		4,743	1,761
Farberdegruben	3	232	1,485	1,674	786
Kieselkreidegruben	0	304		3,114	1,571
Schwerspatgruben	24	1,595	3,020	2,585	1,643
Speckstein und Talkumgruben	0	85		3,913	1,419
Feldspatgruben und -werke	2	126	460	3,771	1,653
Rohton und Bleicherdegruben	1,061	3,710	3,877	3,155	1,515
Kaolingruben (einschl. Aufbereitungs-anlagen)	863	957	4,198	3,188	1,473
Kalkindustrie	4,414	16,474	3,993	3,809	1,638
Magnesitgruben und -werke	0	0			1,039
Zementindustrie	2,857	14,162	7,825	7,728	2,072
Gipsindustrie	1,226	1,571	3,407	3,065	1,519
Mörtelwerke	275	345	7,340	9,634	2,214
Edelputzwerke	150	323	4,302	4,274	1,539
Ziegelindustrie	39,119	71,619	2,276	2,480	1,527
Kalksandsteinindustrie	1,459	3,374	3,819	3,912	1,629
Bimsbaustoffindustrie	6	5,389	1,089	3,308	1,771
Schlackenindustrie	1,360	3,046	3,587	3,427	1,890
Betonwaren und Betonwerksteinindustrie	5,308	9,894	2,584	2,848	1,521
Asbestzementindustrie	126	1,628	6,280	5,386	1,905
Leichtbauplattenindustrie	193	1,834	3,033	5,164	1,560
Steinholzindustrie	384	1,259	4,098	5,235	1,868
Herstellung von Korkstein- u. Kieselgur-waren und sonstigen Erzeugnissen für Temperatur- und Schallschutz	411	1,850	4,229	4,821	1,777
Industrie feuer- und säurefester Erzeugnisse	2,341	14,186	3,160	3,750	1,838
Steinzeugindustrie	1,253	3,106	3,977	5,194	1,822
Feinkeramische Industrie	32,750	42,093	2,571	2,681	1,369
Schleifmittelindustrie	1,403	4,228	5,841	6,830	2,188
Glashüttenindustrie	22,012	24,512	2,976	3,855	1,579
Hohlglas veredelnde und Glas verarbeitende Industrie	6,132	1,186	3,602	3,047	1,131
Flachglas veredelnde Industrie	1,871	3,828	2,887	3,417	1,413

Annex C Industrial Census 1936	Sales Value			Value Added	
	East Germany	West Germany	$F(x)$	East Germany	West Germany
Basic and Fabricated Metal Products					
Hochofenwerke	11,598	818,567	0.251	2,911	205,460
Flussstahlwerke (einschl. der damit verbundenen Stahlformgiessereien	97,724	1400,583	0.199	19,447	278,716
Schweissstahlwerke	0	2,393	0.333	0	797
Warmwalzwerke (einschl. der damit verbundenen Hammer- und Presswerke)	173,039	2384,152	0.277	47,932	660,410
Kupfer-, Blei- und Silberhütten	45,468	133,185	0.156	7,093	20,777
Kupferraffinerien und -elektrolysen	46,526	125,710	0.082	3,815	10,308
Gold- und Silberscheideanstalten	27,517	98,140	0.089	2,449	8,734
Zinkhütten	12,558	23,868	0.390	4,898	9,309
Zinkhütten und Entzinnungsanstalten	140	15,301	0.264	37	4,039
Tonerdefabriken	13,365	26,462	0.474	6,335	12,543
Aluminiumhütten	66,242	73,910	0.352	23,317	26,016
Gewinnung von Nickel und Kobalt	6,813	10,982	0.265	1,805	2,910
Gewinnung von Wolfram, Molybdän u. anderes	45,275	9,917	0.470	21,279	4,661
Herstellung von Ferrolegierungen, Elektrokorund, Karboround	34,524	48,031	0.445	15,363	21,374
Walz-, Press-und Hammerwerke der Nichteisenmetallindustrie	213,627	532,063	0.371	79,256	197,395
Herstellung von Warmpressteilen der Nichteisenmetallindustrie	18,341	30,269	0.381	6,988	11,532
Metallschmelzereien	5,039	31,166	0.244	1,230	7,604
Eisen-, Temper-, und Stahlgiessereien	171,208	657,587	0.674	115,394	443,213
Metallgiessereien	45,050	172,134	0.520	23,426	89,510
Drahtwarenindustrie	59,386	417,747	0.485	28,802	202,607
Werkzeugindustrie	31,909	142,782	0.700	22,336	99,948
Blechwarenindustrie	95,038	318,416	0.505	47,994	160,800
Schloss- und Beschlägeindustrie	8,584	107,512	0.706	6,060	75,904
Feine Schneidewarenindustrie (einschl. Schlägeindustrie)	3,330	100,039	0.708	2,358	70,828
Fahrzeugteileindustrie	90,948	285,336	0.631	57,388	180,047
Herd- und Ofenindustrie	22,678	121,099	0.568	12,881	68,784
Schusswaffenindustrie	44,889	72,889	0.759	34,071	55,322
Sonstige Zweige der Eisen- und Stahlwarenindustrie	160,235	563,891	0.553	88,610	311,832
Stahlbau	55,209	308,975	0.532	29,371	164,375
Waggonbau	16,151	62,204	0.534	8,625	33,217
Feld- und Werkbahnwagenbau	224	32,080	0.409	91	13,121
Schiffbau	15,390	473,661	0.543	8357	257,198
Machinery and Transport					
Werkzeugmaschinenindustrie	201,386	431,761	0.678	136,540	292,734
Textilmaschinenindustrie	122,321	53,538	0.641	78,408	34,318
Herstellung von Maschinen für das Bekleidungsgewerbe	44,741	85,414	0.702	31,408	59,960
Landmaschinenindustrie	57,359	196,099	0.540	30,974	105,893
Herstellung von Maschinen und Apparaten für die Papierherstellung, Papierverarbeitung und für das graphische Gewerbe	60,696	72,572	0.680	41,273	49,349
Büromaschinenindustrie	90,329	52,330	0.830	74,973	43,434
Herstellung von Maschinen und Apparaten für Müllerei, Nahrungsmittel- und Genussmittelindustrie u.ä.	49,362	111,908	0.672	33,171	75,202
Armaturenindustrie	64,281	103,043	0.599	38,504	61,723
Sonstiger Maschinenbau	438,965	1418,104	0.635	278,743	900,496

Annex C Industrial Census 1936	Employment		Labour Productivity		
	East Germany	West Germany	East Germany	West Germany	Average wages
Basic and Fabricated Metal Products					
Hochofenwerke	437	25,372	6,662	8,098	2,422
Flussstahlwerke (einschl. der damit verbundenen Stahlformgiessereien	4,288	38,341	4,535	7,269	2,409
Schweissstahlwerke	0	226		3,526	2,345
Warmwalzwerke (einschl. der damit verbundenen Hammer- und Presswerke)	8,551	118,448	5,605	5,576	2,386
Kupfer-, Blei- und Silberhütten	2,442	5,740	2,905	3,620	2,328
Kupferraffinerien und -elektrolysen	700	1,139	5,450	9,050	2,558
Gold- und Silberscheideanstalten	290	396	8,445	22,057	2,608
Zinkhütten	1,118	3,354	4,381	2,775	2,428
Zinkhütten und Entzinnungsanstalten	7	689	5,280	5,863	2,746
Tonerdefabriken	639	1,295	9,914	9,686	2,558
Aluminiumhütten	2,142	3,211	10,886	8,102	2,268
Gewinnung von Nickel und Kobalt	532	354	3,394	8,221	2,379
Gewinnung von Wolfram, Molybdän u. anderes	2,335	760	9,113	6,133	2,487
Herstellung von Ferrolegierungen, Elektrokorund, Karboround	1,474	1,762	10,423	12,130	2,283
Walz-,Press-und Hammerwerke der Nichteisenmetallindustrie	10,531	2,7867	7,526	7,083	2,234
Herstellung von Warmpressteilen der Nichteisenmetallindustrie	1,099	2,067	6,359	5,579	2,147
Metallschmelzereien	146	1,029	8,421	7,390	1,905
Eisen-, Temper-, und Stahlgießereien	32,509	103,474	3,550	4,283	1,888
Metallgiessereien	5,738	19,839	4,083	4,512	1,876
Drahtwarenindustrie	11,572	51,102	2,489	3,965	1,665
Werkzeugindustrie	7,173	26,254	3,114	3,807	1,558
Blechwarenindustrie	17,717	61,829	2,709	2,601	1,549
Schloss- und Beschlägeindustrie	1,651	18,636	3,670	4,073	1,596
Feine Schneidewarenindustrie (einschl. Schlägeindustrie)	1,035	14,899	2,278	4,754	1,616
Fahrzeugteileindustrie	13,379	35,705	4,289	5,043	1,875
Herd- und Ofenindustrie	4,217	21,210	3,055	3,243	1,742
Schusswaffenindustrie	9,891	8,959	3,445	6,175	1,903
Sonstige Zweige der Eisen- und Stahlwarenindustrie	24,788	117,482	3,575	2,654	1,731
Stahlbau	6,259	36,420	4,693	4,513	2,123
Waggonbau	3,675	10,148	2,347	3273	1,838
Feld- und Werkbahnwagenbau	31	4,173	2,949	3,144	1,676
Schiffbau	3,166	69,912	2,639	3,679	2,144
Machinery and Transport					
Werkzeugmaschinenindustrie	31,007	5,7441	4,404	5,096	2,097
Textilmaschinenindustrie	19,940	9,222	3,932	3,721	1,982
Herstellung von Maschinen für das Bekleidungsgewerbe	9,672	12,993	3,247	4,615	1,850
Landmaschinenindustrie	8,573	25,781	3,613	4,107	1,790
Herstellung von Maschinen und Apparaten für die Papierherstellung, Papierverarbeitung und für das graphische Gewerbe	11,630	12,155	3,549	4,060	2,059
Büromaschinenindustrie	17,360	8,146	4,319	5,332	2,140
Herstellung von Maschinen und Apparaten für Müllerei, Nahrungsmittel- und Genussmittelindustrie u.ä.	9,284	17,899	3,573	4,201	1,947
Armaturenindustrie	9,555	13,181	4,030	4,683	1,806
Sonstiger Maschinenbau	61,309	180,827	4,547	4,980	2,159

Annex C Industrial Census 1936	Sales Value			Value Added	
Cont. Machinery and Transport	East Germany	West Germany	$F(x)$	East Germany	West Germany
Kessel- und Apparatebau	45,318	164,354	0.568	25,741	93,353
Kraftfahrzeugindustrie	320,000	1,087,477	0.439	140,480	477,403
Herstellung von Kraftfahrzeuganhängern und Kraftfahrzeugaufbauten	101,026	149,364	0.528	53,342	78,864
Fahrradindustrie und Herstellung von Kinderwagen	47,863	80,481	0.473	22,639	38,068
Flugmotorenbau	133,286	140,100	0.571	76,106	79,997
Flugzeugzellenbau	406,696	204,778	0.603	245,238	123,481
Electrical Equipment					
Herstellung von elektrischen Maschinen, Apparaten und Zubehör der Stark- und Schwachstromindustrie	329,622	1,229,757	0.654	215,573	804,261
Kabelindustrie	102,603	245,280	0.526	53,969	129,017
Elektrokohleindustrie	12,382	25,139	0.624	7,727	15,687
Batterie- und Elementeindustrie	9,958	9,963	0.574	5,716	5,719
Akkumulatorenindustrie	14,054	37,706	0.571	8,025	21,530
Glühlampen- und Leuchtröhrenindustrie	54,208	32,887	0.788	42,716	25,915
Optics and Fine Mechanics					
Optische, fein- und medizinmechanische Industrie	142,995	228,008	0.712	101,813	162,341
Herstellung von orthopädischen Erzeugnissen und hygienischen Bandagen	10,128	13,355	0.716	7,252	9,562
Grossuhrenindustrie	383	53,873	0.608	233	32,755
Taschen- und Armbanduhrenindustrie	3,875	31,483	0.556	2,155	17,504
Metallwarenindustrie	417,531	523,411	0.389	162,420	203,607
Bronzefarbenindustrie	0	12,665	0.466	0	5,902
Herstellung von metallischen Überzügen	5,225	24,445	0.540	2,822	13,200
Schriftgiessereien	2,288	9,826	0.836	1,912	8,215
Herstellung von Stempelapparaten und Gummistempeln	3,544	4,986	0.865	3,066	4,313
Edelmetall- und Schmuckwarenindustrie	4,404	103,823	0.542	2,387	56,272
Füllfederhalterindustrie	4,696	9,517	0.603	2,832	5,739
Bearbeitung technischer Diamanten	127	2,630	0.530	67	1,394
Bearbeitung von Edel-, Halbedel- und synthetischen Edelsteinen	0	22,385	0.887	0	19,855
Kleinmusikinstrumenteindustrie	20,897	14,905	0.631	13,186	9,405
Herstellung von Saiten aller Art	3,851	1,222	0.629	2,422	768
Herstellung von Sprechmaschinen	322	5,533	0.648	208	3,586
Herstellung von Schallplatten	1,181	2,392	0.793	936	1,897
Spielwarenindustrie (einschl. Herstellung von Christbaumschmuck)	26,997	46,805	0.593	16,009	27,755
Utilities					
Elektrizitätswerke	471,438	1,051,970	0.565	266,363	594,363
Gaswerke	154,449	393,781	0.694	107,187	273,284
Wasserwerke	60,150	184,916	*0.645*	38,797	119,271
Construction	1,777,572	3,371,525	0.600	1,066,543	2,022,915
Total	**17,721,191**	**43,937,227**		**9,105,066**	**21,586,854**

Annex C Industrial Census 1936	Employment		Labour Productivity		
Cont. Machinery and Transport	East Germany	West Germany	East Germany	West Germany	Average wages
Kessel- und Apparatebau	5,318	16,556	4,840	5,639	2,055
Kraftfahrzeugindustrie	23,683	85,149	5,932	5,607	2,373
Herstellung von Kraftfahrzeuganhängern und Kraftfahrzeugaufbauten	12,982	22,528	4,109	3,501	1,944
Fahrradindustrie und Herstellung von Kinderwagen	7,931	10,386	2,855	3,665	1,742
Flugmotorenbau	15,997	15,636	4,758	5,116	2,250
Flugzeugzellenbau	60,485	32,208	4,055	3,834	2,317
Electrical Equipment					
Herstellung von elektrischen Maschinen, Apparaten und Zubehör der Stark- und Schwachstromindustrie	53,629	186,341	4,020	4,316	2,163
Kabelindustrie	9,418	19,893	5,730	6,486	2,109
Elektrokohleindustrie	1,808	3,371	4,274	4,653	1,938
Batterie- und Elementeindustrie	1,477	1,401	3,870	4,082	1,598
Akkumulatorenindustrie	1,589	2,887	5,050	7,458	2,559
Glühlampen- und Leuchtröhrenindustrie	6,308	3,309	6,772	7,832	1,969
Optics and Fine Mechanics					
Optische, fein- und medizinmechanische Industrie	2,6267	41,875	3,876	3,877	2,023
Herstellung von orthopädischen Erzeugnissen und hygienischen Bandagen	3,057	3,113	2,372	3,072	1,434
Grossuhrenindustrie	116	12,137	2,008	2,699	1,509
Taschen- und Armbanduhrenindustrie	1,402	7,521	1,537	2,327	1,431
Metallwarenindustrie	65,147	81,823	2,493	2,488	1,538
Bronzefarbenindustrie	0	1,038		5,686	1,787
Herstellung von metallischen Überzügen	1,288	5,572	2,191	2,369	
Schriftgiessereien	356	1,492	5,372	5,506	2,746
Herstellung von Stempelapparaten und Gummistempeln	1,028	1,296	2,982	3,328	1,677
Edelmetall- und Schmuckwarenindustrie	359	22,244	6,648	2,530	1,313
Füllfederhalterindustrie	806	1,604	3,513	3,578	1,326
Bearbeitung technischer Diamanten	23	425	2,934	3,279	1920
Bearbeitung von Edel-, Halbedel- und synthetischen Edelsteinen	0	7,637		2,600	1,298
Kleinmusikinstrumenteindustrie	4,223	3,797	3,122	2,477	1,347
Herstellung von Saiten aller Art	957	255	2,531	3,013	1,148
Herstellung von Sprechmaschinen	56	1,172	3,721	3,059	1,393
Herstellung von Schallplatten	104	266	9,005	7,131	2,520
Spielwarenindustrie (einschl. Herstellung von Christbaumschmuck)	7,425	10,581	2,156	2,623	1,197
Utilities					
Elektrizitätswerke	29,730	69,868	8,959	8,507	2,643
Gaswerke	14,506	32,802	7,389	8,331	2,497
Wasserwerke	4,026	11,421	9,637	10,443	2,570
Construction	322,673	604,247	3,305	3,348	
Total	**2,308,910**	**5,014,443**	**3,943**	**4,305**	

Sources and notes:
BArch R3102/ 3309; 'Beschäftigte' and 'Absatz'
BArch R3102/ 5922; Absatzwert (= 1) minus "Rohstoffe, Halbfabrikate, Kraftstoffe" (= $F(x)$); and the average wages.

This benchmark is based on archive material of the Bundesarchiv in Berlin-Lichterfelde on the industrial census of 1936. It was traced there by Rainer Fremdling and the author of this research. It allows major improvements in comparison with the official publication „Die deutsche Industrie" of the *Reichsamt für wehrwirtschaftliche Planung* (Berlin 1939) as one can start from a lower aggregation level. Firstly, this makes it possible to separate Anhalt from the other „Länder" that were in the category „sonstige Länder". Secondly, there are fewer aggregations on behalf of the „Betriebsgeheimnisse". Finally, it is possible to distinguish 300 industries, in comparison to only 122 in „Die deutsche Industrie". A more elaborate discussion of the census is in Jaap Sleifer, „Separated Unity: The Industrial Sector in 1936 in the Territory of the German Democratic Republic and the Federal Republic of Germany" in: *Jahrbuch für Wirtschaftsgeschichte* 2001/1

The territorial composition of East and West Berlin is the following:
East Berlin: Berlin-Mitte, Prenzlauer Berg, Horst Wessel, Treptow, Köpenick, Lichtenberg, Weissensee, Pankow

West Berlin: Kreuzberg, Zehlendorf, Schöneberg, Steglitz, Tempelhof, Neukölln, Tiergarten, Charlottenburg, Spandau, Wilmersdorf, Wedding, Reinickendorf

The territorial composition of East Germany and West Germany is the following:
East Germany: Mecklenburg, Brandenburg, Sachsen (Provinz), Thüringen, Sachsen, Anhalt, Berlin-Ost

West Germany: Bayern, Württemberg, Baden, Hessen-Nassau, Hessen, Saarland, Rheinprovinz, Westfalen, Hannover, Hamburg, Schleswig-Holstein, Bremen, Oldenburg, Braunschweig, Lippe, Schaumburg-Lippe, Berlin-West

There are some difficulties concerning the border between East Germany and Poland. Before World War II the Oder-Neisse was not an important division line between administrative units. It divided the pre-war *Länder* Pommern, Brandenburg and Schlesien. The East German territory in this study includes Brandenburg, although some parts of it are east of the Oder-Neisse. This is compensated by the omission of the territories of the *Länder* Pommern and Schlesien. Annex D shows a map.

Annex C.2. East German and West German industries in 1954

Production

East German quantities were obtained from the Staatlichen Zentralverwaltung für Statistik, *Statistisches Jahrbuch der deutschen demokratischen Republik 1955* (Berlin-Ost 1956). West German quantities and sales values were obtained from Statistisches Bundesamt, *Die Industrie der Bundesrepublik Deutschland – Reihe 3 – Die industrielle Produktion. Jahreszahlen 1954 bis 1958* (Stuttgart/Mainz 1958).

	Unit	EG	WG	WG-value	EG-value
Mining					
Steinkohle	th t	2,648	65,140	3,293,484	133,883
Rohbraunkohle	th t	181,913	87,813	192,935	399,683
Braunkohlenbriketts	th t	46,886	15,951	483,448	1,421,036
Braunkohlenschwelkoks	th t	6,240	686	16,910	153,817
Eisenerz eff.	th t	1,470	13,036	227,538	25,658
Kalisalze auf K2O	th t	1,463	1,936	324,535	245,245
Schwefelkies	th t	130.1	596.4	25,340	5,528
Total				**4,564,190**	**2,384,850**
Food, Beverages, Tobacco					
Mehl aller sorten, Mahlmühlen-erzeugnisse	th t	1,308.2	3,725.2	1,864,956	654,927
Nährmittel aller Sorten	th t	134.1	319.4	650,496	273,111
Fleisch und Wurstwaren	th t	193.8	174.6	745,549	827,534
Fleisch und Wurstconserven	t	128,362	47,255	208,658	566,792
Margarine	th t	144.3	589.9	960,031	234,841
Butter	th t	108.7	229.9	129,0410	610,124
Verbrauchszucker	t	733,198	1,098,964	941,850	628,376
Malz	t	137,445	188,404	140,990	102,855
Bier	th hl	10,617	27,479	1,741,405	672,823
Alkoholfreie Getränke	th l	154,260	509,166	199,639	60,484
Rauchtabak	t	2,865	15,706	185,700	33,874
Zigaretten	Mill P	16,999	39,499	941,670	405,262
Total				**9,871,354**	**5,071,003**
Textiles, Wearing Apparel					
Kunstseide (Reyon)	t	20,897	59,795	4,311	1,507
Garne	t	243,275	637,186	34,454	13,154
Gewebe, Rohgewebe	th qm	483,310	617,732	733,553	573,928
Möbelstoffe	th qm	7,484	54,681	279,330	38,231
Teppiche und Läufer	th qm	4,668	15,677	285,006	84,864

	Unit	EG	WG	WG-value	EG-value
Tüll und Gardinen	th qm	38,177	55,177	100,362	69,441
Strumpfe und Socken	th pares	146,586	182,741	482,483	387,025
Untertrikotagen (Leibwäsche)	th P	119,135	196,434	524,036	317,822
Obertrikotagen (Oberbekleidung)	th P	13,460	30,429	415,923	183,980
Total				**2,859,458**	**1,669,952**
Leather Products and Footwear					
Schuhe	th pares	19,374	93,774	1,448,541	299,273
Wood Products and Furniture					
Schnittholz und Schwellen	th cbm	3,446.3	6,881.6	982,647	492,109
Furniere	cbm	21,230	312,708	105,735	7,178
Hartfaserplatten (Holzfaserplatten)	cbm	13,434	163,180	63,182	5,202
Pianos und Flügel	P	6,136	7,147	15,836	13,596
Total				**1,167,400**	**518,085**
Paper and Printing					
Zellstoff aller Sorten (atro)	th t	302.3	629.3	381,707	183,363
Papier aller Sorten	th t	391.4	1,706.6	1,491,917	342,164
Karton und Pappe	th t	216.2	581.4	289,486	107,649
Papiersäcke	t	26,292	131,484	160,583	32,111
Tüten und Beutel	t	21,669	78,636	142,551	39,282
Kartonagen	t	76,185	192,169	241,963	95,926
Wellpappe und -erzeugnisse	t	51,189	208,713	188,725	46,287
Total				**2,896,932**	**846,782**
Chemicals, Rubber, Plastic and Oil Refining					
Schwefelsäure ber auf SO_3	th t	433.7	1,708	1,364,934	346,588
Ätznatron ber auf Na OH	t	227,699	498,155	398,096	181,964
Salzsäure ber auf HCl	t	80,318	144,586	115,545	64,186
Calciumcarbid	t	735,374	803,935	642,458	587,668
Stickstoffdünger ber auf N	t	276,681	696,032	687,414	273,255
Phosphordünger ber auf P_2O_5	t	79,203	490,783	261,019	42,124
Essigsäure	t	28,196	83,033	66,355	22,533
Waschpulver	t	67,813	176,083	254,086	97,854
Lacke und Anstrichmittel	t	95,096	272,267	695,481	242,914
Kraftfahrzeugdecken	th P	1,139.7	5,902	248,825	48,049
Kraftfahrzeugschläuche	th P	1,128	5,011	26,658	6,001
Fahrraddecken	th P	4,951.9	15,395	57,085	18,362
Fahrradschläuche	th P	5,005	13,491	16,699	6,195
Total				**4,834,655**	**1,937,693**

	Unit	EG	WG	WG-value	EG-value
Stone, Clay, Glass					
Gebrannter Kalk	th t	2,303	6,757	278,355	94,872
Zement	th t	2,635	15,618	831,653	140,313
Dachziegel	th P	181,381	1,011,718	205,397	36,824
Schamotteerzeugnisse	th t	593.6	296.5	17,568	35,172
Haushaltsporzellan	t	17,511	65,068	248,308	66,824
Total				**1,581,281**	**374,005**
Basic and Fabricated Metal Products					
Roheisen	th t	1,317.8	12,512	6,685,996	704,188
Rohstahl in Blöcken	th t	2,330.5	16,960	9,062,859	1,245,342
Walzstahl, ohne Walzbleche	th t	2,552.2	7,953	3,891,907	1,248,953
Walzbleche	th t	666.8	3,494	2,006,072	382,842
Bandagen	th t	34.6	52	216,168	143,835
Drahtgeflechte	t	3,288	85,708	76,335	2,928
Total				**21,939,337**	**3,728,088**
Machinery and Transport					
Rohrleitungen	t	45,815	81,791	148,561	83,216
Traktoren-Sä- und -Drillmaschinen	P	6,807	15,837	11,650	5,007
Grasmäher	P	400	7,534	7,076	376
Mähdrescher	P	3,376	5,210	48,355	31,333
Heu- und Strohpressen	P	53,861	9,209	16,169	94,568
Dampflokomotiven	P	87	273	90,222	28,752
Personenkraftwagen	P	19,677	518,190	1,397,608	53,071
Lastkraftwagen	P	12,222	113,146	457,748	49,446
Motorräder	P	50,270	256,869	346,400	67,792
Fahrräder	th P	728.4	890.2	101,134	82,752
Nähmaschinen für den Hausbedarf	P	199,718	526,429	152,317	57,786
Total				**2,777,240**	**554,099**
Electrical Equipment					
Glühlampen	th P	71,437	78,658	50,579	45,936
Radioempfänger	P	896,674	2,632,801	442,945	150,857
Fernsehempfänger	P	40,565	128,930	78,964	24,844
Total				**572,488**	**221,637**
Optics and Fine Mechanics					
Armbanduhren	th P	1,732	5,859	142,821	42,220
Taschenuhren	th P	675.4	557	3,702	4,489
Wecker	th P	1,156.3	8,407	44,696	6,148
Fotoapparate	P	804,087	3,009,210	194,168	51,883
Buchungsmachinen	P	5,113	32,388	85,481	13,495
Total				**470,868**	**118,235**

Annex C.2. (Cont.) Adjustment for the Gerschenkron effect

The table below shows the output value of the matched products in West German prices in column (a) and column (c). The total output values per branch in the own currency's, that are in column (b) and column (d) were derived from the official statistics. Column (e) hides the underlying assumption that the quantity relationship between matched output in the two countries applies to the entire branch. Finally the implicit unit value ratio was derived from the columns (d) and (e).

The "plain" benchmark and the Implicit Unit Value Ratio for 1954

	West Germany		Implicit UVR OM/DM	East Germany		
	Matched DM	Total DM		Matched DM	Total OM	Total DM
	(a)	(b)	(d)/(e)	(c)	(d)	(e)
Mining	4,564.19	7,718.10	0.48	2,384.85	1,928.1	4,032.81
Manufacturing:	*50,419.55*	*132,666.10*	*0.83*	*15,338.84*	*38,034.90*	*45,634.69*
Food, Beverages, Tobacco	9,871.35	22,343.10	0.60	5,071.00	6,933.4	11,477.85
Textiles, Wearing Apparel	2,859.46	16,240.80	0.65	1,669.95	6,177.6	9,484.78
Leather Products, Footwear	1,448.54	2,969.60	1.60	299.27	982.9	613.53
Wood Products, Furniture	1,167.40	5,543.80	0.73	518.09	1,797.5	2,460.31
Paper, Printing	2,896.93	6,252.40	0.70	846.78	1,281.9	1,827.59
Chemicals, rubber, plastic, oil refining	4,834.66	16,885.90	0.99	1,937.69	6,705.2	6,767.73
Stone, Clay, Glass	1,581.28	5,938.20	1.01	374.01	1,416.7	1,404.51
Metal, Machinery, Transport	24,716.58	47,046.70	1.13	4,282.18	9,214.8	8,150.92
Electrical equipment	572.49	7,906.80	0.89	221.64	2,727.5	3,061.09
Optics, Fine mechanics	470.87	1,538.80	2.06	118.23	797.4	386.39
Total		140,384.20	0.80		39,963.0	49,667.50

Source: Annex B, Column (d) is from Staatlichen Zentralverwaltung für Statistik, *Statistisches Jahrbuch der Deutschen Demokratischen Republik 1955* (Berlin 1956) pp 154, 155

The Fisher index is the geometric average of the Laspeyres index that is shown above (0.80) and the Paasche index that can be calculated by weighting the implicit UVRs at East German weights (column d). This makes the Paasche UVR (0.89) and the Fisher index at (0.85).

Using the Fisher UVR the total value of industrial output in East Germany amounts to (39,963/0.85) = 47,015.29 DM. The Laspeyres index summed up to 49,667.50 DM. The Fisher/Laspeyres ratio was calculated as follows: (47,015.29/49,667.50) = 0.9466. This ratio was used to adjust the Laspeyres results in column e.

Annex C.3. Industrial labour productivity in regions in 1936, 1950

The data is based on three different sources: one source for 1936 and two sources for 1950. Firstly the source for 1936, which is the underlying archive material of the industrial census in 1936 (see also Annex C.1). Secondly the sources for 1950. For East Germany the figures are based on the statistical yearbook of 1955, for West Germany for the statistical yearbook of 1952. The main difficulties are the following:

a) Different currency's, between East and West Germany;
b) Changes of regional borders between 1936 and 1950.

The East German Ost-Mark values in 1950 are valued in West German currency by means of the calculated PPP for 1954 (see Annex C.2). It is based on the following regions.

East Germany

Regions 1936	Regions 1950	LP 1936	LP 1950
Mecklenburg	Rostock, Schwerin, Neubrandenburg	7,348	9,403
Brandenburg	Potsdam, Frankfurt, Cottbus	7,832	9,349
Sachsen-Anhalt	Magdeburg, Halle	8,518	12,427
Thüringen	Erfurt, Gera, Suhl	6,835	8,120
Sachsen	Dresden, Leipzig, Karl-Marx-Stadt	6,990	8,991
Berlin-Ost	Berlin-Ost	8,731	10,912

West Germany

Regions 1936	Regions 1950	LP 1936	LP 1950
Schleswig-Holstein	Schleswig-Holstein	10,413	21,370
Hamburg	Hamburg	11,166	27,005
Hannover, Oldenburg, Schaumburg-Lippe, Braunschweig	Niedersachsen	9,092	17,563
Westfalen, Rheinprovinz (50 %)	Nordrhein-Westfalen	9,400	15,640
Bremen	Bremen	9,900	22,236
Hessen, Hessen-Nassau	Hessen	8,135	14,730
Württemberg	Württemberg-Baden	6,946	14,870
Nordbayern, Sudbayern	Bayern, incl. Lindau	7,321	14,408
Rheinprovinz (50%), Pfalz	Rheinland-Pfalz	10,247	15,661
Baden	Baden	7,918	13,937
Unweighted average of Württemberg and Hohenzollern	Württemberg-Hohenzollern	6,646	13,119
West Berlin	West Berlin	8,731	10,717

These regions show discontinuity with regard to Mecklenburg, which for 1936 is smaller than in 1950, Brandenburg which for 1936 is larger than in 1950. Furthermore there are some rough solutions with regard to the split up of Rheinprovinz and the region Württemberg-Hohenzollern.

Annex C.4. Agricultural labour productivity in 1936

Products	Unit	Unit value (prices 1936)	Quantity East	Quantity West
Pflanzliche Erzeugnisse				
Roggen	t	64.93	2,070,178	3,117,742
Weizen und Spelz	t	126.70	1,552,844	2,522,056
Sommergerste	t	66.88	605,058	1,161,044
Wintergerste	t	66.88	423,059	543,815
Hafer	t	20.33	1,587,453	2,866,930
Menggetreide	t	51.46	191,542	341,844
Lupinen	t	51.46	27,558	3,860
Spätkartoffeln	t	11.80	13,146,408	19,172,532
Frühkartoffeln	t	11.80	503,018	828,961
Zuckerrüben	t	42.37	5,460,783	4,120,875
Futterrüben	t	51.46	7,889,826	22,013,212
Kohlrüben	t	51.46	1,737,893	3,756,625
Futtermöhren	t	51.46	156,667	137,064
Flachs (Lein)	t	51.46	25,525	59,695
Hanf	t	51.46	19,404	8,253
Raps und Rübsen	t	51.46	33,121	39,824
Heu	t	51.46	6,198,400	22,484,540
Tierische Erzeugnisse				
Kuhmilch	Th t	85,904.31	4,940	15,019
Schweinefleisch	t	1,154.16	449,398	1,002,404
Rindfleisch	t	1,130.69	212,711	642,304
Kalbfleisch	t	1,508.88	47,742	129,564
Schaffleisch	t	1,403.55	16,012	15,926
Total East German output (West Germany = 100)				41.9

Employment	
	Ohne Kind < 14
Bayern	1,867,909
Hohenzollerische Lande	32,158
Württemberg	654,939
Baden	568,139
Saarland	99,925
Hessen	290,621
Hessen-Nassau	580,957
Bremen	4,336
Rheinprovinz	784,272
Westfalen	605,776
Lippe	39,746
Schaumburg-Lippe	13,949
Hannover	792,053
Braunschweig	77,082
Oldenburg	123,191
Hamburg	16,114
Schleswig-Holstein	189,943
West Germany	6,741,110

Employment	
	Ohne Kind < 14
Mecklenburg	136,084
Brandenburg	479,257
Sachsen (Prov)	512,492
Anhalt	37,124
Thüringen	331,041
Sachsen	289,478
East Germany	1,785,476
WG = 100	26.49

Thus East German labour productivity in agriculture was at 158 per cent of West Germany.
Source: Länderrat des Amerikanischen Besatzungsgebiets, *Statistisches Handbuch von Deutschland 1928–1944* (München 1949)

Annex D.: Miscelleneous

Annex D.1. Map of the changing shapes of Germany

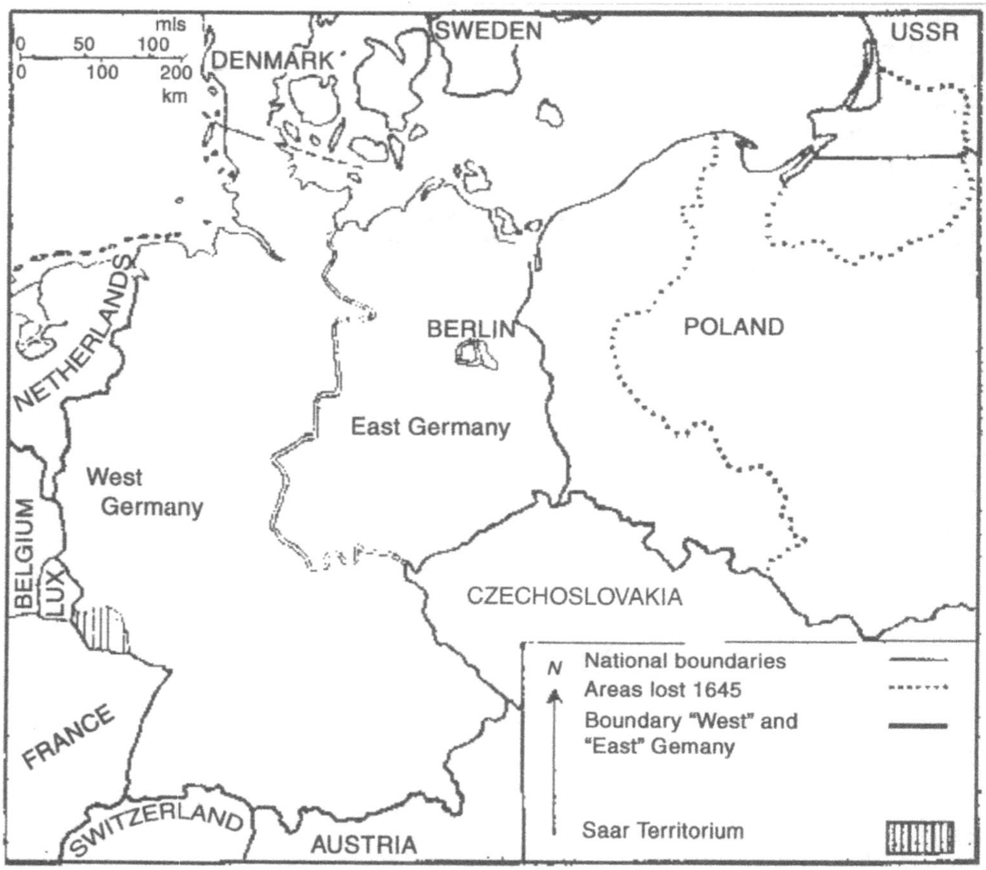

Sources: Own adjustments on T. H. Elkins, *Germany* (London 1968)

Annex D.2. Quality: East and West German exports to Yugoslavia in 1967

Food, beverages, tobacco

Product	NR	East Germany		West Germany		
		Quantity	Value	Quantity	Value	Quality
Meat, fresh, chilled or frozen	n011	1,476	947	170	89	1.23
Sugar and honey	n061	15,033	1,183	224	41	0.43
Beer, including ale, stout, porter	n112.3	2,683	321	340	96	0.42
Animal oils, fats and greases, excluding lard	n411.3	40	23	1,119	197	3.27
Average						1.34

Textiles, wearing apparel

Product	NR	East Germany		West Germany		
		Quantity	Value	Quantity	Value	Quality
Clothing of text fabric, not knitted crocheted	n841.1	66	151	2	22	0.21
Clothing accessories of text., not knitted/croch	n841.2	19	109	16	162	0.57
Clothing and accessories, knitted or crocheted	n841.4	814	1,737	49	284	0.37
Yarn and thread of synthetic fibres	n651.6	3	17	663	1,887	1.99
Yarn and thread of regenerated fibres	n651.7	167	129	494	720	0.53
Cotton fabrics, woven, other than grey	n652.2	39	80	82	353	0.48
Woolen fabrics, woven	n653.2	72	282	206	1,015	0.79
Fabrics, woven, of synthetic fibres	n653.5	47	222	917	2,524	1.72
Fabrics, woven, of regenerated fibres	n653.6	700	1,463	341	887	0.80
Knitted or crochd fabrics not elast nor rubberd	n653.7	2	41	602	2,143	5.76
Tulle, lace, embroidery, ribbons, trimmings	n654	80	666	85	764	0.93
Coated or impregnated textile fabrics & prod.	n655.4	267	416	241	555	0.68

Product	NR	East Germany		West Germany		
		Quantity	Value	Quantity	Value	Quality
Tarpaulins, tents, awnings, sails, etc.	n656.2	22	45	3	7	0.88
Blankets, travelling rugs and coverlets	n656.6	675	1,077	15	16	1.50
Made-up articles of textile materials	n656.9	180	518	45	266	0.49
Linoleum and similar floor coverings	n657.4	1,179	344	1,631	547	0.87
Average						1.16

Wood products, furniture

Product	NR	East Germany		West Germany		
		Quantity	Value	Quantity	Value	Quality
Musical instruments	n891.8	103	458	18	129	0.62
Childrens toys, indoor games etc.	n894.2	391	702	12	30	0.72
Other sporting goods	n894.4	39	199	19	119	0.81
Average						0.72

Paper, printing

Product	NR	East Germany		West Germany		
		Quantity	Value	Quantity	Value	Quality
Books and pamphlets, printed	n892.1	41	99	40	108	0.89
Other printing and writing paper, machine-made	n641.2	121	56	951	537	0.82
Machine-made paper & paperboard, simply fnsh	n641.5	196	28	276	123	0.32
Paper and paperboard in rolls or sheets	n641.9	177	97	1,182	832	0.78
Paper bags, paperboard boxes & other containers	n642.1	3	3	164	79	2.08
Average						0.98

Stone, clay, glass

Product	NR	East Germany		West Germany		
		Quantity	Value	Quantity	Value	Quality
Clay and refractory construction materials	n662	119	48	7,013	1,057	2.68
Mineral manufactures	n663	70	46	1,346	1,494	0.59
Glass in rectangles surface ground or polished	n664.4	46	30	28	5	3.65
Glass carboys, bottles, jars, stoppers, etc.	n665.1	3,626	404	103	24	0.48
Glass tableware etc for household hotel etc	n665.2	191	87	12	16	0.34
Articles made of glass	n665.8	76	111	13	68	0.28
Porcelain or china household ware	n666.4	671	770	85	119	0.82
Pearls and precious and semi-precious stones	n667	5	5	41	22	1.86
Average						1.34

Chemicals, rubber, plastic, oil refining

Product	NR	East Germany		West Germany		
		Quantity	Value	Quantity	Value	Quality
Petroleum products	n332	2	315	2	312	1.01
Organic chemicals	n512	7,113	2,332	26,480	8,405	1.03
Inorg.chemicals-elems., oxides, halogen salts-	n513	1,015	190	12,203	2,582	0.88
Other inorg. Chemicals	n514	6,417	654	7,705	1,700	0.46
Synth.organic dyestuffs, natural indigo & lakes	n531	26	96	682	2,370	1.06
Prepared paints, enamels, lacquers, etc.	n533.3	61	3	2,837	2,292	0.87
Penicillin streptom. Tyrocidine & oth. Antibiot	n541.3	5	127	1	53	0.48
Medicaments	n541.7	39	131	149	2,594	0.19
Essential oils, perfume and flavour materials	n551	3	31	17	167	1.05
Perfumery, cosmetics, dentifrices, etc.	n553	19	37	77	173	0.87
Surface-acting agents and washing preparations	n554.2	178	128	505	269	1.35
Nitrogenous fertilizers and materials	n561.1	4,280	325	76,456	3,032	1.91

Product	NR	East Germany		West Germany		
		Quantity	Value	Quantity	Value	Quality
Potassic fertilizers and materials	n561.3	74,798	2,404	15,343	674	0.73
Prods of condensation, polycond. & polyaddition	n581.1	1,029	251	2,475	1,214	0.50
Products of polymeriza-tion and copolymerization	n581.2	1,305	458	3,429	1,767	0.68
Regen. Cellulose and vulcanized fibre	n581.3	1	1	1,494	1,406	1.06
Insecticides, fungicides, disinfectants	n599.2	1	4	479	1,224	1.57
Starches, inulin, gluten, albumin, substances, glues	n599.5	129	167	883	1,072	1.07
Rubber tyres & tubes for vehicles and aircraft	n529.1	265	296	1,899	1,994	1.06
Photo. Film etc & develpd film other than cine	n862.4	113	809	89	554	1.15
Average						0.95

Machinery, transport

Product	NR	East Germany		West Germany		
		Quantity	Value	Quantity	Value	Quality
power generator	n711	234	470	1,390	4,302	0.65
agricultural machinery	n712.1	109	121	2,724	3,376	0.90
Typewriters	n714.1	92	581	36	251	0.91
Accounting Machines	n714.2	137	3,050	92	1,376	1.49
Machine Tools for Metal Working	n715.1	475	1,021	1,341	4,695	0.61
Other Metalworking ma-chinery	n715.2	1,291	2,243	1,847	1,820	1.76
Textile machinery	n717.2	265	940	2,511	9,263	0.96
Sewing machines	n717.3	80	378	247	2,003	0.58
Paper mill and pulp mill machinery	n718.1	113	422	422	1,537	1.03
Printing and bookbinding machinery	n718.2	317	1,305	630	2,375	1.09
Food Processing Machines	n718.3	61	243	539	1,954	1.10
Construction and mining machinery	n718.4	3,055	2,945	897	1,641	0.53
Mineral crushing etx. & glass-working machinery	n718.5	110	260	469	4,589	0.24
Heating and cooling equipment	n719.1	283	568	634	1,829	0.70

Product	NR	East Germany		West Germany		
		Quantity	Value	Quantity	Value	Quality
Pumps and centrifuges	n719.2	301	548	1,076	3,797	0.52
Mechanical handling equipment	n719.3	853	831	1,698	2,240	0.74
Domestic Appliances, non-electrical	n719.4	62	98	17	39	0.69
Powerd tools	n719.5	328	687	806	3,614	0.47
Other non electrical machines	n719.6	254	810	1,439	6,279	0.73
Ball, roller or needle-roller bearings	n719.7	61	192	369	1,373	0.85
Machinery and mechanical appliances	n719.8	1,307	1,945	4,055	6,776	0.89
Parts and accessories of machinery	n719.9	53	120	829	3,101	0.61
Railway vehicles	n731	765	616	575	619	0.75
Passenger motor cars, other than buses	n732.1	1,478	1,737	22,377	34,123	0.77
Bodies & parts motor vehicles ex motorcycles	n732.8	13	40	633	1,663	1.17
Motorcycles, motorized cycles and their parts	n732.9	453	694	162	373	0.67
Bicycles & other cycles, not motorized &parts	n733.1	40	56	112	153	1.02
Trailers & other vehicles not motorized, & parts	n733.3	21	27	226	215	1.35
ships and boats, other than warships	n735.3	7	11	2,637	1,070	3.87
Average						0.95

Basic and fabricated metal

Product	NR	East Germany		West Germany		
		Quantity	Value	Quantity	Value	Quality
Pig iron, including cast iron	n671.2	6,269	336	550	44	0.67
Wire rod of iron or steel	n673.1	782	74	13,023	1,113	1.11
Bars and rods of iron or steel, ex wire rod	n673.2	13,172	1,578	3,058	601	0.61
Angles etc. of iron or steel, less than 80 mm	n673.5	3,421	387	2,664	459	0.66
Universals etc of iron or steel, over 4.75 mm	n674.1	12,283	1,321	19,392	2,603	0.80

Product	NR	East Germany		West Germany		
		Quantity	Value	Quantity	Value	Quality
Medium plates etc. of iron or steel, 3–4.75 mm	n674.2	798	87	1,630	301	0.59
Plates etc of iron or steel uncoated under 3 mm	n674.3	2,450	317	41,328	6,355	0.84
Tinned plates and sheets	n674.7	130	26	3,219	754	0.85
Hoop and strip of iron or steel	n675	1,865	303	6,084	1,151	0.86
Iron and steel wire, excluding wire rod	n677	847	95	5,543	1,487	0.42
Tubes and pipes of iron or steel, seamless	n678.2	1,086	276	4,451	1,418	0.80
Tubes and pipes of iron or steel, welded, etc.	n678.3	141	28	3,021	659	0.91
Copper and alloys of copper, worked	n682.2	78	111	1,079	1,839	0.83
Tin and tin alloys, unwrought	n687.1	22	34	229	766	0.46
Metal containers for storage and transport	n692	341	151	417	384	0.48
Average						0.73

Electrical equipment

Product	NR	East Germany		West Germany		
		Quantity	Value	Quantity	Value	Quality
Electic Power Machinery	n722.1	153	356	587	1,911	0.71
Apparatus for electrical circuits	n722.2	247	1,137	300	2,298	0.60
Insulated wire and cable	n723.1	57	117	2,561	2,981	1.76
Television broadcast receivers	n724.1	112	777	75	382	1.36
Radio broadcast receivers	n724.2	4	8	48	479	0.20
telecommunications equipment	n724.9	20	361	148	4,068	0.66
Domestic electrical equipment	n725	322	697	724	1,671	0.94
Elec. Apparatus for medic. Purp, radiological ap.	n726	21	200	21	406	0.49
Electric lamps	n729.2	54	100	14	236	0.11
Thermionic valves and tubes, transistors, etc.	n729.3	7	92	211	1,268	2.19
Automotive electrical equipment	n729.4	99	314	277	1,257	0.70

Product	NR	East Germany		West Germany		
		Quantity	Value	Quantity	Value	Quality
Electrical measuring and controlling instruments	n729.5	67	522	87	1,796	0.38
Electro mechanical hand tools	n729.6	6	32	47	450	0.56
Average						0.82

Optics, fine mechanics

Product	NR	East Germany		West Germany		
		Quantity	Value	Quantity	Value	Quality
Binoculars, microscopes & other optical instruments	n861.3	9	167	6	101	1.10
Photographic cameras and flashlight apparatus	n861.4	9	96	27	270	1.07
Photographic & cinematographic equipment	n861.6	6	37	16	170	0.58
Medical instruments	n861.7	21	368	23	576	0.70
Watches, watch movements and cases	n864.1	15	178	4	26	1.83
Clocks, clock movements and parts	n864.2	12	135	6	89	0.76
Average						1.01

Source: OECD Series C, Commodity trade: imports detailed analysis by products 1967

Annex D.3. Abbreviations

BArch	Bundesarchiv (Berlin-Lichterfelde)
DIW	Deutsches Institut für Wirtschaftsforschung (Berlin)
ICOP	International Comparisons of Output and Productivity project (at Groningen Growth and Development Centre)
IWH	Institut für Wirtschaftsforschung Halle
MIT	Massachusetts Institute of Technology
NBER	National Bureau of Economic Research
OECD	Organisation for Economic Co-operation and Development
WIIW	Wiener Institut für Internationale Wirtschaftsvergleiche

References

Abelshauser, Werner, "Markt und Staat. Deutsche Wirtschaftspolitik im langen 20. Jahrhundert" in: Reinhard Spree ed., *Geschichte der deutschen Wirtschaft im 20. Jahrhundert* (München 2001)

Abelshauser, Werner, *Wirtschaftsgeschichte der Bundesrepublik Deutschland 1945–1980* (Frankfurt/M 1983)

Abelshauser, Werner, *Deutsche Wirtschaftsgeschichte seit 1945* (München 2004)

Abramovitz, M., *Thinking about Growth and Other Essays on Economic Growth and Welfare* (Cambridge 1989)

Abramovitz, M., "Resource and Output Trends in the United States Since 1870" in: *American Economic Review* 46 (1956) pp. 5–23

Ahrens, Ralf, *Gegenseitige Wirtschaftshilfe? Die DDR im RGW. Strukturen und handelspolitische Strategien 1963–1976* (Köln 2000)

Akerlof, George A., Andrew K. Rose, Janet L. Yellen, Helga Hessenius, "East Germany in from the Cold: The Economic Aftermath of the Currency Union" in: *Brookings Papers on Economic Activity* (1991/1)

Alton, Thad P. ed., *Growth of East German industrial output 1936, 1946, 1948, and 1950–1967* (New York 1972) OP-35

Alton, Thad P., *et al.*, *Statistics on East European Economic Structure and Growth* (New York 1975) OP-48

Alton, Thad P., *et al.*, *Economic Growth in Eastern Europe 1965–1979* (New York 1980) OP-59

Alton, Thad P., *et al.*, *The Structure of Gross National Product* (New York 1981) OP-64

Alton, Thad P. et al., *Economic Growth in Eastern Europe 1975–1989* (New York 1990) OP-110

Ark, Bart van, "Convergence and Divergence in the European Periphery: Productivity in Eastern and Southern Europe in Retrospect" in: B. van Ark, N.F.R. Crafts eds., *Quantitative Aspects of Post-War European Economic Growth* (Cambridge 1996)

Ark, Bart van, "The Manufacturing Sector in East Germany: A Reassessment of Comparative Productivity Performance, 1950–1988" in: *Jahrbuch für Wirtschaftsgeschichte* 1995/2

Ark, Bart van, *International Comparisons of Output and Productivity. Manufacturing Productivity Performance of Ten Countries from 1950 to 1990* (Groningen 1993)

Ark, Bart van, Marcel Timmer, "Industry Productivity Comparisons" in: *De Economist* 150 (2002) No. 1

Baar, Lothar, Rainer Karlsch, Werner Matschke, "Kriegsschäden, Demontagen und Reparationen" in: Enquete-Kommission (Frankfurt/M 1995)

Baar, Lothar, Uwe Müller, Frank Zschaler, "Strukturveränderungen und Wachstumsschwankungen. Investitionen und Budget in der DDR 1949 bis 1989" in: *Jahrbuch für Wirtschaftsgeschichte* 1995/2

Baar, Lothar, Dietmar Petzina *eds.*, *Deutsch-Deutsche Wirtschat 1945 bis 1990. Strukturveränderungen, Innovationen und regionaler Wandel. Ein Vergleich* (St. Katharinen 1999)

Bähr, Johannes, Dietmar Petzina *eds.*, *Innovationsverhalten und Entscheidungsstrukturen. Vergleichende Studien zur wirtschaftlichen Entwicklung im geteilten Deutschland 1945–1990* (Berlin 1996)

Balassa, Bela, *The Theory of Economic Integration* (Yale 1961)

Barrell, R. and D.W. te Velde, "Catching-up of East German Labour Productivity in the 1990s" in: *German Economic Review* (2000) Volume 1, Issue 3

Barro, R. and X. Sala-I-Martin, "Convergence across States and Regions" in: *Brookings Papers on Economic Activity* 1991/1

Barthel, Horst, *Die wirtschaftlichen Ausgangsbedingungen der DDR. Zur Wirtschaftsentwicklung auf dem Gebiet der DDR 1945–1949/50* (Berlin-Ost 1979)

Bauer, Reinhold, *Pkw-Bau in der DDR. Zur Innovationsschwäche von Zentralverwaltungswirtschaften* (Frankfurt/M 1999)

Bentley, Raymond, *Research and Technology in the Former German Democratic Republic* (Boulder 1992)

Bergson, Abram, *The Real National Income of Soviet Russia since 1928* (Cambridge 1961)

Berthold, Rudolf, *Produktivkräfte in Deutschland 1917/18 bis 1945* (Berlin-Ost 1988)

Boltho, Andrea, Wendy Carlin, Pasquale Scaramozzino, "Will East Germany become a new Mezzogiorno?" in: *Journal of comparative economics* 24 (1997)

Boretsky, Michael, "The Tenability of the CIA Estimates of Soviet Economic Growth" in: *Journal of Comparative Economics* 11 (1987)

Böse, Christian, Wilhelm Henrichsmeyer, "Preis- und Einkommenspolitik: Auswirkungen der veränderten Rahmenbedingungen und Anforderungen an die Politikgestaltung" in: Stephan Merl and Eberhard Schinke eds., *Agrarwirtschaft und Agrarpolitik in der ehemaligen DDR im Umbruch* (Berlin 1991)

Brabant, Jozef M. van, *Adjustment, Structural Change, and Economic Efficiency. Aspects of Monetary Cooperation in Eastern Europe* (Cambridge 1987)

Brada, Josef C., "Privatization Is Transition – Or Is It?" in: *Journal of Economic Perspectives* 10/2 (1996) pp. 67–87

Brakman, S., H. Garretsen, M. Schramm, *The relevance of modern trade theory for convergence between East and West Germany* (Groningen 1999)

Brakman, Steven, Harry Garretsen, Marc Schramm, "The Spatial Distribution of Wages and Employment: Testing the Helpman-Hanson model for Germany" forthcoming (2002)

Buck, Hansjörg F., "Forschungs- und Technologiepolitik in der DDR" in: G. Gutmann et al., *Das Wirtschafts-system der DDR* (Stuttgart 1983)

Buck, Hansjörg, "Öffentliche Finanzwirtschaft im SED-Staat und ihre Transformationsprobleme" in: *Enquete-Kommission* (Frankfurt/M 1999)

Bundesministerium für innerdeutsche Beziehungen, *Bericht und Materialien zur Lage der Nation* (Kassel 1971)

Bundesministerium für innerdeutsche Beziehungen, *Materialien zum Bericht zur Lage der Nation* (Berlin 1974)

Bundesministerium für innerdeutsche Beziehungen, *Materialien zum Bericht zur Lage der Nation im geteilten Deutschland* (Bonn 1987)

Burda, Michael, Michael Funke, "Eastern Germany: Can't We Be More Optimistic?" in: *ifo Studien. Zeitschrift für empirische Wirtschaftsforschung* 3 (1995)

Cameron, Rondo, Larry Neal, *A Concise Economic History of the World. From Paleolithic Times to Present* (New York 2003, forthcoming)

Carlin, Wendy, "West German growth and institutions" in: Nicholas Crafts and Gianni Toniolo, *Economic Growth in Europe since 1945* (Cambridge 1996)

Chenery, Hollis, Sherman Robinson, Moshe Syrquin, *Industrialization and Growth: A Comparative Study* (Oxford 1986)

Ciesla, Burghart, Helmuth Trischler, "Die andere 'Verkehrsnot'. Verkehrspolitik und Leistungsentwicklung des ostdeutschen Verkehrssystems" in: Lothar Baar, Dietmar Petzina eds., *Deutsch-Deutsche Wirtschaft 1945 bis 1990. Strukturveränderungen, Innovationen und regionaler Wandel. Ein Vergleich* (St. Katharinen 1999) pp. 153–192

Collier, Irwin L., *The Estimation of Gross Domestic Product and Its Growth Rate for the German Democratic Republic* (Washington 1985) World Bank Staff Working Papers No. 773

Crafts, N.F.R., *Development history* (London 2000) Working papers in economic history 54/00

Crafts, Nicholas, Gianni Toniolo *eds.*, *Economic Growth in Europe since 1945* (Cambridge 1996)

Czirjak, Laszlo, Jaroslav Dusek, *Growth of East German Industrial Output*, OP-35

Dietz, Raimond, *The Impact of the Unification on the East German Economy* (Vienna/WIIW 1991) No. 172

Dietzenbacher, Erik, Hans-Jürgen Wagener, "Prices in the Two Germanies" in: *Journal of Comparative Economics* 27 (1999)

DIW, "Der Werkzeugmaschinenbau in der DDR" in: *Wochenbericht* 29/82 (22-07-1982)

DIW, "Die chemische Industrie in der DDR. Renaissance einheimischer Rohstoffe durch Beschränkung der Erdölimporte?" in: *Wochenbericht* 47/80 (21-11-1980)

DIW, "Zur Entwicklung des Produktionspotentials in Ostdeutschland" in: *Wochenbericht* 47/91 (1991)

Easterly, William, Stanley Fischer, *The Soviet Economic Decline: Historical and Republican Data* (Cambridge 1994) NBER Working Paper 4735

Eckart, Karl, *Die Eisen- und Stahlindustrie in den beiden deutschen Staaten* (Stuttgart 1988)

Eidem, Rolf, Staffan Viotti, *Economic Systems: How Resources are Allocated* (Oxford 1978)

Elkins, T.H. *Germany* (London 1968)

Elliott, John E., *Comparative Economic Systems* (Belmont 1985)

Feldenkirchen, Wilfried, "Germany: The Invention of Interventionism" in: James Foreman-Peck and Giovanni Federico, *European Industrial Policy. The Twentieth-Century Experience* (Oxford 1999)

Fiege, U., L. Hinners-Tobrägel, "Die Transformation landwirtschaftlicher Unternehmen in Ostdeutschland: ein Modellfall für den EU-Beitritt Polens und Ungarns?" in: *IAMO* (2002)

Fink, Gerhard, Peter Havlik, *Problems of East-West GDP Comparisons* (Vienna 1989) WIIW Forschungsberichte, No. 152

Fischer, Wolfram, Herbert Hax, Hans Karl Schneider eds., *Treuhandanstalt. Das Unmögliche wagen* (Berlin 1993)

Foster, Lucia, John Haltiwanger, C.J. Krizan, *Aggregate Productivity Growth: Lessons from Microeconomic Evidence* (Cambridge 1998, NBER Working Paper 7849)

Franz, Wolfgang, Viktor Steiner, *Wages in the East German Transition Process – Facts and Explanations* (Mannheim/ZEW 1999)

Freeman, Chris, Francisco Louçã, *As time goes by. From the Industrial Revolutions to the Information Revolution* (Oxford 2002)

Fremdling, Rainer, *Van voorsprong en achterstand naar divergentie en convergentie. Denkbeelden in de economische geschiedenis* (Groningen 1990)

Fremdling, Rainer, "De Duitse Democratische Republiek. Economische uitgangspunten na 1945 en hedendaagse toetredingsproblemen met de Bondrepubliek Duitsland" in: *Groniek* (1997)

Fremdling, Rainer, Reiner Stäglin, "Die Industrieerhebung von 1936: Ein Input-Output-Ansatz zur Rekonstruktion der volkswirtschaftlichen Gesamtrechnung für Deutschland im 19. und 20. Jahrhundert – ein Arbeitsbericht" in: *Vierteljahrschrift für Sozial- und Wirtschaftsgeschichte* (2003) Heft 4

Fritz, Wolfgang, "Historie der amtlichen Statistiken der Erwerbstätigkeit in Deutschland. Ein fragmentarischer Abriß: Darstellungen, Quellen, Daten, Definitionen, Chronik" in: *Historical Social Research Supplement 13* (Köln 2001)

Fritsch, Michael, Horst Brezinski eds., *Innovation and Technological Change in Eastern Europe* (Cheltenham 1999)

Gales, Ben, *Ondergronds Bovengronds. Techniek en markt van de Limburgse steenkolenmijnbouw gedurende de achttiende en negentiende eeuw* (Ridderkerk 2002)

Gayko, Axel, *Investitions- und Standortpolitik der DDR an der Oder-Neiße-Grenze 1950–1970* (Frankfurt/M 2000)

Gerschenkron, A., *Economic Backwardness in Historical Perspective* (Cambridge 1962)

Giersch, Herbert, Karl-Heinz Paqué, Holger Schmieding, *The Fading Miracle. Four decades of market economy in Germany* (Cambridge 1994)

Gleitze, Bruno, *Die Wirtschaftsstruktur der Sowjetzone und ihre gegenwärtigen sozial- und wirtschaftsrechtlichen Tendenzen* (Bonn 1951)

Gleitze, Bruno, *Ostdeutsche Wirtschaft. Industrielle Standorte und volkswirtschaftliche Kapazitäten des ungeteilten Deutschland* (Berlin 1956)

Gomulka, Stanislaw, *Growth, Innovation and Reform in Eastern Europe* (Oxford 1986)

Görzig, Bernd, *Produktion und Produktionsfaktoren in Ostdeutschland* (Berlin/DIW 1991)

Görzig, Bernd, Martin Gornig, *Produktivität und Wettbewerbsfähigkeit der Wirtschaft der DDR* (Berlin 1991) DIW, Heft 121 Beiträge zur Strukturforschung

Grünig, Ferdinand, "Volkswirtschaftliche Bilanzen 1936 und 1947. Ein Beitrag zur Analyse der Wirtschaftslage" in: *Vierteljahreshefte zur Wirtschaftsforschung* 1948, Heft 1

Guttman, Gernot, "Kreditwesen, Geld- und Währungssystem in der DDR und seine Umstellung im Zuge der Währungsunion" in: *Enquete-Kommission* (Frankfurt/M 1999)

Harberger, Arnold C., "A Vision of the Growth Process" in: *The American Economic Review* (1998) March

Harmssen, G., *Am Abend der Demontage: Sechs Jahre Reparationspolitik* (Bremen 1951)

Hascher, Michael, Stefan Zeilinger, "Verkehrsgeschichte Deutschlands im 19. und 20. Jahrhundert. Verkehr auf Straßen, Schienen und Binnenwasserstraßen. Ein Literaturüberblick über die jüngsten Forschungen" in: *Jahrbuch für Wirtschaftsgeschichte* 2001/1

Haustein, Heinz-Dieter, "Die notwendige Beschleunigung des Wachstumstempos der industriellen Arbeits-produktivität und die Bewertung der lebendigen Arbeit" in: *Wirtschaftswissenschaft* 38 (1990) 2

Hefele, Peter, *Die Verlagerung von Industrie- und Dienstleistungsunternehmen aus der SBZ/DDR nach Westdeutschland* (Stuttgart 1998)

Heimann, Christian, *Systembedingte Ursachen des Niedergangs der DDR-Wirtschaft. Das Beispiel der Textil- und Bekleidungsindustrie 1945–1989* (Frankfurt/M 1997)

Heske, Gerhard, "Preisstatistische Daten rückrechnen?" in: Statistisches Bundesamt, *Rückrechnungen gesamtwirtschaftlicher Daten für die ehemalige DDR: Beiträge zu einer Statistiktagung in Berlin* (Stuttgart 1993)

Hitchens, D.M.W.N., K. Wagner, J.E. Birnie, *East German productivity and the transition to the market economy* (Avebury 1993)

Hoffmann, Dierk, *Aufbau und Krise der Planwirtschaft. Die Arbeitskräftelenkung in der SBZ/DDR 1945 bis 1963* (München 2002)

Horlings, Edwin, Bart van Ark, *Benchmark Comparisons of Manufacturing Productivity in Eastern Europe, 1937-1989* (Paper for the Sevilla Pre-Conference on "Historical Benchmark Comparisons of Output and Productivity, 1750-1990", Leuven 1996)

ICOP-database, http://www.eco.rug.nl/ggdc/dseries/Data/Sectoral/BV-Germany.xls (07-11-2002)

ICOP Industry Database, http://www.eco.rug.nl/GGDC/icop.html (07-11-2002)

IWH, *Gesamtwirtschaftliche und unternehmerische Anpassungsfortschritte in Ostdeutschland* (Halle 1999) Forschungsreihe, Neunzehnter Bericht, p. 126

IWH, *Zehn Jahre Deutsche Einheit Bilanz und Perspektiven – Tagungsband* – (Halle 2001)

Jasiński, Piotr, Cathryn Ross, "The Use of Policies for Competition in the Promotion of Structural Change in Transforming Economies", in: *Post-Communist Economies* (Vol. 11, No. 2, 1999)

Jong, Herman J. de, *Catching up twice. The nature of Dutch industrial growth during the 20th century in a comparative perspective* (Berlin 2003)

Judt, Matthias, Burghart Ciesla *eds.*, *Technological Transfer Out of Germany After 1945* (Amsterdam 1996)

Karlsch, Rainer, *Allein bezahlt? Die Reparationsleistungen der SBZ/DDR 1945–53* (Berlin 1993)

Karlsch, Rainer, Jochen Laufer *eds.*, *Sowjetische Demontagen in Deutschland 1944–1949. Hintergründe, Ziele und Wirkungen* (Berlin 2002)

Klodt, Henning, Jürgen Stehn et al., *Standort Deutschland: Strukturelle Herausforderungen im neuen Europa* (Tübingen 1994)

Kopstein, Jeffrey, *The Politics of Economic Decline in East Germany, 1945–1989* (London 1997)

Kornai, János, *The Socialist System. The Political Economy of Communism* (Princeton 1992)

Kouwenhoven, Remco, *A Comparison of Soviet and US Industrial Performance: 1928–90* (Groningen 1997) Research memorandum GD-29

Krengel, Rolf, *Anlagevermögen, Produktion und Beschäftigung der Industrie im Gebiet der Bundesrepublik von 1924 bis 1956* (Berlin 1958)

Krugman, Paul, *Geography and Trade* (Leuven 1991)

Kudrov, Valentin, *Soviet Economic Performance in Retrospect. A Critical Re-examination* (Groningen 1998)

Kühr, Rüdiger, "Die Folgen der Demontagen bei der Deutschen Reichsbahn (DR)" in: Rainer Karlsch and Jochen Laufer *eds.*, *Sowjetische Demontagen in Deutschland 1944–1949. Hintergründe, Ziele und Wirkungen* (Berlin 2002)

Länderrat des Amerikanischen Besatzungsgebiets, *Statistisches Handbuch von Deutschland 1928–1944* (München 1949)

Landes, David, *The Wealth and Poverty of Nations. Why Some are So Rich and Some So Poor* (London 1999)

Lange, T. and G. Pugh, *The economics of German unification* (Cheltenham 1998)

Lazarcik, Gregor, *East German Agricultural Production, Expenses, Gross and Net Product, and Productivity, 1934–38 and 1950–1970* (New York 1972) OP-36

Leptin, Gert, *Deutsche Wirtschaft nach 1945. Ein Ost-West-Vergleich* (Opladen 1980)

Leptin, Gert, Manfred Melzer, *Economic Reform in East German Industry* (Oxford 1978)

Lindblom, Charles E., *The Market System. What It Is, How It Works, and What To Make of It* (Yale 2001)

Lindlar, Ludger, Wolfgang Scheremet, *Germany's Slump. Explaining the Unemployment Crisis of the 1990s* (Amsterdam 1998) DIA/Duitsland Cahier 3

Lippe, Peter von der, "Die gesamtwirtschaftlichen Leistungen der DDR-Wirtschaft in den offiziellen Darstellungen. Die amtliche Statistik der DDR als Instrument der Agitation und Propaganda der SED" in: Enquete-Kommission (Frankfurt/M 1995)

Loose, Brigitte, Udo Ludwig, *Überregionale Absatztätigkeit der ostdeutschen Industrie – eine empirische Analyse anhand der Daten des IAB-Betriebspanels* – (Halle 2001) Diskussionspapiere Nr. 153

Ludwig, Udo, Reiner Stäglin, *Verflechtungsanalysen für die Volkswirtschaft der DDR am Vorabend der deutschen Vereinigung* (Berlin 1996)

Maddison, Angus, *Dynamic Forces in Capitalist Development. A Long-Run Comparative View* (Oxford 1991)

Maddison, Angus, *Monitoring the World Economy 1820–1992* (Paris 1995)

Maddison, Angus, *The World Economy: a Millennial Perspective* (Paris 2001)

Mahlich, Wolfgang, *Die Herausbildung der Landwirtschaftlichen Produktionsgenossenschaften in der DDR* (Berlin 1999)

Maier, Wilfried, *Untersuchung zur Preisbildung und Preispolitik in der DDR* (Berlin 1997)

Marer, Paul, *Dollar GNPs of the U.S.S.R. and Eastern Europe* (Washington 1985)

Melzer, Manfred, *Anlagevermögen, Produktion und Beschäftigung der Industrie im Gebiet der DDR von 1936 bis 1978 sowie Schätzung des künftigen Angebotspotentials* (Berlin 1980)

Melzer, Manfred, Reiner Stäglin, "The Role of Economic Statistics in the German Unification Process" in BLS, Eurostat, *Economic Statistics for Economies in Transition: Eastern Europe in the 1990's* (Washington 1991)

Memorandum, dated June 30, 1948, by U.S. Central Intelligence Agency, to President Harry S. Truman, http://www.trumanlibrary.org/whistlestop/study_collections/berlin_airlift/large/cia/bal48-2.htm (10/06/2002)

Merkel, Wilma, Stefanie Wahl, *Das geplünderte Deutschland. Die wirtschaftliche Entwicklung im östlichen Teil Deutschlands von 1949 bis 1989* (Bonn 1991)

Merl, Stephan, Eberhard Schinke eds., *Agrarwirtschaft und Agrarpolitik in der ehemaligen DDR im Umbruch* (Berlin 1991)

Mühlfriedel, Wolfgang, Klaus Wießner, *Die Geschichte der Industrie der DDR bis 1965* (Berlin-Ost 1989)

Müller, Gerhald, *Smaller Productivity Gap between German Regions when Different Producer Prices are Taken into Account* (Halle 1999) IWH-Diskussionspapiere, No. 89

Müller, Ralf, *Humankapital in der Transformation – das Beispiel der neuen Länder –* (Halle 2000) IWH-Diskussionspapiere, No. 126

Müller-Krumholz, Karin, "Erfahrungen beim Versuch der Rückrechnung einer Volkswirtschaftlichen Gesamtrechnung für die ehemalige DDR" in: Statistisches Bundesamt, *Rückrechnungen gesamtwirt-schaftlicher Daten für die ehemalige DDR: Beiträge zu einer Statistiktagung in Berlin* (Stuttgart 1993)

Nettl, J. Peter, *Die deutsche Sowjetzone bis Heute* (Frankfurt/M 1953)

North, Douglass C., *Institutions, Institutional Change and Economic Performance* (Cambridge 1990)

Nötzold, Jürgen, "Wirtschaftspolitische Massnahmen der Ostblock-Industriestaaten von 1945 bis Heute"

O'Brien, Patrick K., Leandro Prados de la Escosura, "Agricultural productivity and European industrialisation, 1890–1980" in: *Economic History Review* XLV, 3 (1992) pp. 514–536

OECD, *Measuring Capital. A Manual on the Measurement of Capital Stocks, Consumption of Fixed Capital and Capital Services* (Paris 2001a)

OECD, *OECD Productivity Manual: A Guide to the Measurement of Industry-level and Aggregate Productivity Growth* (Paris 2001b)

OECD, *Series C, Commodity trade*

OECD, *The OECD STAN Database for Industrial Analysis*

Ofer, Gur, "Soviet Economic Growth: 1928-85" in: *Journal of Economic Literature* 25/4, pp. 1767–1833

Oldenburg, Fred, *Die Implosion des SED-Regimes. Ursachen und Entwicklungsprozesse* (Köln 1991)

Overall Economic Effects Division, *The United States Strategic Bombing Survey: The Effects of Strategic Bombing on the German War Economy* (1945)

Pollard, Sidney ed., *Region und Industrialisierung: Studien zur Rolle der Region in der Wirtschaftsgeschichte der letzten zwei Jahrhunderte* (Göttingen 1980)

Pryor, Frederic L., *A Guidebook to the Comparative Study of Economic Systems* (New Jersey 1985)

Ragnitz, Joachim, *Lagging Productivity in the East German Economy – A Summary of Research Findings* – (Halle 2001)

Reichsamt für wehrwirtschaftliche Planung, *Die deutsche Industrie* (Berlin 1939)

Ritschl, Albrecht O., "An exercise in futility: East German economic growth and decline, 1945–89" in: Nicholas Crafts and Gianni Toniolo, *Economic Growth in Europe since 1945* (Cambridge 1996)

Ritschl, Albrecht, "Aufstieg und Niedergang der Wirtschaft der DDR: Ein Zahlenbild 1945-1989" in *Jahrbuch für Wirtschaftsgeschichte* 1995/2

Ritschl, Albrecht, Mark Spoerer, "Das Bruttosozialprodukt in Deutschland nach den amtlichen Volkseinkommens- und Sozialproduktsstatistiken 1901–1995" in: *Jahrbuch für Wirtschaftsgeschichte* 1997/2

Ritschl, Albrecht, "Deficit Spending in the Nazi Recovery, 1933–1938: A Critical Reassessment" in: *Journal of the Japanes and International Economies* 16 (2002) pp. 559–582

Rostas, L., *Comparative Productivity in British and American Industry* (Cambridge 1948)

Schneider, Jürgen, "Von der nationalsozialistischen Kriegswirtschaftsordnung zur sozialistischen Zentralplanung in der SBZ/DDR" in: Jürgen Schneider, Wolfgang Harbrecht eds., *Wirtschaftsordnung und Wirtschaftspolitik in Deutschland 1933–1993* (Stuttgart 1996)

Schrettl, Wolfram, "Economic and monetary integration of the two Germanies" in: *Economic Systems* 15 (1991)

Schretzenmayr, Martina, "Wohnungsbau in der ehemaligen DDR" in: *DISP* (1998)

Schröter, H., *Ölkrisen und Reaktionen in der chemischen Industrie beider deutsche Staaten: Ein Beitrag zur Erklärung wirtschaftlicher Leistungsdifferenzen* (Berlin 1994)

Schröter, Harm G., "Handlungspfadverengung bis zur 'Selbstzerstörung'? Oder: Warum die chemische Industrie der DDR im Vergleich zu der der Bundesrepublik zwischen 1945 und 1990 so hoffnungslos veraltete" in: Lothar Baar, Dietmar Petzina eds., *Deutsch-Deutsche Wirtschaft 1945 bis 1990. Strukturveränderungen, Innovationen und regionaler Wandel. Ein Vergleich* (St. Katharinen 1999)

Schultz, Helga, "Die sozialistische Industrialisierung – toter Hund oder Erkenntnismittel?" in: *Jahrbuch für Wirtschaftsgeschichte* 1999/2

Schumpeter, Joseph A., *Capitalism, Socialism and Democracy* (London 1961)

Schwarzer, Oskar, "Die Währung der DDR beruht auf der gesunden Grundlage der sozialistischen Gesellschaftsordnung. Wechselkurse zwischen Mark der DDR und D-Mark" in: Jürgen Schneider, Wolfgang Harbrecht eds., *Wirtschaftsordnung und Wirtschaftspolitik in Deutschland (1933–1993)* (Stuttgart 1996)

Schwarzer, Oskar, *Sozialistische Zentralplanwirtschaft in der SBZ/DDR. Ergebnisse eines ordnungspolitischen Experiments (1945–1989)* (Stuttgart 1999)

Seton, Francis, *The Economics of Cost, Use and Value* (Oxford 1992)

Sinn, Gerlinde, Hans-Werner Sinn, *Jumpstart: the economic unification of Germany* (MIT 1992)

Sinn, Hans-Werner, "Zehn Jahre deutsche Wiedervereinigung – Ein Kommentar zur Lage der neuen Länder" in: *ifo Schnelldienst* 26–27 (2000) 29 September

Sinn, Hans-Werner, Frank Westermann, *Two Mezzogiornos* (Cambridge 2001) NBER Working Paper 8125

Sleifer, Jaap, "Separated Unity: The Industrial Sector in 1936 in the Territory of the German Democratic Republic and the Federal Republic of Germany" in: *Jahrbuch für Wirtschaftsgeschichte* 2001/1

Solow, Robert M., "Technical Change and the Aggregate Production Function" in: *Review of Economics and Statistics* 39 (1957) pp. 312–320

Solow, Robert M., "A Contribution to the Theory of Economic Growth" in: *Quarterly Journal of Economics* 70 (1956) pp. 65–96

Spree, Reinhard ed., *Geschichte der deutschen Wirtschaft im 20. Jahrhundert* (München 2001)

Staatlichen Zentralverwaltung für Statistik, *Statistisches Jahrbuch der Deutschen Demokratischen Republik,* various issues (Berlin-Ost)

Statistisches Bundesamt, *Die Industrie der Bundesrepublik Deutschland – Reihe 3 – Die industrielle Produktion. Jahreszahlen 1954 bis 1958* (Stuttgart/ Mainz 1958)

Statistisches Bundesamt, *Produzierendes Gewerbe. Fachserie 4. Reihe 3.1 Produktion im Produzierenden Gewerbe 1992* (Wiesbaden 1993)

Statistisches Bundesamt, *Rückrechnungen gesamtwirtschaftlicher Daten für die ehemalige DDR: Beiträge zu einer Statistiktagung in Berlin* (Stuttgart 1993)

Statistisches Bundesamt, *Sonderreihe mit Beiträgen für das Gebiet der ehemaligen DDR. Heft 4 Produktion ausgewählter Erzeugnisse des Produzierenden Gewerbes 1980 bis 1990 (ohne Baugewerbe)* (Wiesbaden 1993)

Statistisches Bundesamt, *Sonderreihe mit Beiträgen für das Gebiet der ehemaligen DDR. Heft 14 Erwerbstätige 1950 bis 1989* (Wiesbaden 1994)

Statistisches Bundesamt, *Sonderreihe mit Beiträgen für das Gebiet der ehemaligen DDR. Heft 33 Entstehung und Verwendung des Bruttoinlandsprodukts 1970 bis 1989* (Wiesbaden 2000)

Statistisches Bundesamt, *Statistisches Jahrbuch für die Bundesrepublik Deutschland,* various issues (Wiesbaden)

Statistisches Bundesamt, *Volkswirtschaftliche Gesamtrechnungen Fachserie 18 Reihe S. 15 Revidierte Ergebnisse 1950 bis 1990* (Wiesbaden 1991)

Statistisches Landesamt Baden-Württemberg, Arbeitskreis "Volkswirtschaftliche Gesamtrechnungen der Länder", http://www.statistik-bw.de/volkspreise/arbeitskreisvgr/bip95.asp (05-07-2002)

http://www.statistik-bw.de/VolkswPreise/ArbeitskreisVGR/bip_p95.asp (08-14-2002)

Statistisches Landesamt Baden-Württemberg, Arbeitskreis "Volkswirtschaftliche Gesamtrechnungen der Länder", http://www.statistik-bw.de/volkspreise/arbeitskreisvgr/einwohner.asp (05-23-2002)

Statistisches Landesamt Baden-Württemberg, Arbeitskreis "Volkswirtschaftliche Gesamtrechnungen der Länder", http://www.statistik-bw.de/volkswpreisvgr/elaender.asp (05-21-2002)

Statistisches Landesamt Baden-Württemberg, Arbeitskreis "Volkswirtschaftliche Gesamtrechnungen der Länder", http://www.statistik-bw.de/volkspreise/arbeitskreisvgr/bip_jp.asp (05-15-2002)

Steiner, André, *Die DDR-Wirtschaftsreform der sechziger Jahre. Konflikt zwischen Effizienz- und Machtkalkül* (Berlin 1999)

Steiner, André, *Von Plan zu Plan. Eine Wirtschaftsgeschichte der DDR.* (München 2004)

Stiglitz, Joseph E., *Whither Socialism?* (Cambridge 1994)

Stokes, Raymond G., *Constructing Socialism. Technology and Change in East Germany 1945–1990* (Baltimore 2000)

Stolper, Wolfgang F., "The Labor Force and Industrial Development in Soviet Germany" in: *The Quarterly Journal of economics* (Cambridge 1957)

Stolper, Wolfgang F., *The Structure of the East German Economy* (Cambridge 1960)

Sturm, Peter Hans, *A Comparison of Aggregate Production Relationships in East and West Germany* (Yale 1974)

Sturm, Peter Hans, "The System Component in Differences in per Capita Output between East and West Germany" in: *Journal of Comparative Economics* 1 (1977) pp. 5–22

Svennilson, Ingvar, *Growth and Stagnation in the European Economy* (Geneva 1954)

Timmer, Marcel, *The Dynamics of Asian Manufacturing: A Comparative Perspective, 1963–1993* (Eindhoven 1999)

Timmer, Marcel, "Climbing the Technology Ladder Too Fast? New Evidence on Comparative Productivity Performance in Asian Manufacturing" in: *Journal of Japanese and International Economies* 16 (2002) pp. 50–72

Tipton Jr., Frank B., *Regional Variations in the Economic Development of Germany During the Nineteenth Century* (Conneticut 1976)

Tooze, J. Adam, *Statistics and the German State, 1900–1945. The Making of Modern Economic Knowledge* (Cambridge 2001)

U.S. Bureau of Labor Statistics and Eurostat, *Economic Statistics for Economies in Transition: Eastern Europe in the 1990's* (Washington 1991)

Unger, Stefan, *Eisen und Stahl für den Sozialismus: Modernisierungs- und Innovationsstrategien der Schwarzmetallurgie in der DDR von 1949 bis 1971* (Berlin 2000)

United Nations, *International Standard Industrial Classification of all Economic Activities* (New York 1990) Series M/No. 4, Rev. 3

Vertrag über die Schaffung einer Währungs-, Wirtschafts- und Sozialunion zwischen der Bundesrepublik Deutschland und der Deutschen Demokratischen Republik (Bonn, Mai 18th 1990)

Vincentz, Volkhart, *Privatization in Eastern Germany. Principles and Practice* (München 1991)

Working Paper 146 Osteuropa-Institut München

Viscusi, W. Kip, John M. Vernon, Joseph E. Harrington Jr., *Economics of Regulation and Antitrust* (Lexington 1992)

Vogeler, Ingolf, "State Hegemony in Transforming the Rural Landscapes of Eastern Germany: 1945–1994" in: *Annals of the Association of American Geographers* 86/3 (1996) pp. 432–458

Wagener, Hans-Jürgen, "Zur Innovationsschwäche der DDR-Wirtschaft" in: Johannes Bähr, Dietmar Petzina eds., *Innovationsverhalten und Entscheidungsstrukturen. Vergleichende Studien zur wirtschaftlichen Entwicklung im geteilten Deutschland 1945–1990* (Berlin 1996)

Wagener, Hans-Jürgen, *Zur Analyse von Wirtschaftssystemen. Eine Einführung* (Berlin 1979)

Wagenführ, Rolf, Die deutsche Industrie im Kriege 1939–1945 (Berlin 1963)

Wallich, Henry C., *Mainsprings of the German Revival* (Yale 1955)

Weber, Adolf, "Zur Agrarpolitik in der ehemaligen SBZ/DDR: Rückblick und Ausblick" in: Stephan Merl and Eberhard Schinke eds., *Agrarwirtschaft und Agrarpolitik in der ehemaligen DDR im Umbruch* (Berlin 1991)

Wilczinsky, J., *The Economics of Socialism* (London 1970)

Wilkens, Herbert, *Das Sozialprodukt der Deutschen Demokratischen Republik im Vergleich mit dem der Bundesrepublik* (Berlin 1976)

Wilkens, Herbert, *The Two German Economies. A Comparison between the National Product of the German Democratic Republic and the Federal Republic of Germany* (Westmead 1981)

Winiecki, Jan, "An inquiry into the Early Drastic Fall of Output in Post-communist Transition: an Unsolved Puzzle" in: *Post-Communist Economies* (2002) Vol. 14. No. 1

World Bank, *Historically Planned Economies. A Guide to the Data* (Washington 1993)

Yeager, Timothy J., *Institutions, Transition Economies, and Economic Development* (Boulder 1999)

Zank, W., *Wirtschaft und Arbeit in Ostdeutschland 1945-1949: Probleme des Wiederaufbaus in der Sowjetischen Besatzungszone Deutschlands* (München 1987)

Zimbalist, Andrew, Howard J. Sherman, *Comparing Economic Systems: A Political-Economic Approach* (London 1984)

Zimmerman, Hartmut, *ed.*, *DDR Handbuch* (Köln 1985)

www.ingramcontent.com/pod-product-compliance
Lightning Source LLC
LaVergne TN
LVHW081334011026
849161LV00013BB/2919